Landmarks in Linguistic Thought II

'... fills a long-standing need for an intellectually solid survey of thought about language that bridges the divide between language philosophy and linguistics. ... Should be required reading in virtually any academic course, graduate or undergraduate, that deals to any extent with language.'

Paul Hopper, Carnegie Mellon University, USA

Landmarks in Linguistic Thought II introduces the major issues and themes that have determined the development of Western thinking about language, meaning and communication in the twentieth century.

Each chapter contains an extract from a 'landmark' text followed by a commentary, which places the ideas in their social and intellectual context. The book is written in an accessible and non-technical manner.

The book summarizes the contribution of the key thinkers who have shaped modern linguistics. These include:

• Austin	• Bruner	• Chomsky	• Derrida
• Firth	• Goffman	• Harris	• Jakobson
• Labov	• Orwell	• Sapir	• Skinner
• Whorf	• Wittgenstein		

The second volume follows on from *Landmarks in Linguistic Thought I*, which introduces the key thinkers up to the twentieth century. The series is ideal for anyone with an interest in the history of linguistics or of ideas.

John E. Joseph is Professor of Applied Linguistics at the University of Edinburgh, UK. **Nigel Love** is Associate Professor of Linguistics at the University of Cape Town, South Africa. **Talbot J. Taylor** is L.G.T. Cooley Professor of English and Linguistics at the College of William and Mary, Virginia, USA.

ROUTLEDGE HISTORY OF LINGUISTIC THOUGHT SERIES

Consultant Editor: Talbot J. Taylor

College of William and Mary, Williamsburg, Virginia

Landmarks in Linguistic Thought I
The Western tradition from Socrates to Saussure
Roy Harris and Talbot J. Taylor

Landmarks in Linguistic Thought II
The Western tradition in the twentieth century
John E. Joseph, Nigel Love and Talbot J. Taylor

Landmarks in Linguistic Thought III
The Arabic linguistic tradition
Kees Versteegh

Language, Saussure, and Wittgenstein
How to play games with words
Roy Harris

Ideology and Linguistic Theory
Noam Chomsky and the deep structure debates
Geoffrey J. Huck and John A. Goldsmith

Linguistics, Anthropology and Philosophy in
the French Enlightenment
A contribution to the history of the relationship
between language theory and ideology
Ulrich Ricken, translated by Robert Norton

Linguistics in America 1769–1924
A critical history
Julie Tetel Andreson

Generative Linguistics
A historical perspective
Frederick J. Newmeyer

Landmarks in Linguistic Thought II

The Western tradition in the twentieth century

John E. Joseph, Nigel Love
and Talbot J. Taylor

London and New York

First published 2001
by Routledge
11 New Fetter Lane, London EC4P 4EE

Simultaneously published in the USA and Canada
by Routledge
29 West 35th Street, New York, NY 10001

Routledge is an imprint of the Taylor & Francis Group

Typeset in Times
by Florence Production Ltd, Stoodleigh, Devon

Printed and bound in Great Britain by
TJ International, Padstow, Cornwall

British Library Cataloguing in Publication Data
A catalogue record for this book is available from
the British Library

Library of Congress Cataloging in Publication Data
Joseph John Earl.
   Landmarks in linguistic thought 2: the Western tradition in the
   twentieth century / John E. Joseph, Nigel Love, and Talbot J. Taylor.
      p. cm.   (Landmarks in linguistic thought; 2)
   Includes bibliographical references and index.
   Contents: Sapir on language, culture, and personality—Jakobsen
and structuralism—Orwell on language and politics—Whorf on
language and thought—Firth on language and context—Wittgenstein
on grammatical investigations—Austin on language as action—
Skinner on verbal behavior—Chomsky on language as biology—
Labov on linguistic variation—Goffman on the communicating
self—Brunner on the child's passport into language—Derrida on the
linguistic sign and writing—Harris on linguistics without
languages—Kanzi and human language.
      ISBN 0–415–06396–5   0–415–06397–3 (pbk)
   1. Linguistics—History—20th century.   I. Love, Nigel.
II. Taylor, Talbot J.   III. Title.   IV. Series.
P77.J67 2001
410′.9′0904—dc21   2001019241

ISBN 0–415–06396–5 (hbk)
ISBN 0–415–06397–3 (pbk)

Contents

Acknowledgements

Chapter 10 is a revised version of an unpublished essay by Dr Ana Deumert. The authors gratefully acknowledge her contribution.

The authors and publishers are grateful for permission to reprint extracts from *Philosophical Investigations*, Ludwig Wittgenstein © Blackwell Publishers, 1967.

The authors and publishers are grateful to Roy Harris for the permission to reprint extracts from 'On redefining linguistics', © Roy Harris, 1990.

The authors and publishers are grateful for permission to reprint extracts from *Language, Thought and Reality*, Benjamin Whorf, © 1956, by the Massachusetts Institute of Technology.

The authors would also like to extend their heartfelt thanks to Joy Martin, of the College of William and Mary, who worked tirelessly yet cheerfully on the manuscript in its final stages. Without her contribution the book would never have seen the light of day.

Talbot J. Taylor thanks the National Endowment for the Humanities and the College of William and Mary for funding and research leave in support of this project.

Introduction

This book presents twentieth-century linguistic thought as a continuation of the ideas and arguments that have made up the warp and weft of the Western tradition in linguistic thought since its beginnings in Classical Greece. In this respect it is unlike most books on the history of twentieth-century linguistics, in particular those that take linguistic theory at the close of the century to be the end of the story, a story seen with hindsight and told as a matter of 'how we got to where we are today'. The co-authors of this book do not view linguistic thought as a matter of progress towards the theories that have now attained the status of academic standards. Instead, in contrast to such a 'progressivist' perspective, we offer a 'continuist' alternative, according to which twentieth-century thinking about language continued to debate and develop the same themes, questions, issues, concepts and arguments that have preoccupied Western thinking about language since its inception.

Since we look at twentieth-century linguistic thought from the vantage point of the past – that is, as a continuation of pre-twentieth-century thought – we include in our discussion a number of writers and theorists who have not typically been classified as 'linguists'. Again, this is unlike the typical history of linguistics. Beginning with Saussure's *Cours de linguistique générale*, a characteristic feature of the twentieth century was the attention given to establishing and policing the borders of linguistics as a field of inquiry. What counts as 'linguistics' – or as a 'linguistic' study of language – has been an important ideological issue, strongly influencing the ways that language is studied and written about, within as well as without the walls of the professional institutions of learning.

However, this is not to say that the matter of intellectual terri-torial borders was ignored prior to the twentieth century. As Michel Foucault made abundantly clear (see, for example, Foucault 1971), in all fields of intellectual inquiry – although perhaps in language inquiry more than most – issues of disciplinary territoriality have often been regarded as inseparable from the inquiry itself: that is, issues such as what counts as the subject of study, what are legiti-mate questions to ask about the subject, what methods and tools are appropriate in searching for their answers, and how subject, questions, methods, and answers relate to those of other fields of inquiry. Moreover, historical context, in the broadest terms, has always determined – and doubtless always will – how these discipline-defining issues are addressed and who is seen as quali-fied to address them. As regards linguistic thought, this much should be clear from the first volume of this series: *Landmarks in Linguistic Thought: the Western tradition from Socrates to Saussure* (Harris and Taylor 1989). What was distinctive about the twentieth (and to some extent the nineteenth) century was the desire of professional, academic linguists to have their questions, methods and theories – in other words, what the discipline of linguistics *is* – seen as autonomous and scientific. There are many persuasive, practical-professional motivations for linguistic inquiry to seek this status: funding, institutional politics and respect in the academic community are merely the most obvious ones. Disciplinary autonomy was already a part of Saussure's goal in identifying *langue* as the scientific object proper to linguistics and independent of the scientific objects of other disciplines such as psychology and sociology.

Unfortunately, in the twentieth century this 'disciplinary' perspective on linguistic thought led to the exclusion of many scholars and theorists who have written on language not only with great knowledge and insight but also with significant impact on the thinking of non-linguists and laymen alike – and, by this means, on public policies regarding language. Our book is based on the premise that these writers need to be recognized and included among the important contributors to the century's linguistic thought, no less so than those who have worked within the confines of academic linguistics: 'linguistics proper' as it is often called. If, as we try to do here, one looks at twentieth-century linguistic thought free from the blinkers of academic-professional territori-alism, it becomes clear the extent to which 'extra-disciplinary' reflection on language shaped – and responded more effectively to – what in general cultural discourse has been taken to be of importance and significance in language, i.e. to be in need of discussion, investigation, explanation and action. (For an extended discussion of this point, see Cameron 1995.)

In this sense, then, the perspective taken in this book is not only 'continuist', it is also – in contrast to that of disciplinary linguistics – 'inclusive'. Included herein are chapters on the linguistic ideas not only of professional linguists but also of psychologists (Bruner, Skinner), anthropologists (Sapir), sociologists (Goffman), critical theorists (Derrida), philosophers (Austin, Wittgenstein) and even a fire insurance engineer (Whorf) and a novelist (Orwell). There is also a chapter on the implications for language theory of the efforts by primatologists to teach language to apes. A less inclusive history of twentieth-century linguistic thought would have placed the writings of most of these thinkers on the periphery, if within sight at all.

But although 'inclusive' in the sense of not being restricted to linguistics proper, this book is hardly all-inclusive. Limitations of space have enforced selective coverage of the subject matter, and many readers will notice gaps. Just *what* is missing is a function partly of considered authorial choices, and partly of the presentational format of the *Landmarks* collection – essentially, extended commentary on key passages from key writers. Very likely a mere difference of expository framework would have resulted in a substantially different book. That said, however, we do at least hope to have provided a broader-based foundation for serious study of the subject than is at all common in comparable introductory texts.

The continuist and inclusive characters of our presentation are complementary. For it is by adopting an inclusive perspective on twentieth-century linguistic thought that its continuity with pre-twentieth-century linguistic thought is more easily recognizable. Instead of seeing modern disciplinary linguistics as a completely new field – invented by Saussure and the American descriptivists – it emerges as merely one of the threads of development that twentieth-century theorists have woven into the centuries-old fabric of Western linguistic thought.

Nevertheless, we are not claiming that our own perspective is free from the influence of the intellectual and historical context in which we write. On the contrary, we acknowledge that the way we have conceived and written this book has been shaped by our firm conviction that contemporary work on language should resist the efforts by disciplinary linguistics to determine what is relevant and worthy of study in language. There is much more to language than can be recognized or investigated from a purely 'linguistic' perspective, as is illustrated by the chapters in this volume and the one that preceded it. Language is too important, and in too many ways, to be left in the possession of a single disciplinary field. It is our hope that intellectual re-fertilization – both from the past and from outside the boundaries of disciplinary linguistics – can help to open up language theory to new influences, new concerns, new approaches and new applications. Accordingly, our goal has been to produce a book that will be of use not only to students of linguistics but also to students from the wide range of fields to which linguistic thought is relevant, including anthropology, sociology, cultural studies, rhetoric, public policy, communication studies, psychology, literary studies and philosophy. Linguistic thought, in other words, we take to be an essentially *interdisciplinary* endeavour. It always has been. It is our acknowledged goal in writing this book to make sure that this continues to be recognized.

At the same time, we would not want the continuist approach that we adopt to lead to misunderstanding. We are not denying that there were new ideas and original problems in the twentieth century. The facts clearly point to the opposite conclusion. A great deal in twentieth-century linguistic thought was new and original. The sources of these new ideas were many and various, but for convenience's sake the ideas may be categorized as coming from three general sources:

- within linguistics itself, from the radical ideas of Saussure's *Cours de linguistique générale* (see Volume I, Chapter 16), combined with the impact of North American work on Native American languages;
- from changes in the intellectual and ideological context brought about by the two world wars, the propaganda battles of the Cold War and the globalization of Euro-American culture and economy;
- from developments in neighbouring fields of inquiry, particularly psychology, philosophy, anthropology, neurology, sociology and literary studies.

Nevertheless, we do not take the new ideas and questions that these sources have introduced into linguistic thought as intellectual isolates, existing independently of the intellectual and discursive contexts in which they emerged and prospered. On the contrary, we view them as new threads woven into an already-existing tapestry. The material and colour of these new threads may well be original, but the threads are integrated into the fabric of Western linguistic thought, a fabric whose pattern of ideas and issues has an unbroken continuity from the very beginning of the Western cultural tradition.

As an example, we might cite one of the century's most pervasive linguistic topics. As is illustrated in many of the chapters herein, the twentieth century – from beginning to end – was preoccupied with the question of whether language influences thought and, if it does, how it does so and what the implications are. Our chapters on Sapir, Whorf, Austin, Orwell, Wittgenstein and Derrida all show this to be one of their central concerns. In Derrida's case, for instance, the way the issue is raised bears the hallmark of Saussure's influence. What then matters are the implications of Saussure's claim that it is the differential structure of *langue* which gives shape to thought and that, before the introduction of linguistic structure, thought is indeterminate, 'like a swirling cloud where . . . no ideas are established in advance and nothing is distinct' (Saussure 1916: 155). While Saussurean influence is also detectable in their views, the study of Native American languages and cultures leads Sapir and Whorf to aim for quite different goals in discussing how language influences thought. The topic arises for Austin and Wittgenstein from an entirely different direction: namely, the attempts by analytic philosophers to determine the foundations of logic and reasoning (see Volume I, Chapter 15). Whereas Orwell's concern with how language influences thought stems primarily from his experience of the ideological battles of the 1930s and 1940s and the ways that propaganda was used to shape and manipulate public opinion. And yet, each writer approaches the topic in a way that both takes for granted and makes use of certain features of the long-running discourse on the relationship between language and thought, a discourse whose threads may be traced back to the very beginning of the Western cultural tradition. The various ways that the twentieth century discussed the topic of the influence of language on thought rely entirely on the Western tradition's conception of the topic's components – thought, language, reality, self – and the possibilities of their interaction. The twentieth century played the 'linguistic influence' game in original ways, using techniques motivated by concerns and developments that are specific to the historical context. But the game and the pieces used remain the same.

As the first volume of this series shows, the Western tradition has been focused on a fairly broad, but not unlimited, range of topics and issues that, for cultural, political, religious and technological reasons, have been thought to require scholarly attention. The issue of the relationship between language and thought is just one. Others include what the origins of language are, what its parts are, and what its purpose is, how language conveys meaning, how language can represent reality and do so truly or falsely, what the implications are of language diversity, what properties are shared by all languages and why this is, how language makes understanding possible, and how language can be used as a cultural and interpersonal tool. Western thinking about these issues provides the subject matter for each of the chapters in the first volume of this collection, as it does for all the chapters in this volume.

It might be thought that one topic that was wholly new to twentieth-century reflection on language is what might be called 'the reflective turn': that is, the growing interest in and criticism of the foundations of Western linguistic thought itself. We mean by this questions such as the following. Why does Western linguistic thought focus on a family of related issues and topics? Why are particular sorts of concepts, problems, arguments, assumptions, methods, puzzles and solutions characteristic of Western thinking about language? What is the way to solve these issues once and for all, or to break free from the rhetorical spell that they cast? These sorts of questions, characteristic of the reflective turn in the Western tradition, are central to at least three chapters herein, those on Wittgenstein, Derrida and Harris. They are reflected also in the dramatic challenge to the Western linguistic tradition that is presented by those who claim to have taught an impressive range of linguistic skills to non-human primates. Yet even this reflective turn in linguistic thought is not an entirely new development, but is continuous with a trend that goes back at least to the Renaissance. In part, this crisis in linguistic confidence was the combined effect of two historical developments: (1) the 'second babelization' that seemed to be augured by the decline of Latin as a universal language of Europe along with the increased use of the vernacular languages and (2) the impact of printing technology (see Volume I, Chapter 7). Today the Western world is clearly in the throes of another techno-linguistic revolution. A major source of this revolution is the accelerated development and exploitation of new technologies for electronic communication (see Baron 2000). At the same time, what some see as a new 'universal' language is rapidly emerging, taking on the role that Latin once had in the European world. What the consequences will be for the development of linguistic thought in the twenty-first century is hard to predict. Will twenty-first-century linguistic thought continue to focus on the same family of related issues and topics? Will the preceding century's characteristic questions, problems, arguments and puzzles finally be 'solved'? Or will they lose their charm and be forgotten, only to be replaced by others? A major shift in linguistic thought may indeed be looming, in which case the twentieth century, which this volume attempts to cover, will in fact prove to have been a remarkably self-contained unit of intellectual history.

Chapter 1

Sapir on language, culture and personality

It is of course true that in a certain sense the individual is pre-destined to talk, but that is due entirely to the circumstance that he is born not merely in nature, but in the lap of a society that is certain, reasonably certain, to lead him to its traditions. Eliminate society and there is every reason to believe that he will learn to walk, if, indeed, he survives at all. But it is just as certain that he will never learn to talk, that is, to communicate ideas according to the traditional system of a particular society. Or again, remove the new-born individual from the social environment into which he has come and transplant him to an utterly alien one. He will develop the art of walking in his new environment very much as he would have developed it in the old. But his speech will be completely at variance with the speech of his native environment. Walking, then, is a general human activity that varies only within circumscribed limits as we pass from individual to individual. Its variability is involuntary and purposeless. Speech is a human activity that varies without assignable limit as we pass from social group to social group, because it is a purely historical heritage of the group, the product of long-continued social usage. It varies as all creative effort varies – not as consciously, perhaps, but nonetheless as truly as do the religions, the beliefs, the customs, and the arts of different people. Walking is an organic, an instinctive, function (not, of course, itself an instinct); speech is a non-instinctive, acquired, 'cultural' function.

(Sapir 1921: 2)

The Great War of 1914–18 marked a turning point in global intellectual history. Since early in the nineteenth century the study of language had been dominated by Germany, and the rest of the world largely followed the lead of the centres of linguistic study at Berlin and Leipzig (see Volume I, Chapter 14). With Germany's defeat in the war, it was as though a spell was broken. Linguists in both Europe and America were ready for a new start, a modern approach that they could make their own.

A strikingly new approach had been promulgated in the courses in general linguistics given before the war by Ferdinand de Saussure at the University of Geneva (see Volume I, Chapter 16). But the compilation of his lectures was not published until 1916, the middle of the war, and did not then attract the widespread notice it would receive following publication of a slightly revised second edition in 1922. A year before that, however, a new book appeared by an American linguist-cum-anthropologist which was the first post-war general study of language to attract wide notice. It was a rich and readable account of language embedded in culture, written by a man with field experience to match his intellectual and literary gifts. Significantly for the degree of confidence it expressed in its subject matter, it had as its main title the single word *Language* (Sapir 1921).

Somewhat ironically, in view of the break from German linguistic thought it represented, the book's author, Edward Sapir (1884–1939), had been born in Germany, though his parents emigrated when he was still a small boy. What is more, the teacher who most directly shaped his approach to language was another German *émigré* to America, Franz Boas (1858–1942), who specialized in the anthropology of North America.

After a short period of teaching in Berlin, Boas settled in the United States in the late 1880s. What made him the founder of a large and productive school of linguistic research was his work as organizer, under the aegis of the Smithsonian Institution, of a survey of the indigenous languages of America north of Mexico. *The Handbook of American Indian Languages* was published in 1911. Boas's introduction to it contains a good summary of the approach to language that came to be known as 'American descriptivism'. Several of the chapters on individual languages were written by Boas, and he trained those who investigated the others. For decades, subsequently, all the great names in American linguistics learned their subject from Boas at first or second hand (Sampson 1980: 58).

The native languages of America are in many respects radically different from the various forms of Indo-European with which Western language studies had hitherto been primarily concerned: whatever their European heritage may have been, it availed Boas and Sapir little in the day-to-day anthropological work of recording and analysing the dozens, indeed hundreds, of languages of the American Indian tribes of North America. One of Boas's main contributions to American linguistics was to develop a method of transcribing these languages that relied as little as possible on categories and designations familiar from the languages of Europe, and to train generations of anthropologists in its use. In so far as they were anthropologists, the object of this exercise was to equip them with a prerequisite for understanding the culture whose vehicle a given language was. But in so far as they were linguists, description came to be seen as an end in itself, not just as a source of data for the construction of a general theory of language. It is true that the most eminent of the descriptivists are well known because they did theorize about language in general, but in all cases their general theories were backed up by intensive research on the detailed structure of various 'exotic' languages, and many of their less famous colleagues and followers preferred to take theories for granted and concentrate on the data.

Once the languages were recorded, Boas's interest in them – apart from the anthropological content of the stories and songs that made up many of the linguistic samples – lay in determining the historical affiliations of the various American Indian language groups. The problem was that, whereas for European languages there were written records dating back into the distant past that might reveal their historical affinities, there was nothing comparable available for American Indian languages. If sufficient similarities existed, a common ancestor was reconstructed by comparing them, in the way historical linguists attempted to reconstruct the proto-Indo-European parent language, but with a much shallower time-depth in the recorded sources. Moreover, whereas German-dominated Indo-European linguistics approached languages as discrete, organic wholes in which laws of sound-change operated with near-perfect regularity (distorted only by processes of analogy, a kind of psychological interference), Boas's experience with American Indian languages suggested that they did not develop in isolation and that similarities among them did not necessarily point to a common genetic origin. Rather, he argued that similarities were more the product of linguistic contact among peoples, and that this affected all levels of language structure, including phonology, vocabulary and grammar.

> While I am not inclined to state categorically that the areas of distribution of phonetic phenomena, of morphological characteristics, and of groups based on similarities of vocabularies are absolutely distinct, I believe this question must be answered empirically before we can undertake to solve the general problem of the history of modern American languages. If it should prove true, as I believe it will, that all these different areas do not coincide, then the conclusion seems inevitable that the different languages must have exerted a far-reaching influence on one another. If this point of view is correct, then we have to ask ourselves in how far the phenomena of acculturation extend also over the domain of languages.
>
> (Boas 1940[1920]: 215)

That last sentence is a direct challenge to the German neogrammarian linguistic establishment (see Volume I, Chapter 14), and takes up the resistance to their approach that had been steadfastly maintained by a minority of linguists. These included Hugo Schuchardt (1842–1927), whose interest in contact phenomena led him to initiate the serious study of pidgins and creoles, and Otto Jespersen (1860–1943), whose work included inquiry into the symbolic functions of language for nations and individuals.

Although Boas had an abiding interest in language, his skills as a descriptive linguist were self-taught and outshone by those of his protégé Sapir, who came to be regarded as *the* linguist of Boasian anthropology (Darnell 1990: xii). Sapir, the most eminent student of American Indian languages of his time, began his career in charge of the anthropological division of the Canadian Geological Survey; in 1925 he moved to the University of Chicago and in 1931 to Yale.

Sapir's own anthropological background and bias are evident from the quotation from *Language* (Sapir 1921) which opens this chapter, where he insists upon the social and cultural nature of human speech. The neogrammarian linguistic science of the late nineteenth century took as its objects speech sounds and forms in abstraction from the human beings who produced them and the cultures within which those human beings lived. Language was studied as the essentially natural mechanics of the human unconscious. Sapir developed a theory of language drift that in some ways mediated between Boasian acculturation and neogrammarian mechanics. He did not dispute that the production of speech involves a number of unconscious functions in the brain and the vocal tract, but he denied that this is where language (or speech) is located. These are simply the means by which we realize language, the essence of which is in the conscious will. Speech, according to Sapir, is an extremely complex and ever-shifting network of adjustments – in the brain, in the nervous system, and in the articulating and auditory organs – tending towards the desired end of communication (Sapir 1921: 7). That desire, the will, is neither physical nor mechanical, but the cultural product of the society in which the speaker lives.

Note that when Sapir introduces the word 'cultural' near the end of the opening citation, it is in quotation marks. He does not explain why, and clues to the reason do not come until the penultimate chapter of the book. The problem is the word 'culture' itself, which over the previous century had become heavily charged with overtones, initially Romantic and spiritual, and increasingly political (this was even more true of the German cognate, *Kultur*). Sapir did not want to be misunderstood as implying that cultures embody a 'national spirit' which determines their history and is inseparably bound up with the form of their language. This was the view put forward in the writings of such German Romantics as Herder (1744–1803), about whom Sapir wrote his 1905 MA thesis (Sapir 1907), and Humboldt (see Volume I, Chapter 13); and it implied that the *value* of a culture, its level of intellectual development, was directly correlated with the structure of its language.

> Rightly understood, such correlations are rubbish. The merest *coup d'oeil* verifies our theoretical argument on this point. Both simple and complex types of language of an indefinite number of varieties may be found spoken at any desired level of cultural advance. When it comes to linguistic form, Plato walks with the Macedonian swineherd, Confucius with the head-hunting savage of Assam.
>
> (Sapir 1921: 234)

Sapir added the quotation marks to 'cultural' to signal that in using that word he was implying nothing about what we sometimes call 'culture with a capital C'. For the anthropologist, all cultures are equally good, in the sense of being inherently of equal value as objects of study. The anthropological and Romantic senses of 'culture' are responsible for the tension in Sapir's *Language* between statements such as, on the one hand, 'speech is ... a "cultural" function' (Sapir 1921: 2, 10) and 'Language and our thought-grooves are inextricably interwoven, are, in a sense, one and the same' (Sapir 1921: 232) and, on the other, 'Nor can I believe that culture and language are in any true sense causally related' (Sapir 1921: 233) and 'we shall do well to hold the drifts of language and of culture to be non-comparable and unrelated processes' (Sapir 1921: 234). In his writings for more specialized audiences of anthropologists and linguists, Sapir usually took for granted that he could treat language as being embedded in culture without danger of being misunderstood.

But that is not to say that linguists or even anthropologists recognized all the implications of the notion that language is embedded in culture, in Sapir's view. Linguists undertaking the study of a previously unanalysed language had to ask themselves, for example, whether they could assume that they would find in it nouns, verbs, adjectives, prepositions and the other word classes that traditionally formed part of the grammatical analysis of European languages. What if there was no direct evidence that in this language the words that corresponded to nouns and to verbs in English were distinguishable from one another? In Western languages, nouns and verbs are morphologically differentiated. In some non-Western languages, such as Chinese, this is not so. By applying the distributional method to such languages (see Chapter 9), we may find that word classes can be distinguished on the basis of what other classes of word they do or do not follow – thus in the case of Chinese we can label as 'nouns' those words that can follow a particular set of forms we call 'classifiers', which 'verbs' never follow. The results we obtain in this way will rarely show an exact correspondence with the traditional Western grammatical categories.

Moreover, from his own field experiences Sapir knew that the linguist must not imagine that the results obtained by use of the distributional method constituted an objective truth about the structure of a language that was somehow superior to the native speaker's own understanding of it. He notably insisted on this point with reference to the phoneme – phonemes, for Sapir, unlike many descriptive linguists, were not artificial, abstract products of a distributional analysis of sound-segments but psychological realities in the minds of speakers which it is the linguist's task to discover.

In 1923 Sapir read a book that had a profound impact on his thinking about language: *The Meaning of Meaning* (1923) by C. K. Ogden and I. A. Richards. Drawing on a number of sources, including the Cambridge analytic philosophers (Russell, Whitehead, Wittgenstein), Ogden and Richards argued that language has a shaping influence on thought, of a largely negative character, preventing thought from being logical by setting metaphysical traps that have been encoded in the language for generations. As we have seen, Sapir (1921) had suggested that our language creates 'thought-grooves' which guide our thinking. But it did not occur to him before reading Ogden and Richards that these thought-grooves might be an obstacle to logical thought, and that linguistics might contribute to its removal. The idea recurs in his writings from 1924 on that the scientific status of linguistics rests upon its ability to show the rest of the human sciences their way around the traps of language.

> Human beings do not live in the objective world alone, nor alone in the world of social activity as ordinarily understood, but are very much at the mercy of the particular language which has become the medium of expression for their society. It is quite an illusion to imagine that one adjusts to reality essentially without the use of language and that language is merely an incidental means of solving specific problems of communication or reflection. The fact of the matter is that the 'real' world is to a large extent unconsciously built up on the language habits of the group. No two languages are ever sufficiently similar to be considered as representing the same social reality. The worlds in which different societies live are distinct worlds, not merely the same world with different labels attached. . . . We see and hear and otherwise experience very largely as we do because the language habits of our community predispose certain choices of interpretation.
> . . . From this standpoint we may think of language as the symbolic guide to culture.
>
> (Sapir 1949: 162)

. . . [A]s our scientific experience grows we must learn to fight the implications of language. 'The grass waves in the wind' is shown by its linguistic form to be a member of the same relational class of experiences as 'The man works in the house'. As an interim solution of the problem of expressing the experience referred to in this sentence it is clear that the language has proved useful, for it has made significant use of certain symbols of conceptual relation, such as agency and location. If we feel the sentence to be poetic or metaphorical, it is largely because other more complex types of experience with their appropriate symbolisms of reference enable us to reinterpret the situation and to say, for instance, 'The grass is waved by the wind' or 'The wind causes the grass to wave'. The point is that no matter how sophisticated our modes of interpretation become, we never really get beyond the projection and continuous transfer of relations suggested by the forms of our speech . . . Language is at one and the same time helping and retarding us in our exploration of experience.

(Sapir 1949: 10–11)

The new perspective on the influence of language on thought that Ogden and Richards revealed to Sapir – i.e. that it is a *problem* – provided him with a way out of the dilemma discussed earlier in connection with his 1921 book, where he wanted to describe language as 'cultural' but worried about the Romantic associations that might be read into that. Treating language as a source of metaphysical traps was a modern philosophical approach which eliminated the danger that Sapir might be read as implying an association between 'great' cultures and the classical Western languages, *à la* Herder and Humboldt.

Sapir (1921) had raised the question whether thought is possible without speech (for 'speech' in this context read 'language'). This is a question, he says, that has been plagued by misunderstandings. First, whether or not thought requires speech, speech does not necessarily require thought: someone who says 'I had a good breakfast this morning' is probably not 'in the throes of laborious thought'; he or she is doing no more than transmitting 'a pleasurable memory symbolically rendered in the grooves of habitual expression'. In such a case it is 'somewhat as though a dynamo capable of generating enough power to run an elevator were operated . . . to feed an electric doorbell'. In this view, thought is the 'highest latent or potential content of speech, the content that is obtained by interpreting each of the elements in the flow of language as possessed of its very fullest conceptual value' (Sapir 1921: 14); and this potential is, on most occasions of speech, neither attained nor aspired to. Language is 'an instrument originally put to uses lower than the conceptual plane', and 'thought arises as a refined interpretation of its content' (Sapir 1921: 15). Thus, language does not necessarily embody thought, but thought is an outgrowth from language.

Thus stated, Sapir's case may appear vulnerable to a contrary idea, on the face of it at least as plausible, which may be most simply stated by claiming that, when someone speaks, the words used (unless he or she happens to be talking about words themselves) must be determined by something that is not words. As a recent champion of this view rhetorically puts it: 'when I say something (or think or say words in my head), what is it that decides what I say? Why do I say "duck" and not "tiger"? What "chooses" that particular word? It is my thought, in this case the picture in my head of a duck' (Gethin 1990: 195). Furthermore, Gethin continues, the thing that 'decides what I say' may occasionally be stumped for a word altogether. One often thinks about things that one does not know the word for. 'There must be quite a few people, for instance, who have thought about the thing that has the word *pelmet* associated with it, without knowing that word' (Gethin 1990: 195).

Sapir's response to this line of argument rests on his somewhat rarefied conception of 'thought'. We must, he says, distinguish between imagery and thought: what precedes speech, in the kind of case Gethin mentions, is not thought but an image. Sapir concedes that images, in themselves, are or may be pre-linguistic, but when we start to perform mental operations on images, words ineluctably come into play: 'no sooner do we try to put an image into conscious relation with another than we find ourselves slipping into a silent flow of words' (Sapir 1921: 15). Here we come up against a fundamental difficulty bedevilling any attempt to assess Sapir's views on language and thought: the slipperiness of the concept 'thought' itself.

A rather different claim commonly made by those who believe that thought is independent of language is that there are modes of reasoning – demanding, in their highest manifestations, all the power the mental dynamo is capable of generating – that are not inherently tied to language at all. Musical and mathematical thought are examples, and the case can be bolstered by citing the testimony of practitioners themselves. 'The physicists Einstein and Sakharov', Gethin declares, 'have both said that in their work they did not think in language' (Gethin 1990: 198). Given that Sapir was himself an accomplished musician, it is odd that he does not appear to have addressed this point directly; and it is difficult to reconstruct from what he does say an altogether convincing Sapirian response to it. It is clear enough, however, that 'thought', for Sapir, has to do with concepts; and it may be that a 'concept' is to be understood as something intrinsically verbal. In which case it begins to look as though the case for the language-dependence of thought is being made, at least in part, by definitional fiat.

However well or badly Sapir makes it, the case that thought depends on language in general (*langage*) is no more than a pre-requisite for what would come to be known as the Sapir–Whorf hypothesis, which, roughly speaking, is that thought depends on the particular language (*langue*) that one speaks. That Sapir's profound knowledge of languages structurally very different from his own led him to believe this too is evident from passages such as the following:

> Language ... not only refers to experience largely acquired without its help but actually defines experience for us by reason of its formal completeness and because of our uncon-scious projection of its implicit expectations into the field of experience ... Such categories as number, gender, case, tense ... are not so much discovered in experience as imposed upon it because of the tyrannical hold that linguistic form has upon our orientation in the world.
>
> (Sapir 1931: 578)

But it was left to Sapir's student Benjamin Lee Whorf to develop this idea into something approaching a systematic doctrine (see Chapter 4 below).

For Sapir himself, his new perspective on language and thought gave rise to a new tension. If it is the case that 'we see and hear and otherwise experience very largely as we do because the language habits of our community predispose certain choices of interpretation', then how is it that speakers of the same language do not all think exactly alike? How is *individuality* possible?

Already in 1917 Sapir had become engaged in a debate in the journal *American Anthropologist* with another Boas-trained anthropologist, Alfred L. Kroeber (1876–1960), over an article Kroeber had written on the 'superorganic' nature of culture. By this Kroeber meant that culture is something detached from the physical ('organic') reality of the individuals who make it up. To Sapir (who seems to have read more into Kroeber's term than Kroeber intended) this was unacceptable, because it denied that in the final analysis cultures are produced by individuals, ordinary as well as extraordinary ones, and that individuals, society and culture are not distinct entities but different aspects of the same entity. A recent reconstruction of Sapir's May 1934 lecture on t his topic (based on students' notes, but with the editor's additions in brackets) shows that this remained a concern throughout his career:

> [I have said on several occasions that one must begin] with a study of the cultural patterns in the individual's milieu. [No matter how interested we may be in individuals in their own right, we must not forget that] the individual in isolation from society is a psychological fiction ... On the other hand, the personality needs culture in order to give it its fullest meanings. It is the culture of the group that gives the meanings to symbolisms without which the individual cannot function, either in relation to himself or to others.
>
> From one point of view, however, culture is the agreed-upon ghost in the [machine], that catches up the individual and moulds him according to a predetermined form and style. [This is the view of culture as the] impersonal, pageant-like 'superorganic', as Kroeber [termed it and against which I have engaged in some] polemic. Culture, like truth, is what we make it. [It does not seem to me necessary or suitable to construct as unbridgeable a chasm between individual and culture as there seems to be between the organic and the social.] Social science is not psychology, not because it studies the resultants of a superpsychic or superorganic force, but because its terms are differently demarcated.
>
> (Sapir 1994: 244–5; the last sentence
quoted from Sapir 1917)

What Sapir is arguing against above all is any attempt to *reduce* human behaviour to any single level of analysis, be it the individual, the social or the cultural. Yet how exactly to combine these various perspectives was (and remains) the rub.

Sapir's *Language* confines discussion of linguistic individuality to degrees of variation from a prototypical norm:

> This means that there is something like an ideal linguistic entity dominating the speech habits of the members of each group, that the sense of almost unlimited freedom which each individual feels in the use of his language is held in leash by a tacitly directing norm. One individual plays on the norm in a way peculiar to himself, the next individual is nearer the dead average in that particular respect in which the first speaker most characteristically departs from it but in turn diverges from the average in a way peculiar to himself, and so on . . . If all the speakers of a given dialect were arranged in order in accordance with the degree of their conformity to average usage, there is little doubt that they would constitute a very finely intergrading series clustered about a well-defined centre or norm.
>
> (Sapir 1921: 158)

That norm is understood by Sapir to be continuous with, or projected from, the individuals who make it up. But from the mid-1920s Sapir's anthropological and linguistic writings came to focus less on individuals and more directly on *personality* as a necessary dimension in the understanding of human experience. In a 1933 encyclopaedia article which would be his last general statement about language, he wrote about both its power as a social force and its role in the shaping of individual personality:

> Language is a great force of socialization, possibly the greatest that exists. By this is meant not merely the obvious fact that significant social intercourse is hardly possible without language, but that the mere fact of a common speech serves as a peculiarly potent symbol of the social solidarity of those who speak the language. The psychological significance of this goes far beyond the association of particular languages with nationalities, political entities, or smaller social groups . . .

In spite of the fact that language acts as a socializing and uniformizing force, it is at the same time the most potent single known factor in the growth of individuality. The fundamental quality of one's voice, the phonetic patterns of speech, the speed and relative smoothness of articulation, the length and build of the sentences, the character and range of the vocabulary, the scholastic consistency of the words used, the readiness with which words respond to the requirements of the social environment, in particular the suitability of one's language to the language habits of the person addressed – all these are so many complex indicators of the personality. All in all, it is not too much to say that one of the really important functions of language is to be constantly declaring to society the psychological place held by all of its members.

(Sapir 1933: 15–18)

Sapir died in 1939 before finishing a single one of the series of books he had projected which would put forward his mature vision of language, culture and personality. The recently published compilation of his lectures on the subject of one of those proposed books, *The Psychology of Cultures* (Sapir 1994), makes it appear that he never managed to find a satisfactory framework for scientific inquiry in his nexus of universal, culture-specific and individualistic psychological perspectives, which include the following:

- the structures of languages are real, and exist in the psychology of speakers;
- as a result, all languages have certain universal characteristics by virtue of being psychological realities for their speakers;
- the structure of a person's language shapes the way he or she thinks; therefore;
- cultures that share a language share a way of thinking, which constitutes the psychology of the culture;
- cultures are constituted not by physical attributes but by symbolic values, i.e. meanings;
- cultural unity of language and thought notwithstanding, individual variation in language serves to establish personality, which is one aspect of individual psychology.

Sapir's approach to language did not permit reduction of linguistic phenomena to some simple formula or principle of analysis. It demanded a readiness to appreciate language within culture, conceived both socially and personally, in the richness of all its aspects. Predictably perhaps, Leonard Bloomfield's (1887–1949) rather more streamlined approach to a knowledge of language quite detached from culture appealed to more students of linguistics than Sapir's did during the quarter century between Sapir's death and the ascent of Chomsky (see Chapter 9 below).

It must also be recognized that Sapir's views presented problems and contradictions that he never clearly sorted out. First, if the reality of language structure lies with the speaker rather than the linguist, what about cases where speakers seem by all the evidence to misanalyse or misunderstand some aspect of their own linguistic usage? Are we to say that the speaker's intuition is never faulty? Second, if the value of all cultures is purely relative, how do we justify the activities of anthropology and linguistics, which after all engage in a form of 'scientific' analysis that is historically the product of a particular group of cultures and whose special value has been established in conjunction with the political hegemony of those cultures? Third, the idea that the structure of our language shapes the way we think might be more convincing if 'languages' existed in some uniform state, where words and grammatical features had exactly the same meaning for all speakers. We know this is not so, if only from the everyday experience of arguing about the meanings of particular words. If each of us has to construct meanings for our language, can it also be true that our language is transmitting some kind of overarching structure of meaning to us which a linguistic 'world-view' would represent? Fourth, although Sapir viewed language, culture and personality as existing simultaneously and continuously on the universal, social and individual planes, he never renounced the general ideology of scientific analysis which demands that those planes be separated. He thus made it difficult for those who wished to continue his work to produce 'knowledge' of language and cultures that met general scientific strictures in the fields as they stood after his death. Granted that he could not have been expected to bring about a scientific revolution single-handed, might he not have sought a way out of the universal, social/cultural and individual/personal levels themselves, which represent somewhat artificial and certainly culturally loaded distinctions?

Sapir's interest in the individual psychology of language, minus the cultural aspects, *seems* to have been resurrected by Chomsky, who defines his object of study as the individual's internal knowledge of language. But the individual in whom Chomsky is interested is an 'ideal speaker-listener' (see Chapter 9 below), who being idealized is not invested with personhood but corresponds in effect to the traditional notion of the language community. Furthermore, in Chomsky's 'modular' conception of the mind, the language faculty is autonomous, which is to say that it does not interact with other cognitive faculties, including those presumably responsible for the factors of personality that Sapir believed were intimately bound up with language. So while Chomsky appears to share with Sapir an interest in language and mind, the mind as Chomsky conceives it is not something in which the processes that intrigued Sapir could be imagined to take place.

Alongside Chomsky's linguistics there have, however, continued various strains of anthropological linguistics, still based essentially on the methods developed by Boas, Sapir and their students. Even during the height of Bloomfield's popularity in the 1940s to mid-1960s, anthropological linguists tended to look to Sapir as their hero because of his powerful advocacy of the link between language and culture. Today, Sapir is the one who speaks more directly to readers, whether their interests lie in the study of language and mind or in language embedded in culture. The research programme in the ethnography of communication (see Chapter 11 below) has been formed directly round the language–culture complex, as Sapir defined it. 'Constructionist' approaches to language acquisition, which focus on how the child's language-learning environment interacts with his or her mental 'hardware', have found much common ground with 'cognitive linguistics', which is founded on the interplay between language structure and mental structure, very much in the enduring spirit of Sapir. Furthermore, Sapir's view that the reality of the phoneme lies with the speaker's judgement rather than with the linguist's analysis anticipates by decades developments in post-structuralist anthropology.

As already noted, it was Whorf who would develop Sapir's ideas on how language shapes thought and culture into what became known as the 'Sapir–Whorf hypothesis'. This was not something Sapir himself ever set about investigating; for him it was above all an argument for the importance of linguistics to the other human sciences, starting with anthropology. That it has become the idea with which his name is now most widely associated is unfortunate, in that for Sapir an essential fact about language is that its capacity for shaping societies and cultures is counterbalanced by its intricate role as producer and product of individual psychology and personality.

Chapter 2

Jakobson and structuralism

[W]e discern a rigid REGULARITY in the succession of [the child's] acquisitions, which constitute for the most part a strict and invariable temporal sequence. It has been nearly a century now that this regularity has impressed observers: whether it is a question of French or English children, Scandinavian or Slavic, German or Japanese, Estonian or New Mexican Indian, every careful linguistic description provides equal confirmation of the fact that the RELATIVE CHRONOLOGY of certain innovations remains always and everywhere the same . . .

Ordinarily the vowel system originates in a wide vowel and the consonant system simultaneously in a stop with occlusion at the front of the mouth; usually the vowel is *A* and the consonant is a labial stop. The first opposition within the consonantal system is between nasal and oral, and the second between labials and dentals (*P–T*, *M–N*).

These two oppositions constitute the MINIMAL CONSONANTAL SYSTEM of all the languages of the world.

(Jakobson 1971: 9–10)

The Russian linguist Sergei Karcevski (1884–1955) was among the small audience for Ferdinand de Saussure's (1857–1913) lectures on general linguistics at the University of Geneva (see Volume I, Chapter 16). He returned to Moscow in 1917 and transmitted Saussure's ideas to the members of the Moscow Linguistic Circle, founded two years previously by a nineteen-year-old polymath named Roman Jakobson (1896–1982). With his boundless interests in historical linguistics, folklore and literature, Jakobson stood at the centre of a general 'formalist' movement (as it was dubbed by its critics) embracing the analysis of poetry, art and music as well as their creation. The best-known member of the movement was the poet Vladimir Mayakovsky (1893–1930). After the Russian Revolution, Jakobson went to Czechoslovakia in the employ of the Soviet government. A brief portrait of him from this period could in fact have come from any decade of his long life:

> I think it was in September 1923 that a friend of Mayakovsky arrived in Berlin from Prague. This was red-haired Romka – the linguist Roman Osipovich Yakobson, who worked at the Soviet Representation. Roman was pink faced and blue-eyed, with a squint in one eye; he drank a great deal but his head remained clear, and only after the tenth glass would he button his coat the wrong way. What struck me was that he knew everything: the structure of Khlebnikov's verse, old Czech literature, Rimbaud, the machinations of Curzon and Ramsay MacDonald. Occasionally he made things up, but when anyone tried to catch him out in an inaccuracy, he replied with a grin: 'That was just a working hypothesis of mine'.
>
> (Ehrenburg 1963: 60)

Saussure's impact on Jakobson's thinking would soon become apparent. From 1926 to 1938 he and his principal collaborator, Prince Nikolai Trubetzkoy (1890–1938), who like all royalty had been obliged to flee Soviet Russia, took part in the work of the Prague Linguistic Circle. Jakobson especially exercised an intellectual influence over the Circle's mostly Czech members. Jakobson and Trubetzkoy took inspiration from Saussure's conception of language as a totally self-contained system of elements that functioned purely through their difference from one another, without regard to their phonetic substance. Trubetzkoy undertook to analyse in this way the sound systems of all the world's languages on which he could get adequate information, while Jakobson tried to reconceive the historical development of phonological systems in the light of Saussure's views, as well as drawing out their implications for the study of poetics.

However, by 1930 it would become clear that neither Jakobson nor Trubetzkoy could stay with Saussurean orthodoxy in the analysis of sound systems. Their work suggested, contrary to what Saussure's *Cours* (Saussure 1916) maintains, that the relationships holding among all elements of the linguistic system are not of precisely the same nature. For example, the consonants /t/, /d/, and /f/ are distinctive phonemes in most languages, since they function to distinguish meanings (*tin* versus *din* versus *fin*). Yet it seems obvious that /t/ and /d/ have a closer relationship to one another than either has to /f/. In /t/ and /d/ the vocal organs perform essentially the same action in the same position, except that in /d/ the vocal cords vibrate. In many languages, Jakobson and Trubetzkoy noted, the distinction between /t/ and /d/, and between other pairs of voiced and unvoiced consonants, is 'neutralized' at the end of a syllable or word. Thus the German genitive (possessive) noun *Rades* 'wheel's' has as its nominative (subject) form *Rad*, pronounced not *[rad], but [rat], the same as *Rat* 'council'.

Again, the possibility of such a deeper connection contradicts the Saussurean view that the phonetic substance of /t/ and /d/ is inconsequential, and all that matters is the fact that they differ in some perceptible way. Jakobson and Trubetzkoy proposed the term 'correlation' for the type of relationship holding between /t/ and /d/. Any pair of elements which do not exist in a correlation, such as /d/ and /f/, form instead a 'disjunction'.

As their work progressed, a new perspective developed. They realized that the correlation /t/–/d/ consists of a core of features common to the two sounds, plus a distinguishing element, namely vocal cord vibration (voicing). They created the term 'archiphoneme' for the core of features common to /t/ and /d/ (symbolized /T/). They could then specify that the alternation between German *Rades* and *Rad* does not involve simply a change of phonemes; it is a realization of the same archiphoneme, but with the distinguishing element deleted in word-final position.

On 31 July 1930, while Trubetzkoy was on holiday in France, he wrote to Jakobson with some new reflections on the typology of phonological oppositions which the two had developed over the preceding years. He proposed that certain elements in the linguistic system have an interrelationship that is neither arbitrary nor purely formal, but defined by the fact that one element is distinguished from the other through the addition of an extra feature, a *mark*. When the distinction is neutralized it is always the simple, 'unmarked' member of the opposition that appears. Thus the minimal contrast between the genitive nouns *Rates* 'council's' and *Rades* 'wheel's' is neutralized in the nominative, where, as noted above, both *Rat* 'council' and *Rad* 'wheel' are pronounced with a final /t/ – the unmarked member of the pair.

The 'mark' in this case is the vibration of the vocal cords that differentiates /d/ from /t/, making /d/ the more 'complex' member of the correlation.

Because simplicity as here understood includes the physical elements of articulation and sound, markedness undoes the key Saussurean tenet that language is form, not substance. Trubetzkoy wrote to Jakobson almost casually mentioning the idea. Jakobson immediately saw its broader implications.

> I am coming increasingly to the conviction that your thought about correlation as a constant mutual connection between a marked and unmarked type is one of your most remarkable and fruitful ideas. It seems to me that it has a significance not only for linguistics but also for ethnology and the history of culture, and that such historico-cultural correlations as life ~ death, liberty ~ non-liberty, sin ~ virtue, holidays ~ working days, etc., are always confined to relations a ~ non-a, and that it is important to find out for any epoch, group, nation, etc., what the marked element is. For instance, Majakovskij viewed life as a marked element realizable only when motivated; for him not death but life required a motivation . . . At present in Soviet print there has emerged a slogan; they used to say that 'all those who are not against us are with us', but now they say 'all those who are not with us are against us' . . . I'm convinced that many ethnographic phenomena, ideologies, etc. which at first glance seem to be identical, often differ only in the fact that what for one system is a marked term may be evaluated by the other precisely as the absence of a mark.
>
> (Letter from Jakobson to Trubetzkoy, 26 November 1930, translated in Jakobson and Waugh 1979: 90–1)

This reply moved far beyond Trubetzkoy's modest proposal, to foresee developments in the analysis of literature and culture that would not come to fruition for another two to three decades. But already in 1939 an important paper of Jakobson's on 'The sound laws of child language and their place in general phonology' (Jakobson 1971) convinced many linguists that the new 'hierarchical structuralism' envisaged by him and Trubetzkoy laid the grounds for a unified theory explaining the facts not only of language structure but of linguistic history and typology, the acquisition of language, and its loss when damage occurs to the brain.

Jakobson proposed that a universal hierarchy of sounds was valid across all the languages of the world. This hierarchy could be interpreted in terms of markedness, the vowel /a/ being the maximally unmarked sound. This made sense in terms of articulation, since /a/ is the sound produced with the least amount of closure in the vocal passage. Every degree of closure added to it, whether by raising the tongue to produce a different vowel or by using the lips, tongue or larynx to produce a consonant, could be understood as an articulatory mark superimposed upon the basic sound to create a distinction. The highest degree of distinctiveness was produced by the very first mark acquired by children, the one producing the opposition between /a/ and a labial stop consonant, /p/, /b/ or /m/. Hence the near universal occurrence of words such as *mama*, *papa* and *baba* for denoting the most important beings in the infant's world.

Others had tried to explain the occurrence of these words across languages by invoking a 'principle of least effort' according to which /a/, /m/, /p/ and /b/ are the easiest sounds to produce. But as Jakobson pointed out, in the babbling stage that precedes the production of words, children produce *all* the sounds of all the world's languages, which means that no sound is actually beyond them in articulatory terms. What makes certain sounds 'easier' and others 'harder' to master must therefore lie not in the tongue but in the mind, and specifically in the ease or difficulty with which the mind perceives distinctions among sounds. 'The phonological sequence of stages . . . is rigorously consistent. It follows the principle of MAXIMAL CONTRAST, and it proceeds, in the ordering of oppositions, from the SIMPLE and homogeneous to the COMPLEX and differentiated' (Jakobson 1971: 14). Jakobson noted further that the place of a particular sound in the universal order of phonological acquisition by children corresponded exactly with its degree of distribution among the languages of the world.

> Thus, in the child's phonemic system the acquisition of velar and palatal consonants implies that of labials and dentals, and in the languages of the world the presence of palato-velars implies the simultaneous existence of labials and dentals. This solidarity is irreversible: the presence of labials and dentals does not imply the presence of palato-velars as can be shown, for example, by the total absence of the latter in Tahitian and in the Tatar language of Kasimov . . .

The child's acquisition of fricatives presupposes that of stops, and similarly in the phonological systems of the world's languages the existence of the former implies that of the latter. There are no languages without stops, but on the other hand one finds many languages in Oceania, Africa, and South America without a single fricative.

(Jakobson 1971: 11)

The reason, again, is that labials (p, b, m) and dentals (t, d, n) are more distinctive to the ear than are palatals (ʃ, ʧ) or velars (k, g, ŋ). Stops (p, b, t, d) involve complete closure of the vocal tract, while fricatives (f, v, s, z) involve only partial closure, making them less distinctive from vowels, where there is no closure. Children master strong distinctions before weaker ones. In all languages, successive generations of children will have mastered those distinctions which are universally strongest, while the weaker distinctions will have been taken on in some languages but not others.

Moreover, the 'unmarked' sounds which make up the strong, fundamental distinctions will be less susceptible to change over time than the 'marked' sounds, which are relatively unstable in historical terms. For an individual who loses language in aphasia, sounds will be lost in the reverse order from the one in which they are acquired: the marked sounds are the most susceptible to loss, the unmarked sounds the most likely to endure.

What remains decisive in the correspondence between child language and the languages of the world is exclusively THE IDENTITY OF THE STRUCTURAL LAWS which underlie every modification of language, individual and social. It is, in other words, the same invariable superposition of values which is at the basis of every growth and decline in a phonological system.

(Jakobson 1971: 13)

It is worth assessing at this point how much continuity exists between Saussure and Jakobson, and how far Jakobson's structuralism diverges from Saussure. The key continuity lies in the conception of languages as systems of signs that operate through their distinctiveness from one another. But Saussure imagined this distinctiveness as consisting of 'pure difference', so that no essential change would be made to the language system if, for example, all the dentals were switched with the velars. *A king took out his dagger* is signalled just as effectively by *A tin koot ouk his gadder*, so long as the switch was done in a completely systematic way. Jakobson's perspective, however, would induce us to consider such a remade system as an 'unnatural' language, since it will have reversed the universal order in which classes of sounds are acquired and distributed. While for Saussure language is form, not substance, Jakobson argues that form is inseparable from substance.

Obsessed, despite his searching fervor, by that fear of purposiveness which characterized the decline of the past century, F. de Saussure taught as follows: 'Contrary to the false idea which we like to foist on language, the latter is not a mechanism created and aimed to express concepts'. Now, however, we are in a position to reply to the devastating hypercriticism of the previous era, that it is precisely common sense, and in particular the idea which as talking beings intuitively have about language, is the most realistic: language is indeed a tool regulated and aimed to express concepts. It efficiently masters the sound matter and transforms these physical objects into oppositive attributes capable of bearing meaning. One of the proofs for this statement are the rules of phonological structure sketched above.

(Jakobson 1971: 20)

The remark about 'fear of purposiveness' seems strange in reference to a time when Darwinian evolution was in the process of becoming the dominant scientific paradigm, but Jakobson was thinking particularly of theories of language change. In the last quarter of the nineteenth century the study of language was dominated by the 'neogrammarians' of Leipzig, Saussure's teachers, who, as Viel (1984: 39n) has put it, occupied the first rank in Jakobson's personal 'demonology'. They took the firm position that the sound changes that occur over the history of a language follow their own internal laws, impervious to any considerations of the 'functional' sort Jakobson is putting forward here (see Volume I, Chapter 14). But, contrary to what Jakobson implies, it did not take half a century of further discoveries to put us 'in a position to reply to' the neogrammarians. Their view and

Jakobson's represent two sides of an argument that has been going on since antiquity, over whether the shape of languages is controlled and determined by something external to them, or is the accidental product of a series of wilful human actions.

This was in fact one of the questions at the heart of Plato's *Cratylus* (Plato 1995; see Volume I, Chapter 1). When Jakobson declares above that 'language is indeed a tool regulated and aimed to express concepts', he is saying essentially the same thing as Socrates (Plato 1995: 388b13): 'A word, then, is an instrument for teaching about something, and for distinguishing among realities, just as a shuttle does with the woven cloth'.

> SOCRATES: Having discovered the instrument naturally suited to a particular purpose, one must render it out of the material one is working with, not in whatever way one wishes, but in the natural way. It is as though one must know how to put into iron the drill naturally suited to each particular job.
>
> HERMOGENES: Of course.
>
> SOC.: And into the wood the shuttle naturally suited to each job.
>
> HERM.: That's right.
>
> SOC.: Because by nature there seems to be a particular shuttle for each particular type of cloth, and likewise for the other things.
>
> HERM.: Yes.
>
> SOC.: Well then, my good friend, isn't there also a word suited by nature for each thing, which the lawgiver must know how to put into sounds and syllables? . . .
>
> HERM.: Of course.
>
> (Plato 1995: 389c4–390a4)

Unlike Socrates and Plato, Jakobson does not believe that languages are the work of 'lawgivers', but instead takes them, as the neogrammarians did, to be the product of a continuous evolution extending backward into prehistory all the way to the beginning of humankind. Now, if one imagines a lawgiver (or any other rational individual, human or divine) purposely fashioning a language, there is little problem in ascribing to him or her the intentions Socrates does. If on the other hand one imagines language as the product of an infinite evolutionary regress starting from a stage prior to the development of the sort of rational thought that already requires language as a prerequisite, then there is little problem in picturing it as a neogrammarian-style series of blind accidents.

What Jakobson wants us to believe in, however, is conceptually much more difficult: evolution without rational intent but nevertheless with a functional purpose. The very fact that language exists in order to represent concepts would impose precise and universal limits on the shape it can take. It is something like the 'invisible hand' in Adam Smith's theory of economics.

Another problem for Jakobson was Saussure's principled separation of linguistic diachrony (history) from synchrony (the operation of the system at a given point in time). How could this be reconciled with Jakobson's belief that the functional development of language over time was the key to understanding its present shape? The notion of the mark offered a resolution. Saussure's *Cours* (Saussure 1916) identified the arbitrariness of the link between signifier (sound pattern) and signified (conceptual meaning) as the first principle of the linguistic sign. But it went on to point out that this arbitrariness was significantly limited by the 'relative motivation' within many signs, one of his examples being the French word for the number 19, *dix-neuf* (literally 'ten-nine'), which he noted is not arbitrary in the same way as is the word for 20, *vingt*, since the latter cannot be broken down into any smaller units. Moreover, Saussure maintained that, however arbitrary most linguistic signs may be, the link between signifier and signified is maintained in such a strong form by the *social* nature of language that no one can change it. In normal usage, designating something as 'arbitrary' is a statement about its past – that it took the form it did without motivation – and an opinion about its future, that there is no obstacle in principle to changing it. Saussure's arbitrariness principle, however, applies to linguistic signs whether they are 'relatively motivated' or not, and declares them immutable. It thus denies them both a past and a future, and treats them strictly 'synchronically', in line with the avowed purpose of Saussure's programme.

The mark allowed Jakobson to reintegrate history into the synchronic analysis of the linguistic signifier. The position of a sound on the markedness hierarchy determines not only its present value but its past history and its future stability. Jakobson did not restrict this type of analysis to sounds; already by 1932 he was extending the idea of the mark to morphology, to suggest for example that the reason a plural noun such as *doctors* or a possessive such as *doctor's* is phonologically longer, hence more complex, than the corresponding singular non-possessive *doctor*, is that the latter is *conceptually* simpler. This conceptual simplicity (or unmarkedness) is signalled 'iconically' at the level of sound. Jakobson came to believe that such iconicity is a general principle running through all languages. It means that signifiers are not as arbitrarily connected to signifieds as Saussure had suggested. Rather, *parallelism* between form and meaning is the hidden principle structuring language.

Jakobson's 1939 paper on child language (listed in the bibliography as Jakobson 1971) was written while in flight from the Nazis, whom he had numerous reasons to fear, starting with the fact of his Jewish birth. In 1941 he sailed for America, where he spent the rest of his life. At the start of 1942 he gave two courses on Saussure at the École Libre des Hautes Études organized in New York by fellow refugees. His audience included one of his fellow teachers in the École, the French ethnologist Claude Lévi-Strauss (b. 1908), who previously knew Saussure's *Cours* (Saussure 1916) only superficially (see Lévi-Strauss's preface to Jakobson 1978). In the wake of Jakobson's inspiring presentation of Saussurean theory, including his revolutionary modifications to it, Lévi-Strauss reformulated his approach to ethnology on 'structuralist' grounds. This led to the development in the 1950s of a general intellectual movement of structuralism in France, embracing literary studies and all the 'human sciences', and recognizing Jakobson and particularly Saussure as its founding figures (see Chapter 13 below).

Jakobson's impact on American linguistics would be no less profound. After the war he taught first at Columbia University, then at Harvard, where in the early 1950s he befriended the young Noam Chomsky. Jakobson's belief in universal hierarchies across all the languages of the world laid the groundwork for Chomsky's assertion of an innate 'universal grammar' (see Chapter 9 below). Jakobson's and Trubetzkoy's 'theory of markedness' (as it was renamed in Chomsky and Halle's 1968 *The Sound Pattern of English*, dedicated to Jakobson) not only became the basis for the versions of phonological and syntactic analysis developed at MIT in the 1970s and since, but has also been at the heart of the search for language universals launched by Joseph H. Greenberg (b. 1915) in the early 1960s, work that continues to be carried on with illuminating results.

More recently, Optimality Theory, or OT, which had its origins in phonology, has been applied to virtually every aspect of the study of language. The thrust of OT is that innate universal grammar consists of a set of constraints, each of which can be violated and which are ranked differently in different languages. Even within a language, the constraints can be ranked differently for different speakers – this is the basis of the OT account of language variation. The constraints themselves are 'markedness statements' (Archangeli 1997: 17). Markedness is here defined in terms of the continuum between language-universal and language-specific properties, 'with completely unmarked properties being those found in virtually all languages and extremely marked properties being found quite rarely' (Archangeli 1997: 2).

The main obstacle faced by OT is the same one faced by every attempt to apply the idea of 'markedness' to the analysis of language. It is not clear that any linguistic phenomenon will pose a genuine problem for OT to explain; it is simply a matter of determining plausible constraints (preferably ones that are not ad hoc or language-specific) and ordering them so as to come out with the desired answer. A case that is unusual will turn out to be marked, one with analogues in numerous other languages will be unmarked. Although Jakobson was successful in tying the marked and the unmarked to mental and cerebral structure in a way that was satisfactory to many from the 1930s to the 1960s, our conceptions of those structures has complexified since then, and our 'mapping' of language structure to brain structure has not kept up, though it is making ever greater progress. Without a convincing grounding in something external to language itself, analyses based on the 'marked' and the 'unmarked' are vulnerable to charges of circularity and even vacuity.

Jakobson's exchange of letters with Trubetzkoy in 1930 marked the major turning point in twentieth-century European linguistics, from the kind of radically arbitrary structuralism called for by Saussure towards a new kind of structuralism grounded in the functional nature of the system itself – an idea whose metaphysical quality is at once its greatest attraction and shortcoming. It appeals to those linguists who want to believe that they are unlocking the secret architecture of the human mind, which perhaps mirrors that of the universe, while repelling those who regard unobservables as antithetical to science. Moreover, every attempt at 'universalist' explanation of language has proved in practice to require massive marginalizing of 'inconvenient' data – starting with facts about children's acquisition of phonology that do not follow Jakobson's universal hierarchy, and are carefully tucked away in the qualifiers that accompany all his assertions: 'we discern a rigid REGULARITY in the succession of [the child's] acquisitions, which constitute *for the most part* a strict and invariable temporal sequence' (italics added) (Jakobson 1971: 9). Here we can certainly catch Jakobson out in a rhetorical trick. The absurdity of this statement lies in its attempt to hold on to something 'rigid', 'strict' and 'invariable' in the universal analysis of child language acquisition, but to do it only 'for the most part'. One can formulate an 'invariable' rule about anything, so long as it needs to be applied only most of the time. One can almost hear Jakobson replying with his famous grin: 'That was just a working hypothesis of mine'.

Nevertheless, Jakobson deserves credit for recognizing and attempting to resolve the cognitive dissonance between the arbitrary and the natural as it existed in the programme for structuralism announced by Saussure's *Cours* (Saussure 1916). His resolution was unambiguously on the side of the natural, claiming that finally every linguistic structure, no matter how seemingly arbitrary, is somehow shaped or determined by the very purposes for which language has come into existence. The remaining problem is how to prove this is so in a way that does not ultimately depend on axiomatic declaration or logical circularity, defining the shape by the purpose and the purpose by the shape.

Chapter 3

Orwell on language and politics

Newspeak was the official language of Oceania and had been devised to meet the ideological needs of Ingsoc, or English Socialism . . . The purpose of Newspeak was not only to provide a medium of expression for the world-view and mental habits proper to the devotees of Ingsoc, but to make all other modes of thought impossible . . . This was done partly by the invention of new words, but chiefly by eliminating undesirable words and by stripping such words as remained of unorthodox meanings, and so far as possible of all secondary meanings whatever. To give a single example. The word *free* still existed in Newspeak, but it could only be used in such statements as 'This dog is free from lice' or 'This field is free from weeds'. It could not be used in its old sense of 'politically free' or 'intellectually free', since political and intellectual freedom no longer existed even as concepts, and were therefore of necessity nameless . . . Newspeak was designed not to extend but to *diminish* the range of thought, and this purpose was indirectly assisted by cutting the choice of words down to a minimum.

(Orwell 1949: 312–13)

George Orwell (1903–50) was born Eric Arthur Blair in Motihari, Bengal, where his father was an agent of the British colonial government's bureau for ensuring the purity of the opium it produced for export to China. Young Eric left for England in 1907 with his mother and older sister, a typical pattern for colonial families when the oldest child reached school age. In 1917 Eric won a scholarship to Eton, but did not subsequently win one for university. He decided to return to south Asia in 1922 to serve for five years with the Indian Imperial Police in Burma, an experience that left him strongly anti-imperialist.

He spent the late 1920s and the 1930s between England and the Continent, going to Spain in 1936 to fight for the Republican (leftist) side in the Civil War, and suffering a severe bullet wound in the throat. Before it was over he and other socialists found themselves in less danger from the Fascists they had gone to fight than from their communist 'allies', who accused them of being a Trotskyite Fifth Column secretly in league with the enemy, and ended up imprisoning and even executing many of them. Blair, his wife and a few companions narrowly escaped to France just as the communists were preparing to arrest them.

Between 1933 and 1941 Blair, writing under the pen-name George Orwell, published a book a year, including *Burmese Days* (Orwell 1934) and three other novels, mostly well received, plus five non-fiction books. Some of these earned him still greater acclaim than the novels, especially *The Road to Wigan Pier* (Orwell 1937), documenting the effects of mass unemployment and poor housing in northern England. The book was commissioned by Orwell's leftist publisher Victor Gollancz and selected for his Left Book Club, but so controversial were Orwell's critical assessments of socialist policies that Gollancz himself added a Preface apologizing to readers and disowning Orwell's arguments. When, a year later, Orwell completed *Homage to Catalonia* (Orwell 1938), recounting his experiences in the Spanish Civil War, including his persecution by his communist 'allies', he had to find another publisher.

During the Second World War he wrote profusely for newspapers and journals, was literary editor of a national paper and worked for the BBC Eastern Service, broadcasting by shortwave to India. Although he never again wrote a traditional novel, it was the two fictional works he published after the war, *Animal Farm* (Orwell 1945) and *Nineteen Eighty-Four* (1949), that secured him a unique and enduring status as one of the most powerful voices in world literature of his or any other century. Both are devastating satirical portraits of totalitarian regimes. Even though Orwell never ceased to identify himself as a leftist, the direct target of his critiques was the Stalinist government of the USSR. This was at a time when Western socialists still tended to act as apologists for Stalin in spite of abundant evidence of his ruthless tyranny, which Orwell had had a taste of in Spain.

Leftist faith in the USSR required an idealism alien to Orwell, who had the critical eye of a realist and the deep sensibilities of a traditional, Millsian liberal. Whatever system would allow people the greatest freedom to do and think as they pleased would have his support. While he continued to hope that disparities of wealth between the rich and poor might be limited, he was not willing to let tyranny be the price. A system like Stalin's, which was progressively lowering people's standard of living while claiming to do the opposite, was not truly 'socialist' at all, and even more dangerous than its economics were its attempts to distort and control the truth. In this it had a ready-made weapon at its disposal: language.

Orwell was not alone in the fear that language could be manipulated so as to control people's thoughts, while leaving them under the illusion that they were giving voice to their individual wills. Anxiety about propaganda was widespread in the years surrounding the two world wars. Perhaps, however, no one else saw so clearly how easy such mind control would be for *any* state to carry out and justify to itself. The potential lay within the principle of government itself, indeed within society itself, since even in an anarchic state one group would inevitably try to gain control over the others. Still, recent history had shown Orwell that the more radically a state aimed to perfect society, the more individual freedom of thought and action would necessarily be suppressed in the process.

In 1946, just after the phenomenal success of *Animal Farm* (Orwell 1945), Orwell published an essay on 'Politics and the English language' (Orwell 1946) in the prominent London literary review *Horizon*. Described as 'his most influential essay' by his biographer Michael Shelden (Shelden 1991: 430), it is interesting for the insight it offers into his process as a writer and stylist as well as in how it anticipates the core problem of language he would address so memorably in *Nineteen Eighty-Four* (Orwell 1949). Given that his satirical Newspeak is an engineered language, it may be surprising that the 1946 article opens with an earnest call for conscious action to engineer current English.

> Most people who bother with the matter at all would admit that the English language is in a bad way, but it is generally assumed that we cannot by conscious action do anything about it ... Underneath this lies the half-conscious belief that language is a natural growth and not an instrument which we shape for our own purposes.

... The point is that the process is reversible. Modern English, especially written English, is full of bad habits which spread by imitation and which can be avoided if one is willing to take the necessary trouble. If one gets rid of these habits one can think more clearly, and to think clearly is a necessary first step towards political regeneration.

(Orwell 1946: 252–3)

The linguistic 'bad habits' Orwell refers to, and the 'clear thinking' he opposes to it, have to do with what comes first in the mind of the speaker or writer, words or images. The healthy way is to start from mental pictures, then find words to describe them. For if one does the opposite, it is tempting to let the words string themselves together in well-worn patterns, which lets the words determine the meaning rather than the other way round.

[M]odern writing at its worst does not consist in picking out words for the sake of their meaning and inventing images in order to make the meaning clearer. It consists in gumming together long strips of words which have already been set in order by someone else, and making the results presentable by sheer humbug. The attraction of this way of writing is that it is easy.

(Orwell 1946: 259)

This invasion of one's mind by ready-made phrases ... can only be prevented if one is constantly on guard against them, and every such phrase anaesthetizes a portion of one's brain.

(Orwell 1946: 263)

On one level, Orwell's view is similar to the advice generally offered to students of musical composition. They are warned against working at the keyboard, where it is too easy to let their fingers do the composing by falling into familiar and comfortable patterns. Composing mentally is more likely to produce music that is original rather than derivative, and cerebral rather than emotional. Beyond this, however, Orwell is concerned about the fact that 'if thought corrupts language, language can also corrupt thought' (Orwell 1946: 262). If we begin from mental images, those images will be of *concrete* things, whereas starting from words is likelier to produce purely abstract thinking. Orwell, realist that he is, is not against abstract thinking *so long as it is grounded in observable reality*.

> When you think of a concrete object, you think wordlessly, and then, if you want to describe the thing you have been visualizing, you probably hunt about till you find the exact words that seem to fit it. When you think of something abstract you are more inclined to use words from the start . . . Probably it is better to put off using words as long as possible and get one's meaning as clear as one can through pictures or sensations.
>
> (Orwell 1946: 264)

This discussion has links with the long-standing Western philosophical debate about realism and nominalism – whether what words mean connects to things outside language or not. But where do the 'politics' come in? The answer is that this detachment of language from observable reality is what makes it possible for a political party to maintain an orthodoxy among its followers, and to dupe those whom it wishes to enslave. If the party manages to use language in a way that prevents concrete mental pictures from being called up, people will not understand what is happening to them, and they cannot rebel against what they do not understand.

> In our time it is broadly true that political writing is bad writing. Where it is not true, it will generally be found that the writer is some kind of rebel, expressing his private opinions and not a 'party line'. Orthodoxy, of whatever colour, seems to demand a lifeless, imitative style.
>
> (Orwell 1946: 260–1)

> In our time, political speech and writing are largely the defence of the indefensible . . . Such phraseology is needed if one wants to name things without calling up mental pictures of them.
>
> (Orwell 1946: 261–2)

The linguistic intervention Orwell calls for is not a restructuring of the language, just a change in how its elements are put to use. One should always start with thought rather than words, and with thought about what is concrete and empirically observable, and therefore verifiable. Then and only then can language hope to serve the interests of truth, rather than merely those of power.

Towards the end of the article he makes clear that his call for abstractions to be grounded is by no means to reject them entirely. On the contrary, too great a distrust of abstractions can have catastrophic political consequences of its own. 'Stuart Chase and others have come near to claiming that all abstract words are meaningless, and have used this as a pretext for advocating a kind of political quietism. Since you don't know what Fascism is, how can you struggle against Fascism?' (Orwell 1946: 265). Stuart Chase (1888–1985) was the author of *The Tyranny of Words* (Chase 1938), a widely read book that helped to popularize General Semantics, a movement concerned with how metaphysical traps encoded into language lead us into false modes of thought. The fact that Chase encouraged direct intervention into language use in order to produce clear thinking would seem to link him to Orwell's programme. But, as the preceding quotation suggests, Chase was *so* sceptical about abstract words as to delude himself that their 'tyranny' was more real than Hitler's. Early in his book he writes:

> Abstract terms are personified to become burning, fighting realities. Yet if the knowledge of semantics were general . . . the conflagration could hardly start . . .
>
> . . . Bad language is now the mightiest weapon in the arsenal of despots and demagogues. Witness Dr Goebbels. Indeed, it is doubtful if a people learned in semantics would tolerate any sort of supreme political dictator . . . A typical speech by an aspiring Hitler would be translated into its intrinsic meaning, if any. Abstract words and phrases without discoverable referents would register a semantic blank, noises without meaning. For instance:
>
>> The Aryan Fatherland, which has nursed the souls of heroes, calls upon you for the supreme sacrifice which you, in whom flows heroic blood, will not fail, and which will echo forever down the corridors of history.
>
> This would be translated:
>
>> The blab blab, which has nursed the blabs of blabs, calls upon you for the blab blab which you, in whom flows

blab blood, will not fail, and which will echo blab down the blabs of blab.

The 'blab' is not an attempt to be funny; it is a semantic blank. Nothing comes through. The hearer, versed in reducing high-order abstractions to either nil or a series of roughly similar events in the real world of experience, and protected from emotive associations with such words, simply hears nothing comprehensible. The demagogue might as well have used Sanskrit.

(Chase 1938: 14)

If Chase thought that 'Bad language is now the mightiest weapon in the arsenal of despots and demagogues', Orwell had a neck wound to remind him that the enormous military-industrial complexes Hitler and Stalin possessed were not so easily 'blabbed' away. Hitler's rhetoric and Goebbels's propaganda may have played a key role in the Nazi rise to power, but, now that the power was theirs to lose, the way to combat it was not to proclaim their abstractions empty. On the contrary, the urgent need was to show people how the use of abstract words by despots filled them with concrete and terrible meanings.

In Orwell's *Nineteen Eighty-Four* (Orwell 1949), Newspeak is the re-engineered English of Oceania, a country comprising the Americas, the Atlantic islands including the British Isles, Australasia and the southern portion of Africa. Oceania is perpetually at war with one of the world's other two countries, Eurasia and Eastasia. It is controlled by the Party, whose head, Big Brother, is a symbol rather than an actual person. There is an Inner Party of a privileged two per cent of the population; a larger Outer Party which does not enjoy anything like the same privileges; and the proles, the remaining eighty-five per cent whose lives have not changed radically since before the Revolution, except that in material terms they are considerably worse off. The mind control described in the opening quotation from the novel is directed almost entirely at the members of the Outer Party, and is enforced by the Thought Police, which the Inner Party controls. The proles are considered not worth bothering about.

The idea of re-engineering the English language by reducing its vocabulary had already been prominently put into practice by C. K. Ogden (1889–1957) (see Chapter 1 above). The chapter on definitions in *The Meaning of Meaning* (Ogden and Richards

1923), co-authored by Ogden and I. A. Richards (1893–1979), had led Ogden to formulate the idea of a 'Basic English' that would be capable of expressing anything with a vocabulary of just 850 words. Orwell was interested in Basic and wrote about it on a couple of occasions in the 1940s. The feature of Basic trumpeted most loudly by Ogden, the fact that it had done away with verbs, has a direct parallel in Newspeak (Orwell 1949: 165). Another feature of Basic, its replacement of certain negative adjectives by their positive counterpart preceded by un-, is exaggerated to the point of absurdity in Newspeak, where for example the equivalent of the Oldspeak form 'terrible' is *doubleplus ungood*.

Like the project for *The Meaning of Meaning* (Ogden and Richards 1923) from which it sprang, Basic was an attempt to solve a perceived crisis of meaning in the modern world. In Ogden's view, the First World War was itself the result of the misuse of complex abstract words such as *democracy* and *freedom* for purposes of propaganda, and any hope of future world peace depended upon the ability of thinking people to control the meanings of such words so that they could not be abused. *The Meaning of Meaning* opens with a long historical survey of attempts to do this, including the solution proposed by John Locke (1632–1704) (see Volume I, Chapter 10). Locke classified ideas into the simple and the complex, and among complex ideas he believed that those he called 'mixed modes', including all moral terms, were the likeliest to create misunderstanding – unless they were always carefully defined in terms of the simple ideas, derived from direct sensory experience, that combined to produce them. For essentially the same reason, Ogden believed that paring down the language to 850 words, a large portion of them referring to concrete substances, would make it virtually impossible to use language in such a way as to deceive people for propagandistic purposes.

But Orwell realized that it might actually have the opposite effect. Propaganda can be combated only by rational analysis and argument. This entails rephrasing propagandistic statements in a different form. If such rephrasing were made impossible through the loss of alternative words in which the same idea might be given a different linguistic shape, then it might no longer be possible to question the truth of any statement. Orwell made this into the precise aim of Newspeak: 'to make all other modes of thought impossible'. For instance, according to the Party, $2 + 2 = 5$. The hero of the novel, Winston Smith, realizes from the evidence of his own eyes that this is wrong, but the Party already has enough control over his thought and language that he cannot put together the argument he intuitively knows would prove its falsity. The same is true with the Party's operation for rewriting history, in which Winston himself is engaged, and indeed with its three slogans:

WAR IS PEACE

FREEDOM IS SLAVERY

IGNORANCE IS STRENGTH

Winston's estranged wife Katharine 'had not a thought in her head that was not a slogan' (Orwell 1949: 69) – that is, a collocation of words and thought pre-packaged by the Party. By reducing the number of words and their possible collocations, the Party strictly limits the occurrence of original thought, whether based on empirical observation or individual reasoning. For Winston, this stranglehold on sensory evidence and creativity in combining words represents what is most evil and oppressive about the Party:

> The Party told you to reject the evidence of your eyes and ears. It was their final, most essential command. His heart sank as he thought of the enormous power arrayed against him, the ease with which any Party intellectual would overthrow him in debate, the subtle arguments which he would not be able to understand, much less answer. And yet he was in the right! . . . Stones are hard, water is wet, objects unsupported fall towards the earth's centre. With the feeling that he was . . . setting forth an important axiom, he wrote:
>
> *Freedom is the freedom to say that two plus two make four. If that is granted, all else follows.*
>
> (Orwell 1949: 84)

It is because of the way his command of language has been controlled by the Party that he could not hope to understand or answer the arguments. At the end of the novel, Winston, his mind broken by torture, signals how completely he has submitted to the Party's doctrine when he traces 'almost unconsciously' in the dust on the table: $2 + 2 = 5$ (Orwell 1949: 303).

Newspeak is directly connected to the ideas expressed by Orwell in 'Politics and the English language' (Orwell 1946). As the ultimate language for the suppression of thought, Newspeak represents the horrific end of the road Orwell describes English as travelling, the point at which it is too late to get rid of the linguistic bad habits that prevent clear thinking and political regeneration because they have become structurally ingrained. The appeal of Basic, which Orwell himself had felt, is perhaps just a further symptom of how far this development has gone. Originally proposed as a way of grounding language in observable reality, Ogden's Basic aimed to do this by intervening directly into the structure of English, paring it down to a fraction of its traditional form. But wasn't *this* already a form of linguistic tyranny, limiting rather than expanding people's freedom to speak and think as they pleased? If so, Orwell the interventionist in linguistic usage could not support it any more than Orwell the socialist could stomach the excesses of Stalinism.

The point made at the end of the 1946 essay, about excessive distrust of abstractions leading to an inability to recognize or combat Fascism, is echoed in the description of the word *free* in Newspeak (see the quotation at beginning of the chapter). It has been limited to just its concrete meaning. 'This dog is free from lice' certainly calls up a clearer mental image than does 'politically free' or 'intellectually free'. But again, while abstraction without a concrete anchor remains extremely dangerous, the failure to abstract away from certain key concrete anchors is no less threatening.

In Oceania, only the proles have 'stayed human' (Orwell 1949: 172), and we see from the occasional glimpses of their dialogue that their language is Oldspeak, as in this conversation about the lottery which Winston overhears in a pub:

'Can't you bleeding well listen to what I say? I tell you no number ending in seven ain't won for over fourteen months!'
'Yes it 'as, then!'
'No, it 'as not! Back 'ome I got the 'ole lot of 'em for over two years wrote down on a piece of paper. I takes 'em down reg'lar as the clock. An' I tell you, no number ending in seven —'
'Yes, a seven 'as won! ...'

(Orwell 1949: 88)

Each of the two proles is capable of independent thought, and one of them makes an argument based on historical evidence that would be beyond the ability of any Party member. For its members, the Party is rewriting history every day and making sure they cannot perceive it happening. What is more, the fact that these proles are arguing about numbers contrasts with the inability of Party members to argue about the sum of 2+2. And the numerous non-standard features of their 'Oldspeak' cause it to ring with freedom to Orwell's ears. In his book *The English People* (Orwell 1947) he wrote:

> [P]robably the deadliest enemy of good English is what is called 'standard English'. This dreary dialect, the language of leading articles, White Papers, political speeches, and BBC news bulletins, is undoubtedly spreading: it is spreading downwards in the social scale, and outwards into the spoken language. Its characteristic is its reliance on ready-made phrases – *in due course, take the earliest opportunity, warm appreciation* . . . – which may once have been fresh and vivid, but have now become mere thought-saving devices, having the same relation to living English as a crutch has to a leg. Anyone preparing a broadcast or writing to *The Times* adopts this kind of language almost instinctively, and it infects the spoken tongue as well. So much has our language been weakened that the imbecile chatter in Swift's essay on polite conversation (a satire on the upper-class talk of Swift's own day) would actually be rather a good conversation by modern standards.
>
> (Orwell 1947: 26–7)

The continuation of this passage introduces a further political (or more accurately socio-political) dimension to Orwell's view of language and freedom. The power of language to promote clear thinking and combat tyranny, as discussed in 'Politics and the English language' (Orwell 1946), is *inherent to the language of the working classes*. The tendencies of language and thought he believes must be resisted are those he associates with the educated middle and upper classes.

> The temporary decadence of the English language is due, like so much else, to our anachronistic class system. 'Educated' English has grown anaemic because for long past it has not

been reinvigorated from below. The people likeliest to use simple concrete language, and to think of metaphors that really call up a visual image, are those who are in contact with physical reality... And the vitality of English depends on a steady supply of images of this kind. It follows that language, at any rate the English language, suffers when the educated classes lose touch with the manual workers.

(Orwell 1947: 27)

Part of the reason the proles of Oceania have stayed human is that they have clung to real language. With all its faults, traditional English at least offers the *hope* of free speech and thought, and will do so until these possibilities are standardized out of existence. In the novel, Winston concludes that the only hope for the future lies with the proles, and this conclusion corresponds with Orwell's view on the future of the language as expressed in *The English People* (Orwell 1947). Through Newspeak, Orwell warns the world of the danger that standardization of language goes hand in hand with standardization of thought. In particular, radical attempts to restructure the language, even if aimed at the improvement of thought, could result in tyranny no less than communist revolutions have done. The danger is especially great if, as with Basic, *reduction* of the language is the means by which it is to be brought under control.

The opposition Orwell establishes between the language of different social classes aligns with the difference between empiricist and conventionalist views of language. One well-known modern embodiment of this conflict is Ogden and Richards's (1923) rejection of Ferdinand de Saussure's (1857–1913) conventionalist view of the linguistic sign. Saussure (see Volume I, Chapter 16), in line with one mode of 'relativistic' continental thinking, believed that the meaning of a word is not tied to some physical object in the world around us, but is strictly conceptual and is a part of a given language just as much as is the sound pattern used to signify it. The evidence for this includes the existence of words for abstractions and things such as unicorns that do not exist in the world; the vastly different ways in which languages divide up the world, for instance in terms of the colours they do or do not distinguish, and the various categories (noun genders, for example) into which they place words; metaphorical uses of words; and the occurrence of semantic shift and change.

Ogden and Richards (1923), in the British empiricist tradition, carefully considered Saussure's view and rejected it on the grounds that it was self-negating. For, if the meanings of words are completely cut off from things in the world, there is no possibility of verifying whether or not anything anyone says is true, starting with Saussure's own statement.

> Unfortunately this theory of signs, by neglecting entirely the things for which signs stand, was from the beginning cut off from any contact with scientific methods of verification. De Saussure, however, does not appear to have pursued the matter far enough for this defect to become obvious.
>
> (Ogden and Richards 1923: 8)

Orwell's position is that the English language in the mid-twentieth century is in a perilous state because those who speak and write it do so following the model of Saussure, treating words as though they were unconnected to reality and therefore producing meanings that are arbitrary and internal to the language rather than engaging with the world. At least, this is what educated middle- and upper-class speakers of 'standard English' do. The extract cited above from *The English People* (Orwell 1947) suggests that the working classes instead follow the Ogden and Richards (1923) model, in which meaning is connected to things in the world. True socialist that he was, Orwell believed that the working-class way of signifying was better, healthier, truer than the unverifiable contents of standard English.

No doubt the realist in Orwell recognized the extent to which views such as these represent vast over-generalizations that romanticize the working class and fail to explain how a middle-class Old Etonian like himself could come to understand these things more clearly than any Lancashire coal miner. But such objections would not come to the fore when he felt so strongly the need to make known the dangerous political ramifications of the arbitrariness of language.

In *Nineteen Eighty-Four* (Orwell 1949), Orwell makes manifest his view of the essential difference between standard and working-class English by pushing the tendencies of standardization to their extreme in the form of Newspeak. Despite taking some of its inspiration from Ogden's Basic, Newspeak is completely Saussurean in that its meanings cannot be verified against anything in the real world. What Orwell wants to suggest is that the best hope for the future of humankind lies in *acting as if* language operates as Ogden and Richards (1923) say it must, tying it to observable reality in the way that working-class speakers do, and refusing to be swept up by the conventionalist Saussurean view of language that, alas, describes all too well the dangerous workings of standard English. He believes we can do this because language is not a 'natural growth' but an institution we control. We need scepticism – just enough of it to keep us on guard against those who would take control over us, but never forgetting that one very powerful way they might do this is to encourage us to be *so* sceptical that we do not even believe we are being controlled. If we want to remain free, we must be sceptical about everything, including, paradoxically, scepticism itself. It can be meaningful only so long as we do not paint ourselves into the corner of being sceptical that $2 + 2 = 4$.

This is the corner occupied by members of the Outer Party of Oceania, as well as by 'Stuart Chase and others' who cannot struggle against Fascism because their scepticism about language has blinded them to the reality of abstractions. In the same corner are those who would deny that the sum of 2+2 can be pinned down to anything more precise than 'an arbitrary signified', and who find in this ultra-relativism a liberation from the 'tyranny of words' – not as Chase meant it, but in the sense of a language conceived as the embodiment of logic and truth. No one can ever know the whole of logic or truth, the argument goes; therefore they are mythical. Orwell's message is: forget about this all-or-nothing approach to truth and knowledge. Know what you can, for every bit matters. Know it as simply and directly as you can, and tell it the same way. Above all, know that the metaphorical 'tyranny' of words is all that stands in the way of the very un-metaphorical tyranny of Big Brother.

Chapter 4

Whorf on language and thought

[A]round a storage of what are called 'gasoline drums', behavior will tend to a certain type, that is, great care will be exercised; while around a storage of what are called 'empty gasoline drums', it will tend to be different – careless, with little repression of smoking or of tossing cigarette stubs about. Yet the 'empty' drums are perhaps the more dangerous, since they contain explosive vapor. Physically the situation is hazardous, but the linguistic analysis according to regular analogy must employ the word 'empty', which inevitably suggests lack of hazard. The word 'empty' is used in two linguistic patterns: (1) as a virtual synonym for 'null and void, negative, inert', (2) applied in analysis of physical situations without regard to, e.g., vapor, liquid vestiges, or stray rubbish, in the container. The situation is named in one pattern (2) and the name is then 'acted out' or 'lived up to' in another (1), this being a general formula for the linguistic conditioning of behavior into hazardous forms.

In a wood distillation plant the metal stills were insulated with a composition prepared from limestone and called at the plant 'spun limestone'. No attempt was made to protect this covering from excessive heat or the contact of flame. After a period of use, the fire below one of the stills spread to the 'limestone', which to everyone's great surprise burned vigorously. Exposure to acetic acid fumes from the stills had converted part of the limestone (calcium carbonate) to calcium acetate. This when heated in a fire decomposes, forming inflammable acetone. Behavior that tolerated fire close to the covering was induced by the name 'limestone', which because it ends in '-stone' implies non-combustibility . . .

An electric glow heater on the wall was little used, and for one workman had the meaning of a convenient coathanger. At night a watchman entered and snapped a switch, which action he verbalized as 'turning on the light.' No light appeared, and this result he verbalized as 'light is burned out.' He could not see the glow of the heater because of the old coat hung on it. Soon the heater ignited the coat, which set fire to the building.

... A tannery discharged waste water containing animal matter into an outdoor settling basin partly roofed with wood and partly open. This situation is one that ordinarily would be verbalized as 'pool of water.' A workman had occasion to light a blowtorch nearby, and threw his match into the water. But the decomposing waste matter was evolving gas under the wood cover, so that the setup was the reverse of 'watery.' An instant flare of flame ignited the woodwork, and the fire quickly spread into the adjoining building ...

Beside a coal-fired melting pot for lead reclaiming was dumped a pile of 'scrap lead' – a misleading verbalization, for it consisted of the lead sheets of old radio condensers, which still had paraffin paper between them. Soon the paraffin blazed up and fired the roof, half of which was burned off.

Such examples, which could be greatly multiplied, will suffice to show how the cue to a certain line of behavior is often given by the analogies of the linguistic formula in which the situation is spoken of, and by which to some degree it is analyzed, classified and allotted its place.

(Whorf 1956: 135–7)

In so far as linguists are a subspecies of full-time, paid denizens of academe, Benjamin Lee Whorf (1897–1941) was never a linguist. On the contrary, having taken a degree in chemical engineering, he began a successful career as a fire-prevention inspector with an insurance company in Hartford, Connecticut; and despite several offers of permanent university posts in linguistics he continued to work for the same company until his death at the age of forty-four. He came to be associated with Sapir during the latter's time at Yale, and for one academic year (1937–8) stood in for him as a teacher there. He is famous for the view (the 'Sapir–Whorf hypothesis'; see Chapter 1 above) that how we think is moulded, if not determined, by the language we speak.

Whorf's contribution to the Sapir–Whorf hypothesis was a product not just of his amateur linguistics but of his professional work too. In the course of the latter he had occasion to analyse many reports of fires and explosions on industrial premises. Although primarily interested in the purely physical circumstances surrounding these mishaps (such as defective wiring, presence or lack of air spaces between metal flues and woodwork, and so on), he came to believe that another factor was often involved: the linguistically determined understanding people had of the physical situation, as revealed in the verbal description they gave of it.

The examples Whorf cites to establish the point (see above) are not all equally convincing. It is hard to see, for instance, how any alternative verbalization could have helped the watchman who inadvertently switched on an electric heater concealed from view by a coat: what he was in the first instance mistaken about, presumably, was which switch worked the light. And sometimes ignorance of chemistry seems to be more to blame than inappropriate description. Replacing the putatively misleading term 'limestone' (with its connotation of non-combustibility) by 'calcium carbonate' would not in itself lead anyone to take precautions against fire in the situation Whorf discusses, unless he or she happened to know that acetic acid converts calcium carbonate to calcium acetate, which on exposure to heat yields inflammable acetone. (Incidentally, the fact that many English-speakers these days would substitute 'flammable' for 'inflammable' here is a matter on which Whorf might well have had something to say.) In other cases, though, the point is well made. An 'empty' container, in ordinary parlance, is very often not one that is literally empty, but one whose residual contents are either useless or not worth the bother of retrieving: if the residuum in question is petrol, for instance, this verbal usage is potentially dangerous.

This is an overt, palpable illustration of how the way one talks about a thing may determine how one thinks about it. But Whorf believed that this kind of connection between language and thought had a covert, submerged counterpart: a language may, as it were automatically, categorize experience in ways that its speakers are not consciously aware of. Whorf called such categorizations 'cryptotypes'.

A simple example Whorf offers – albeit not a very good one – is the distribution in English of voiced and voiceless word-initial interdental fricatives. Voiced [ð] occurs initially only in a small class of 'form words' comprising the definite article, demonstratives, certain adverbs and conjunctions, and the old second person singular pronouns and possessives (*this*, *there*, *than*, *thither*, *thou*, *thy* etc. – contrast the 'full' words *thigh*, *think*, *theft, theory, thimble, theatre*). In Whorf's terminology the former class constitutes 'the cryptotype of demonstrative particles'; its reality as a class (i.e. the fact that the distribution is not just accidental) is demonstrated by the 'psychic pressure' that operates against pronouncing *th-* in new or imaginary full words (e.g. *thig, thag, thob, thuzzle*) as [ð] (Whorf 1956: 76). The difficulty here lies not in the classification itself, but in seeing what is supposed to be cryptic about it. Cryptotypes stand in contrast to overt grammatical categorizations ('phenotypes'), such as the distinction between present and past tense in English finite verbs. 'Past' is an overt category, because (a few exceptions such as *cut* aside) it is morphologically marked. But the category 'form word beginning with *th*' would seem to be no less overt, in that it is phonologically marked. It is true that, unlike the past-tense marker, [ð] here would not usually be considered an independently meaningful form; and that, having no orthographic support, the distributional pattern of [ð] and [θ] word-initially is likely to pass unnoticed by many speakers. Still, this is not quite what Whorf appears to mean by 'cryptotype' elsewhere, to judge by other examples he gives.

For instance, place-names in English are a cryptotype because, although they outwardly resemble other nouns, they cannot be reduced to pronouns after the prepositions *in, at, to, from* (Whorf 1956: 92). Thus one can say 'I live in it', when 'it' refers back to a phrase such as *that house* or *the basement*, but not when it refers to *Williamsburg* or *Westphalia* – even though 'I live in Williamsburg', 'I live in Westphalia' are perfectly acceptable. The point is that the class of cases where it is impossible is not in any way overtly marked in speech. A more complex example (Whorf 1956: 70–1) involves the English particle *up*, meaning 'completely', 'to a finish', as in *break it up, cover it up, eat it up, twist it up, open it up*. This, Whorf says, can be used with any monosyllabic verb, or any disyllabic verb with stress on the first syllable – with the exception of those belonging to four cryptotypes. One is the cryptotype of 'dispersion without boundary': hence one does not have *spread it up, drain it up, filter it up*. Another is the cryptotype of 'oscillation without agitation of parts': this rules out *rock up a cradle, wave up a flag, wiggle up a finger, nod up one's head*. The third is the cryptotype of 'non-durative impact': we do not have *whack it up, tap it up, stab it up, slam it up, wrestle him up, hate him up*. The fourth is 'verbs of directed motion': *move, lift*, *pull*, *push*, *put* etc., with which *up* occurs, but only in the sense of 'upward' and its figurative extensions.

When the meaning of a word such as *empty* leads, in a given situation, to a certain (inappropriate) line of thought and action, language, Whorf would say, is controlling one's understanding of reality. Similarly, Whorf's point about cryptotypes is that the language forces its speakers to make the categorizations they embody whether or not they consciously wish or intend to. In both types of example we see, projected on to speakers of what he called 'standard average European', a view of the relation between language and thought that Whorf explored more fully in connection with the striking differences between standard average European and certain American languages – notably Hopi.

In 'An American Indian model of the universe' (Whorf 1956: 57–64), Whorf claims that the Hopi has no general idea of time as a continuum in which everything in the universe proceeds out of a future, through a present, into a past. Time is not regarded as a linear dimension that can be measured and divided into units. This is reflected linguistically in the fact that the Hopi language, according to Whorf, contains no words, grammatical forms, constructions or expressions that refer directly to what we call 'time', or to past, present or future, or to enduring or lasting, or to motion as kinematic rather than dynamic (i.e. as a continuous movement in space and time rather than as a display of dynamic effort in a certain process), or to space in such a way as to exclude that element of extension or duration that we call 'time', and so by implication leave a residue that could be called 'time'. None the less, says Whorf, Hopi is capable of accounting for and describing correctly, in a pragmatic or observational sense, 'all observable phenomena of the universe'.

The everyday metaphysics underlying standard average European (i.e. setting aside the relativistic ideas of twentieth-century science, which have yet to impinge in a substantial way on the non-specialist mind) imposes on the universe the two fundamental concepts of space and time: static, three-dimensional infinite space; and kinetic, one-dimensional uniformly and perpetually flowing time – two separate and unconnected aspects of reality, according to this familiar way of thinking. The flowing realm of time is, in turn, subject to a threefold division: past, present and future. Hopi metaphysics also has its fundamental concepts comparable to these in scale and scope. What are they? What follows is a paraphrase of Whorf's lyrical attempt to express in English his understanding of the relevant aspects of Hopi thinking.

The key distinction is between the 'manifest' and the 'not yet manifest' (or, alternatively, the 'objective' and the 'subjective'). The objective or manifest comprises all that is or has been accessible to the senses – the physical universe both actual and historical, but excluding everything that we call 'future'. The subjective or not-yet-manifest comprises all that we call future, but also all that we call 'mental' – everything that appears or exists in the mind. This is 'the realm of expectancy, of desire and purpose'. It is in a dynamic state, yet not a state of motion: it is not advancing towards us out of a future, but is already with us mentally, evolving without motion from the subjective towards a result that will belong to the objective. In translating into English, the Hopi will say that these entities in the process of becoming 'will come' or that they – the Hopi – 'will come to' them, but in their own language there are no verbs corresponding to our *come* and *go* purely and simply.

This realm of the subjective (i.e. of the process of manifestation), as distinguished from the objective (i.e. the result of this process), includes also an aspect of existence that for us counts as 'present': that which is beginning to emerge into manifestation (i.e. something that is beginning to be done), such as going to sleep or starting to write, but which is not yet in full operation. Thus, this 'nearer edge of the subjective' cuts across and includes a part of our present time, but most of what is temporally 'present' for us belongs in the Hopi scheme to the objective realm and so is not distinguished from our past. The verb *tunatya* – perhaps generally best translated as 'hope' – is the term that crystallizes the Hopi philosophy of the universe in respect of its basic dualism of objective and subjective; it is the Hopi word for 'subjective'. It refers not just to human mental activities but to the idea of a life-force in the universe generally – to whatever is endowed with an immanent capacity to bring about change: 'the Hopi see this burgeoning activity in the growing of plants, the forming of clouds and their condensation in rain, the ... planning ... of the communal activities of agriculture and architecture, and in all human hoping, wishing, striving, and taking thought' (Whorf 1956: 62). The inceptive form of *tunatya* (*tunatyava*) does not mean 'begins to hope', but rather 'comes true, being hoped for'. The inceptive denotes the first appearance of the objective, but the fundamental meaning of *tunatya* is subjective activity or force; the inceptive implies the terminus of such activity.

In standard average European, basically spatial terms are commonly extended to refer to temporal phenomena (*before the door ~ before sunset, between Williamsburg and Newport News ~ between Friday and Sunday, in the kennel ~ in the evening*). According to Whorf, this does not happen in Hopi. On the contrary, space seems to be 'subordinate' to time, and in part understood in terms of it:

The Hopi conceive time and motion in the objective realm in a purely operational sense – a matter of the complexity and magnitude of operations connecting events – so that the element of time is not separated from whatever element of space enters into the operations. Two events in the past occurred a long 'time' apart ... when many periodic physical motions have occurred between them in such a way as to traverse much distance or accumulate magnitude of physical display in other ways. The Hopi metaphysics does not raise the question whether the things in a distant village exist in the same present moment as those in one's own village, for it is frankly pragmatic on this score and says that any 'events' in the distant village can be compared to any events in one's own village only by an interval of magnitude that has both time and space forms in it. Events at a distance from an observer can only be known objectively when they are 'past' (i.e. posited in the objective) and the more distant, the more 'past' (the more worked upon from the subjective side). Hopi, with its preference for verbs, as contrasted with our own liking for nouns, perpetually turns our propositions about things into propositions about events. What happens at a distant village, if actual (objective) and not a conjecture (subjective) can be known 'here' only later. If it does not happen 'at this place', it does not happen 'at this time'; it happens at 'that' place and at 'that' time. Both the 'here' happening and the 'there' happening are in the objective, corresponding in general to our past, but the 'there' happening is the more objectively distant, meaning, from our standpoint, that it is further away in the past just as it is further away from us in space than the 'here' happening.

(Whorf 1956: 63)

One specifically linguistic consequence of this alien conceptualization of time and space is that the Hopi verb does not have anything corresponding to our 'tense'. In 'The relation of habitual thought and behavior to language' (Whorf 1956: 134–59) Whorf discusses another way in which this affects grammar. 'Numbering' in standard average European (i.e. use of cardinal numbers and the grammatical categories 'singular' and 'plural') operates without reference to the distinction between literal aggregations of matter in space and metaphorical extensions of that notion. We say 'ten men' and also 'ten days'. Ten men either are or could be objectively perceived as ten, ten in one group perception – ten men on a street corner, for instance. But 'ten days' cannot be objectively experienced. We experience only one day, today; the other nine (or even all ten) are conjured from memory or imagination. If 'ten days' is regarded as a group it must be as an imaginary, mentally constructed group. Again, when we speak of 'ten steps forward', 'ten strokes on a bell', or any similarly described cyclic sequence, 'times' of any sort, we are doing the same thing as with 'days'. Cyclicity is thought of in terms of imaginary plurals. But the idea of envisaging a cyclical series of events as a collection of objects is by no means simply given to pre-linguistic experience, however familiar and unremarkable it may be to speakers of standard average European; and there is nothing like it encoded in, for instance, Hopi. In Hopi plurals and cardinal numbers are used only for entities that form or can form an objective group. There are no metaphorical or 'imaginary' plurals, but instead ordinals used with singulars. The Hopi equivalent of 'they stayed ten days' might be 'they stayed until the eleventh day' or 'they left after the tenth day'. 'Ten days is greater than nine days' becomes 'the tenth day is later than the ninth'. Standard average European reifies 'lengths of time' in just the way that that phrase suggests, and having done so treats them like any other countable object, whereas 'the Hopi language has not laid down any pattern that would cloak the subjective "becoming later" that is the essence of time' (Whorf 1956: 140).

If, in the way illustrated here, 'we dissect nature along lines laid down by our native language' (Whorf 1956: 213), then it follows that science must be language-relative (assuming, of course, the rather Olympian standpoint from which for example the 'dialects' of Indo-European are insignificantly differentiated versions of one language). This is perhaps the most striking implication of Whorf's thought. However, the way he develops it in 'Science and linguistics' (Whorf 1956: 207–19) is somewhat disappointing.

To say that science is language-relative is not, in Whorf's view, to say that the reality described by science is language-relative. It means, rather, 'that all observers are not led by the same physical evidence to the same picture of the universe, unless their linguistic backgrounds are similar, or can in some way be calibrated' (Whorf 1956: 214). The intellectual product of Western culture that we call 'science' is merely one possible coherent picture of the universe. It is a purely contingent fact, says Whorf, that this particular picture happens to have enjoyed overwhelming world-historical success; and that fact should not disguise the culturally parochial nature of its linguistic foundations. Western physics is based on 'various grand generalizations' to do with 'time, velocity and matter' (Whorf 1956: 216) derived essentially from a categorization of experience embedded in ancient Greek, and thence diffused into standard average European; and these generalizations, according to Whorf, are dispensable.

One obvious difficulty with this view is that in the history of science important conceptual advances have largely consisted in overturning a commonsense view reflected in everyday language. Even so early and simple an acquisition as the idea of heliocentricity runs counter to the wisdom embodied in a sentence such as *the sun rises in the east*. Newtonian mechanics makes nonsense of our ordinary understanding of motion and stasis. And in the twentieth century Western science has so decisively emancipated itself from the world-view enshrined in the language that putatively moulds it as to be incomprehensible to the average speaker without a prolonged course of special training. It takes an unusually elastic imagination to see how, for instance, the deliverances of post-Einsteinian physics might plausibly be treated as continuous with the cosmology latent in standard average European. In contrasting the 'metaphysics' of the latter with that of Hopi, Whorf concedes that Western science has taken a new turn, and that the world-view reflected in contemporary physics must be set aside for purposes of his exposition. What he does not tackle, however, are the implications of modern science for the Sapir–Whorf hypothesis generally.

Another weakness of 'Science and linguistics' is that Whorf is unable to establish his implied case for the equipollence of different pictures of the universe by providing an example of an alternative, 'exotic' picture possessed of anything like the richness and complexity of what we call 'science'. It is true that the indigenous American cultures Whorf is primarily interested in simply lack the material wherewithal for the development of a full-blown rival science. It is less obvious, though, that if their material culture were sufficiently advanced to permit such a thing, the science they developed would not show a suspicious tendency to converge on science as we know it. Whorf does offer what he claims to be a demonstration of how 'a physics constructed along Hopi lines' would work, which runs as follows:

> Hopi grammar, by means of its forms called aspects and modes, makes it easy to distinguish among momentary, continued and repeated occurrences, and to indicate the actual sequence of reported events. Thus the universe can be described without recourse to a concept of dimensional time. How would a physics constructed along these lines work, with no T (time) in its equations? . . . We may have to introduce a new term I, intensity. Every thing and event will have an I, whether we regard the thing or event as moving or just enduring or being. Perhaps the I of an electric charge will turn out to be its voltage or potential. We shall use clocks to measure some intensities, or, rather, some RELATIVE intensities, for the absolute intensity of anything will be meaningless . . .
>
> A scientist from another culture that used time and velocity would have great difficulty in getting us to understand these concepts. We should talk about the intensity of a chemical reaction; he would speak of its velocity or its rate, which words we should at first think were simply words for intensity in his language. Likewise, he at first would think that intensity was simply our own word for velocity. At first we should agree, later we should begin to disagree, and it might dawn upon both sides that different conceptual systems were in play. He would find it very hard to make us understand what he really meant by velocity of a chemical reaction. We should have no words that would fit. He would try to explain it by likening it to a running horse, to the difference between a good horse and a lazy horse. We should try to show him, with a superior laugh, that his analogy also was a matter of different intensities, aside from which there is little similarity between a horse and a chemical reaction in a beaker. We should point out that a running horse is moving relative to the ground, whereas the material of the beaker is at rest.
>
> (Whorf 1956: 217–18)

What we see here, though, is not so much a physics constructed along Hopi lines as a demonstration of how a physics constructed along Western lines might be translated into Hopi.

Whorf is sometimes accused of bolstering his claims about the relationship between language and thought by using deliberately 'unsympathetic' translations. For instance, he explains the Nootka sentence *tlih – is – ma*, which can be used to refer to a state of affairs that might be reported in English as 'the boat is grounded on the beach', by translating it as 'moving pointwise – on the beach – it is' (Whorf 1956: 236). The point of Whorf's rendering is to highlight the fact that the Nootka sentence has no word for 'boat'. The implication seems to be that the Nootka do not think of the situation, as we do, in terms of one material object (the boat) in a stationary relation with another material object (the beach). But if this is indeed Whorf's conclusion, is he not making the simple mistake of confusing thought with its verbal formulation?

A critic might press this accusation by pointing out that, by means of similarly unsympathetic translations, languages much closer to English than Nootka is could be made to yield apparently bizarre patterns of thought. The French say *je me suis lavé les mains* where the English say *I washed my hands*. But an unsympathetic translation of the French sentence might render it as 'I me am washed the hands'. Does this show that French speakers conceive of washing one's hands not as something you do to yourself, but as something that gets done to you by an unknown agency? At its most implausible such a line of argument might lead to supposing that the French mind conceives of the sun (*le soleil*) as male and the moon (*la lune*) as female. In which case we should, presumably, translate *le soleil* as something like 'he, the sun' and *la lune* as 'she, the moon'.

These considerations draw attention to at least three distinct but related issues which are of some importance in modern linguistics. First, since modern linguistics involves a great deal of translation between different languages, there seems to be a hidden assumption that it is legitimate to establish equivalences and non-equivalences between them. But how can we be sure that these interlinguistic equivalences and non-equivalences are valid? And what linguistic assumptions are we making when we accept them in order to support linguistic arguments? Second, if it is granted, as translators and lexicographers maintain, that it is often very difficult to find precise word-for-word correspondences between different languages, does this in itself prove Whorf's point? Or are some of these difficulties unimportant and more or less irrelevant, while others reveal deep incompatibilities between the way speakers of different languages think? If so – that is, if only some translation disparities have any cognitive significance – how can we determine objectively (1) which these significant disparities are, and (2) what exactly any such disparity shows about different modes of thought? Third, if Whorf is taken to be arguing his case, at least in part, on the basis of translation, does not the argument in the end defeat itself? For in order to demonstrate a significant disparity, it has to be shown that certain equivalences which *should* hold (if languages were isomorphic) do not in fact hold. But *ex hypothesi* this demonstration is impossible if thought really is moulded by language. For it requires us to treat as equivalences what are in fact not equivalences. And this should beggar any attempt at demonstration. The 'equivalences' should be as puzzling as the alleged disparities. For instance, we should be simply baffled when a piece of gibberish such as 'moving pointwise – on the beach – it is' is produced as a translation, since it should not correspond to anything in our thought patterns. Or if we think we do understand it, then we are victims of an illusion.

At a certain level of generality, it is clear enough what Whorf's main ideas are. Much of the subsequent attention they have attracted has been directed towards making them more precise. In particular, scholars have been concerned to establish just what exactly the 'Sapir–Whorf hypothesis' is supposed to be, and whether it is, or might be made, empirically testable. What J. B. Carroll (b. 1916) compiled for publication in the 1950s is a posthumous medley of journal articles, papers read to conferences and unpublished manuscripts: nowhere does it contain a precise statement of a specific 'hypothesis'.

The consensus is that lurking behind these writings there are two potential assertions worthy of further investigation: a strong linguistic determinism and a weaker linguistic relativism. Linguistic determinism is the claim that the language we speak determines the kinds of knowledge and the modes of understanding we can aspire to. Linguistic relativism is the claim that, although our language sets no *a priori* limits to our knowledge and understanding, the thought of at least its more unreflective speakers will tend to run in linguistically preordained channels.

Whorf is occasionally held to have espoused determinism, and passages such as the following are cited in support of this:

> How does ... a network of language, culture and behavior come about historically? Which was first: the language patterns or the cultural norms? In main [sic] they have grown up together, constantly influencing each other. But in this partnership the nature of the language is the factor that limits free plasticity and rigidifies channels of development in the more autocratic way. This is so because a language is a system, not just an assemblage of norms. Large systematic outlines can change to something really new only very slowly, while many other cultural innovations are made with comparative quickness.
>
> (Whorf 1956: 156)

But, in so far as this is a testable assertion, the evidence subsequently brought to bear does not seem to support it. Some later writing on problems of cross-cultural communication (e.g. Gumperz 1982, Scollon and Scollon 1981) points to the obvious fact that very different cultural patterns can have as their vehicle one and the same language, so that speakers from different cultural backgrounds may experience consistent and severe communicational difficulties, despite the fact that they are using what, in the usual understanding, would be counted as the same grammatical and lexical resources. Conversely, the grammatical patterns of a language may yield readily to interference from an alien culture: to cite just one example, Hollenbach (1977) has described the reversal of a temporal deictic system in Copala Trique under the influence of Spanish.

In any case, an appraisal of the whole range of Whorf's writings does not support seeing him as a consistent determinist. And, as has often been pointed out, his work itself contains a refutation of determinism, in the strong sense canvassed here: has Whorf not succeeded in using English to explain, for example, his understanding of the Hopi *Weltanschauung*? Some readers might be inclined to respond to this rhetorical question with a resounding negative, but that would point merely to the difficulty of the task. The determinism thesis entails its impossibility.

With linguistic determinism largely discredited, more interest has been shown in the relativistic claim. The main strategy has been to try to establish the limits to variation in grammatical patterning through the exploitation of linguistic universals. The first requirement for such work is accurate descriptive studies of languages, coupled with careful ethnographic accounts of the corresponding cultures. Accordingly, linguists and anthropologists have had occasion to re-examine many of the exotic languages on the peculiarities of whose grammatical structures the twentieth-century renascence of linguistic relativism has been founded. And conspicuous among the 'classic' linguo-anthropological descriptions that have not altogether survived re-scrutiny are Whorf's writings on Hopi. Longacre (1956) suggested that Whorf's grammatical generalizations were often faulty, and more recent work has tended to bear out his suspicions. Whorf's far-reaching claims about the Hopi view of time, as embodied in such linguistic patterns as the non-existence of metaphors that treat time as though it were space, the impossibility of counting units of time, the lack of tenses in the verb, have latterly been rendered at best dubious by investigations such as those of Gipper (1976), Voegelin, Voegelin and Jeanne (1979) and Malotki (1979, 1983) – which present an awkwardly large number of counter-examples to all these assertions about Hopi grammar.

But this may be of little import outside the ranks of specialists in American languages. However inaccurate Whorf's specific linguistic descriptions may be, the very fact that trouble has been taken to establish their inaccuracy testifies to the long-term significance of the Boasian tradition (see Chapter 1 above) in permanently enlarging the subject matter of Western inquiry into language, and more specifically, to the importance of Whorf's own work in rekindling interest in one of the most fundamental questions that can be raised concerning the role of language in human affairs.

Chapter 5

Firth on language and context

Say when!

Quite a number of readers will have lively recollections of the very practical use of those two words. Many Englishmen will at once place themselves in a pleasant situation with good glass, good drink, and good company. The two words fit into the situation. They have their 'psychological' and practical moment in what is going on between two people, whose eyes, hands, and goodness knows what else are sharing a common interest in a bit of life. What do the words 'mean'? They mean what they do. When used at their best they are both affecting and effective. A Martian visitor would best understand this 'meaning' by watching what happened before, during and after the words were spoken, by noticing the part played by the words in what was going on. The people, the relevant furniture, bottles and glasses, the 'set', the specific behaviour of the companions, and the words are all component terms in what may be called the context of situation. Meaning is best regarded in this way as a complex of relations of various kinds between the component terms of a context of situation.

(Firth 1964: 110)

John Rupert Firth was born in 1890. After serving as Professor of English at the University of the Punjab from 1919 to 1928, he took up a post in the phonetics department of University College London. In 1938 he moved to the linguistics department of the School of Oriental and African Studies in London, where from 1944 until his retirement in 1956 he was Professor of General Linguistics. He died in 1960. He was an influential teacher, some of whose doctrines (especially those concerning phonology) were widely propagated and developed by his students in what came to be known as the 'London school' of linguistics.

Firth's chief interest as a linguistic thinker lies in his attempt to resist the idea that linguistics should treat what he calls 'speech events' as no more than a means of access to what really interests most linguists: the language system allegedly underlying them. In so far as a definite conclusion can be drawn from the small body of often cryptic and allusive writings that are all we have to go on, the attempt was a failure. But its failure raises the interesting question of how far the enterprise was ever possible at all, granted the fundamental assumption, overtly stated by Firth himself, that 'the business of linguistics is to describe languages' – a question which, along with other theoretical problems brought fitfully to light in Firth's own work, was to be confronted far more rigorously and systematically a generation later by another British linguist, Roy Harris (see Chapter 14 below).

Like Harris, Firth rejects (or sets out to reject) the idea that linguistic communication is a matter of exchanging messages in a 'fixed code' – that is, a language conceived as a determinate system of form–meaning pairings. What it is to use a language, in this view, may be broadly characterized as follows. Producing an utterance involves selecting forms with appropriate meanings, and uttering representations of those forms. Understanding an utterance involves perceiving representations of forms and matching them up with corresponding meanings. Embedded in this scenario is an answer to the question of how communication by use of language is possible. It is an answer so widely accepted that communication itself is often *defined* as a matter of implementing a system of the kind envisaged by descriptive linguists. For example:

> I shall give COMMUNICATION the following general definition: communication is the manifestation of an abstract message through the medium of a physical signal; particular messages being tied to a specific signal according to conventions shared by the parties to any communicative event. These conventions, or 'rules', allow a sender to encode a meaning in a proper signal and, provided the sender has obeyed the rules, permit a receiver to retrieve the intended meaning from the signal.
>
> (Fowler 1974: 4)

The foregoing may be construed, broadly speaking, as an account of the Saussurean concept of the *langue* (see Volume I, Chapter 16), as it has been subsequently developed within post-Saussurean linguistics, and of how shared possession of the same *langue* by members of a given community is held to permit linguistic communication. The theory or general theoretical stance in evidence here may be dubbed 'psychologistic structuralism'.

Firth objected to psychologistic structuralism, and formulated his objections with reference to Saussure himself. He claimed that Saussure followed Durkheim in treating a language as a set of 'social facts', on a different plane from the phenomena observable as the individual language-user's linguistic behaviour on particular occasions. These social facts constitute a 'silent . . . system of signs existing apart from and over and above the individual as *sujet parlant*' (Firth 1957: 180); and it is this system of signs (the *langue*) that the psychologistic structuralist takes as object of study, not the speech events brought about by particular *sujets parlants* on particular occasions of speech. The language system, in the Saussurean view, is 'a function of *la masse parlante* . . . stored and residing in *la conscience collective*' of a community (Firth 1957: 180). In contrast, Firth takes linguistics to be primarily concerned with the speech events themselves. These speech events are, in a sense, 'concrete', whereas the Saussurean *langue* is 'a system of differential values, not of concrete and positive terms. Actual people do not talk such "a language"'. Language is 'a form of human living rather than merely a set of arbitrary signs and signals' (Firth 1968: 206). He observes that the 'static mechanical structuralism' that Saussure elaborated under the influence of Durkheimian sociology involves regarding the structures as *realia*. 'The structure is existent and treated as a thing. As Durkheim said . . . social facts must be regarded as "*comme des choses*"' (Firth 1957: 181); and in Saussurean and post-Saussurean linguistics instances of *parole* (actual speech) are relegated to the role of providing evidence for the structure.

This is not to deny that dealing with speech events will involve the systematic deployment of analytical constructs and categories, which may in practice turn out to be rather similar to the constructs and categories involved in the analysis of abstract systems underlying speech events. The difference lies in the ontological status accorded to the constructs and categories and, by extension, to the language system itself. 'Our schematic constructs', says Firth, 'have no ontological status, and we do not project them as having being or existence' (Firth 1957: 181). Whereas for the psychologistic structuralist speech comes about through implementation of the speaker's knowledge of a systematic linguistic structure, for Firth the systematic structure is a linguist's fiction, resulting from the attempt to understand speech.

In accordance with his rejection of the idea that *langue* rather than *parole* constitutes the linguist's object of study, Firth rejects the theory of communication implied by psychologistic structuralism, whereby communication is envisaged as the transferring of thoughts from one mind to another in virtue of shared knowledge of a linguistic code. Following the anthropologist Bronislaw Malinowski (1884–1942), he asserted that it is 'a false conception of language' to see it 'as a means of transfusing ideas from the head of the speaker to that of the listener' (Malinowski 1935 vol. 2: 9). Rather, communication involves 'reciprocal comprehension, level by level, stage by stage, in a stated series of contexts of situation' (Firth 1968: 200).

In accordance with his rejection of psychologism, linguistic forms are not, for Firth, in themselves containers of ideas or meanings: 'words do not in any sense "hold" or "contain" or "express" the "meanings" shown against their written form in a dictionary' (Firth 1964: 184). 'I have avoided any attempt to approach individual "reified" words as isolates of conceptual meaning' (Firth 1968: 16). Hence his interest in what he terms 'collocation': he believes that 'the company it habitually keeps' is an important part of the meaning of a word, and illustrates the point with reference, *inter alia*, to the (British) English word *ass*. Having largely lost a competition with *donkey* as a standard term designating the kind of equid, *ass* is nowadays more or less confined to a metaphorical sense, in which it is remarkably restricted as to its collocations: 'there are only limited possibilities of collocation with preceding adjectives, among which the commonest are *silly, obstinate, stupid, awful*, occasionally *egregious*' (Firth 1957: 195).

Hence too the much-discussed Firthian judgement that the example sentences linguists use to illustrate points of grammar are 'nonsense':

I have not seen your father's pen, but I have read the book of your uncle's gardener, like so much in grammar books, is only at the grammatical level. From the semantic point of view it is just nonsense.

The following gives perfectly satisfactory contexts for phonetics, morphology and syntax, but not for semantics: *my doctor's great-grandfather will be singeing the cat's wings.* We make regular use of nonsense in phonetics, and so also do most grammarians. Even the anthropological Sapir offers an example like *the farmer kills the duckling.* Jespersen gives us *a dancing woman charms* and *a charming woman dances,* and Dr Gardiner makes shift with *Pussy is beautiful, Balbus murum aedificavit,* and Paul's example of *the lion roars.*

(Firth 1957: 24)

This passage has puzzled commentators, who tend to take Firth as saying merely that it is difficult to imagine a context in which these might be uttered (see e.g. Sampson 1980: 226). But if that had been his point Firth could surely have contrived more decisive illustrations of it than *the farmer kills the duckling.* Firth's point is that *any* sentence, as such, is an abstraction, and abstractions do not in themselves have meaning. Meaning is to be sought in actual speech events embedded in particular 'contexts of situation'. Moreover, it is not just that *part* of the meaning of an utterance is the context in which it is uttered. One cannot, in Firth's view, allow for the effect of context on meaning by tacking something on to a statement of the meaning of an abstraction, for what abstraction we are dealing with depends on the context. A context of situation is not a static background to speech events, but

a patterned process conceived as a complex activity with internal relations between its various factors. These terms or factors are not merely *seen* in relation to one another. They actively take one another into relation, or mutually 'prehend' one another ... What is said by one man in a conversation prehends what the other man has said before and will say afterwards. It even prehends negatively everything that was not said but might have been said.

(Firth 1964: 110–11)

For Firth, analysing the meaning of speech events is the ultimate task of descriptive linguistics. Although all speech events are unique, they none the less have features in common with other speech events: 'it is clear we see structure as well as uniqueness in an *instance*, and an essential relationship to other *instances*' (Firth 1968: 200); and the quest to state the meaning of instances starts with this perception. 'We must separate from the mush of general goings-on those features of repeated events which appear to be parts of a patterned process, and handle them systematically by stating them by the spectrum of linguistic techniques' (Firth 1957: 187). 'Descriptive linguistics is . . . a sort of hierarchy of techniques by means of which the meaning of linguistic events may be . . . dispersed in a spectrum of specialised statements' (Firth 1957: 183).

Meaning is a function of a linguistic form in a context. However, there is a sense in which forms have 'meaning' at various different descriptive levels: phonological and grammatical as well as semantic. 'Semantic meaning' (an unfortunate phrase, but perhaps necessary, given Firth's recognition of phonological and grammatical meaning as well) is a function of an utterance and its parts in a context of situation. In phonology and grammar the elements and categories set up to describe the patterns of utterances function (i.e. have their meaning) in terms of their relations with other elements belonging to (abstracted at) the same level. Phonological meaning is the function of phonological elements in relation to other phonological elements. Grammatical meaning is the function of grammatical elements in relation to other grammatical elements. Thus speech events are split up for analysis and description into a series of separate functions of elements and forms abstracted by the appropriate criteria at each level.

How in practice is this 'hierarchy of techniques' employed? Firth offers a demonstration of their application to an English form transcribable as [bɔːd], as abstracted from such potential utterances as [wɪtʃbɔːd] *which board?*, [bɔːdəvstʌdɪz] *board of studies*, [bɔːdi] *bawdy*, [bɔːdɪŋ] *boarding*, [bɔːdtədɛθ] *bored to death*.

What is the phonological meaning of the sounds of which [bɔːd] consists? Simply their use in that context in opposition to the other sounds that might have substituted for them. Thus between initial [b] and final [d] fifteen other vowels are possible. Similarly, the meaning of [d] in [bɔːd] is its use there instead of other possibilities such as [t], [l] or [n] in [bɔːt], [bɔːl] or [bɔːn]. And one can state the meaning of [bɔːd] as a whole, on the phonological level, as being its difference from the total set of trisegmental forms arrived at by exhaustively substituting for one, two or all three of its component parts. But, Firth insists, as it stands [bɔːd] has no more meaning than that. It is what he calls a 'neutral' (Firth 1957: 25).

Establishing its grammatical meaning involves considering the contrast it offers with other forms in different series, each series of forms being related to [bɔːd] in such a way as to isolate its grammatical status in that series. Firth offers three examples: (1) [bɔːd], [bɔːdz]; (2) [bɔːd], [bɔːdz], [bɔːdɪd], [bɔːdɪŋ]; (3) [bɔː], [bɔːz], [bɔːd], [bɔːɹɪŋ]. Examination of these series reveals that in (1) [bɔːd] is a singular noun, in (2) the uninflected form of a verb, and in (3) the past-tense form of a verb. However, there is a sense in which [bɔːd] in (1) remains a 'neutral'. The neutrality here can be resolved by extending the series of forms in two different ways: (1a) [bɔːd], [bɔːdz], [bɔːdɹuːm], [bɔːdskuːl]; (1b) [bɔːd], [bɔːdz], [bɔːdi]. 'All this sort of thing', says Firth, 'can be arrived at merely by recollection, or by asking the native speaker, or by collecting verbal contexts' (Firth 1957: 25).

Establishing the semantic meaning of a form requires that it be contextualized in an actual utterance. Imagine an utterance of the question '[bɔːd]?' In different contexts this might elicit such replies as 'Not really' or 'No' with a rising intonation, or 'Go on'. In each case the reply will determine a different relation between '[bɔːd]?' and its context; and it is this relation with a context that Firth distinguishes as what we are here referring to as 'semantic meaning'.

Various questions arise, however. Not the least of these concerns the status of the linguistic entities whose meaning (at the various different levels) Firth's analytic technique is designed to elucidate. As Firth himself observes, 'no two people pronounce exactly alike. The same speaker will employ several variants of the "same word" as required in different situations. There is not one word *have*, there are many *haves*, there is not one *k*, *t*, or *i*, but groups of related variants of these sounds' (Firth 1964: 181–2). Moreover, 'each word when used in a new context is a new word' (Firth 1957: 190). But if that is so, justification is required for the view that spoken English includes a single recurrent phonological invariant, identified by writing the symbols bɔːd within square brackets. Nowhere does Firth explicitly address this issue. He appears to accept without question that application of the transcriptional procedures associated with the use of a phonetic alphabet will automatically yield just those entities that a linguistic description is concerned to describe. The correctness of this assumption may be concluded from the answer he does explicitly give to a further question, namely: given that in normal speech the movement of the vocal organs is continuous, what determines that there are just three discrete 'sounds' in [bɔ:d]? According to Firth, we can simply take it for granted 'that the [speaker-hearer] recognizes a "phone" or separable speech-sound when he hears or makes one, and that he can analyse the stream of speech into a sequence of such phones' (Firth 1964: 159). Furthermore

> a phonetic notation does not attempt to reproduce on paper an exact record of every detail of sound, stress and intonation. It is not a direct sound-script faithfully caught by an acoustic automaton . . . Phonetic notation enables you to represent the language when you know something about the way the native uses his 'sounds' . . . In a sense, therefore, you should record not what a native says, but what he thinks he says.
>
> (Firth 1957: 3)

But this sounds like the basis for an *a priori* psychologistic phonemics of a familiar kind. And that is incompatible with the idea that the abstract structure that emerges from the language-describer's analytic labours is no more than a linguist's fiction. For by taking for granted the putative decisions of language-users as to the identification of recurrent invariants Firth is in effect appealing to the principle that the language-describer's task is to make plain what language-users already know. But that renders untenable his claim to repudiate Saussure-inspired psychologistic structuralism, in as much as he here seems to be doing just what psychologistic structuralists do: eliciting an abstract structure allegedly stored in speakers' heads.

This, as Firth apparently came to recognize, will not do. Elsewhere in his writings one can see attempts to rectify the discrepancy outlined here between his broadest theoretical principles and the analytic practice exemplified with respect to [bɔ:d]. As regards grammar, his remarks to this effect are somewhat sketchy. But none the less they imply rejection of the idea that the artefacts of traditional grammar are *realia* underlying utterances, and to which utterances are to be referred. For instance, he points out that 'the characteristic feature of all spoken language is that native speakers make the fullest use of the perceived situation and of the assumed background of common contexts of experience' (Firth 1964: 174). Speakers effect economies in speech by relying on shared background knowledge: 'the linguistic "economics" of speech are not those of writing' (Firth 1964: 174). But these economies are not to be explicated in terms of 'full' forms from which 'economic' utterances are to be derived by such processes as contraction or ellipsis. 'The use of such terms as "contraction", "mutilation", "ellipsis" in describing normal speech habits is unscientific and unnecessary . . . grammar is logical and makes language amenable to reason. Common speech is, however, not the servant of reason' (Firth 1964: 175). Rapid colloquial utterances such as [aiʃtfθɔ:tsou] or [aiŋənəbaiwʌnfəmisɛlf] present difficulties for grammatical analysis ('What sort of word is [aiŋənə]') (Firth 1968: 122), but it does not follow that they should be analysed as derivations from *I should have thought so* or *I am going to buy one for myself*, for it is inappropriate to think of such utterances as deviant implementations of the grammarian's regularized abstractions. He observes, as another example, that inclusion among the traditional impedimenta of grammatical description of a category called 'the verb' by no means guarantees that one can always identify an exponent of that category:

Somehow or other the game of finding the verb had been mentioned. And, pressed for material, I suggested the sentence: *she kept on popping in and out of the office all the afternoon.* Where's the verb? *Kept*? *Popping*? *Kept popping*? *Kept on popping*? *Kept on popping in* and *kept on popping out* (with forms, as they say, understood), or *kept on popping in and out*, or *kept on popping in and out of*? Is there a tense here? What conjugation does it belong to? How could you set it out?

If you look at the various ways in which what is called the English verb is set out in tabulated paradigms, you will get nowhere at all. It is useful here to distinguish between the verb in English as a part of speech, and what may be called the verbal characteristics of the sentence. The exponents of these characteristics in the sentence quoted . . . are distributed over the sentence structure . . . In noting such verbal characteristics as person, tense, aspect, mood and voice, we cannot expect to find them in any single word called the verb, drawn from a book conjugation.

(Firth 1968: 121–2)

But it was in phonology that Firth made a concerted effort to pursue the location and statement of 'meaning' at the expense, if necessary, of established descriptive practice. The innovatory techniques of phonological description for which he is perhaps best known derive from a dissatisfaction with phoneme-based phonology arising from his idea of what it is to identify meaning at the various (non-semantic) levels of analysis. As a contemporary linguist put it, 'speaking a language is picking one's way through a succession of choices' (Haas 1957: 43). The meaningfulness of an element at any level resides in the possibility of choosing an alternative from the paradigm of its substituents; and since a Firthian description consists in identifying a hierarchy of sets of meaningful elements, the analytic technique employed must be such as to permit the identification of the units which are meaningful in this sense. But not all the units identified by phonemic analysis *are* meaningful in this sense. For instance, the English words *cats* and *cads* would be transcribed /kæts/ and /kædz/ respectively. But there is no possibility of a choice between voiced and voiceless sibilant in these forms: the phonotactics of English demand that a word-final plosive-plus-sibilant cluster be either voiced or voiceless as a whole. A segmental transcription misleads by offering no indication of the impossibility of a choice. To put the point another way, it fails to show that there may be syntagmatic dependencies between the segments. Firth's proposal, in effect, is to recognize 'segments' in two dimensions instead of one. From /ts/ in /kæts/ he would extract a two-segment-long 'prosody' of voicelessness, contrasting here with a prosody of voice, for the cluster as a whole. This prosody determines the pronunciation of the cluster in interaction with segment-sized 'phonematic units' (not 'phonemes') that represent the information that is left when the co-occurrence restriction on the elements of the cluster has been abstracted as a prosody.

In sum, segmental writing, even in the streamlined guise of a phonetic alphabet, is an unreliable guide to what is phonologically 'meaningful':

in actual speech, the substitution elements are not letters, but all manner of things we may analyse out of the living voice in action, not merely the articulation but quite a number of general attributes or correlations associated with articulation, such as length, tone, stress, tensity, voice. The phoneme principle enables a transcriptionist to get down formulas for pronunciation, but lengths, tones, and stresses present many difficulties, both practical and theoretical.

(Firth 1957: 21)

Distrust of the letter leads Firth to recognize as a further problematic aspect of established phonological theory the lack of attention it pays to 'polysystematicity'. He introduces this principle with the following observation:

In print the word *nip* is just *pin* reversed. The letters *p* and *n* occur at the beginning or at the end. But if you had *pin* on a gramophone record and played it backwards you would not get *nip*. You might get something rather like it, but not distinguished from *pin* by the same diacritica as the normal *nip*. So although we identify our sounds by articulation likenesses and represent them by the same letter, this does not really correspond to the facts of speech. An initial element in a spoken word is functionally different, physiologically and grammatically, from a final element.

(Firth 1964: 39)

Adumbrated here is the idea that it may be a mistake to see a language as having one integrated phonological system, identified by the letters of a regularized alphabet, such that one letter represents one sound. Rather, the phonology of a language consists of a number of different subsystems that come into play at different points in a phonological 'piece', and there is no reason to identify the alternants in one subsystem with those of another. Firth suggests as one such subsystem in English the pattern of possibilities for syllable onsets. English syllables may begin with one, two or three consonants. Triconsonantal onsets are very restricted: the first consonant must be [s], the second must be a voiceless plosive [p], [t] or [k], the third must be a liquid or glide [l] [ɹ] [j] or [w]. Additionally, if the second consonant is [t] the third cannot be [l], and if the third is [w] the second must be [k]. Firth suggests that clusters such as these should be regarded as 'group substituents', whose individual components (e.g. the [t] in [stɹaip]), because they have a different function (that is, phonological meaning) from similar sounds in other phonetic contexts (e.g. [t] in [tʰaip]), are not to be identified with such sounds.

The theoretical basis for these descriptive procedures is quite different from that underlying psychologistic phonemics. The rationale for setting up prosodies and phonematic units is not that one reveals thereby phonological abstractions which are 'real' for speakers, but that in doing so one conforms more precisely than is possible with phonemic analysis to the information-theoretic principle of meaning as (context-determined) choice. Thus there is at least a superficial sense in which the phonological system is allowed to emerge from an analysis of phonological 'meaning', rather than being assumed as the basis for that analysis.

But there are a number of issues that remain unresolved by this reformulation of the principles of phonological description. The chief of these is the question, alluded to earlier, of how to identify the abstract invariants whose phonic structure application of the principles is designed to elucidate. Confronted with an utterance that might be somewhat narrowly transcribed as [kʰæts], the phonemicist in effect assumes that the task is merely to regularize the transcriptional system already invoked in citing the utterance, with reference to such principles as contrastive versus complementary distribution. In this particular case, all the tidying-up required is elimination of the phonemically redundant information that [k] is aspirated here, giving a transcription /kæts/. The prosodist, in contrast, makes no assumption that crypto-orthographic [kʰæts] provides even an approximate ready-made guide to the points at which significant choice is possible. But he or she none the less takes it for granted, no less than the phonemicist, that the abstraction [kʰæts] correctly identifies a relevant class of actual or potential utterances, notwithstanding that no two of them are phonetically identical. There is, therefore, a sense in which prosodic analysis is a less thoroughgoing departure from orthodox phonology than might at first sight appear. It is not so much an alternative to segmental analysis as a superimposition on it. For it continues to rely on segmental analysis to reveal the abstractions on which it operates.

The difficulty here is fundamental to any attempt to reconcile the study of speech events with the description of a language, and particularly pressing if one wishes to claim, as Firth does, that the language system under description is no more than the emergent product of an effort to understand speech events. No doubt a given utterance is envisaged by both speaker and hearer as an utterance of an abstraction of some kind (or of a number of abstractions of different kinds). Stating the meaning of speech events therefore involves, among other things, identifying and stating the abstractions. But what is crucially required is a means of ascertaining *what* abstractions an utterance is an utterance of. Firth fails to confront this requirement directly. But his attitude to it is hinted at in the remark that 'in a sense written words are more real than speech itself' (Firth 1964: 40); and the hint is reinforced by a complaint he makes against Malinowski that

> his attitude to words as such is curiously unsatisfactory when we remember his concern with institutions and customs. There is no doubt that, in literate societies such as our own, words and other elements of language are institutionalised, and statements about them in dictionaries and even in common talk are treated with a respect felt to be due to some sort of authority.
>
> (Firth 1968: 155)

For in practice, notwithstanding the distrust of writing underlying the rejection of phonemics, he falls back on the old idea that the writing system in use in a community already offers the necessary identification of the abstractions instantiated by utterances. A phonetic alphabet improves on the ordinary spelling system in eliminating certain obvious inconsistencies. It is true that there are many English-speakers in whose speech there can be detected no systematic differentiation of *board*, *bawd* and *bored*. A spelling [bɔ:d] for all three is, for phonological purposes, therefore preferable. But it is none the less a spelling *of board*, *bawd* and *bored*. A truly radical break with orthography-imposed description would start by asking what guarantees that the spellings *board*, *bawd* and *bored* themselves identify units of the language. Unless this is asked, the claim that it is the meaning of speech events that gives rise to the language system rather than vice versa cannot be made good.

Another departure from orthodoxy that turns out on inspection to be more apparent than real concerns the view implied as to the relation between speakers and the language-system that emerges from the language-describer's analysis. Strict application of the principle of meaning-as-choice yields, for phonology at least, a descriptive statement (of prosodies and phonematic units) which cannot be readily matched up with what a language-user 'thinks he or she says'. The system of contrastive phonic units identified by phonemic analysis gives way to a system of 'choice points'; and the analyst's decisions as to the nature of the units, at any given point, among which a choice is possible, will not necessarily correspond to notions entertained by the language-user. But the fictional system of abstractions thus identified is none the less underpinned by a very familiar idea about the relation between speakers and the language they speak. It is the idea that speakers are constrained to manipulate a system of choices provided for them in advance by the language. That this is so is tacitly hinted at by Firth's failure to answer another question that might be asked about the analysis of [bɔːd]. Why is it that, in discussing the paradigm of potential substituents for [ɔː] in that form, he neglects to mention such possibilities as [ɹɔː] in [bɹɔːd] *broad* or [ɹɪŋəlɛŋkθəvkɔː] in [bɹɪŋəlɛŋkθəvkɔːd] *bring a length of cord*? Why is it not part of the meaning of [ɔː] in [bɔːd] that it contrasts with these sequences? Presumably because to admit such possibilities would be to open floodgates that Firthian descriptive procedures depend for their viability on keeping firmly shut. For the fact is that there is no definite limit to what might fill the gap between [b] and [d] in an utterance [b_____d]. But if to analyse a form at a given level of description is to state an exhaustive paradigm of potential substituents, some definite limit must be imposed. Otherwise its meaning at that level cannot be determined. And if we ask why its meaning at that level should be held to consist in the contrast between what is said and a finite list of things that might alternatively have been said, the answer is that this is simply a fundamental principle of Firth's view of how languages work: that is, of how they offer to their users a means of communication. But this principle is at odds with Firth's explicit repudiation of the psychologistic structuralist's account of communication. For the possibility of communication turns out to depend on interlocutors' shared prior knowledge, for every point in an utterance at which a choice is possible, of a fixed paradigm of substituents.

So Firth's theoretical programme, which at first sight appears to promise an account of the speech event that turns upside-down the orthodox conception of the relation between speech events and language systems, ultimately founders in a series of equivocations and compromises with the orthodoxy. The ambiguity of his theoretical posture is epitomized in the unresolved tension between his respect for words as fixed, institutionalized objects and the dictum that every word when used in a new context is a new word. Resolving that tension would require a more radical re-orientation of linguistic inquiry than Firth ever saw his way clear to making.

Chapter 6

Wittgenstein on grammatical investigations

People are deeply imbedded in philosophical, i.e., grammatical confusions. And to free them from these presupposes pulling them out of the immensely manifold connections they are caught up in. One must so to speak regroup their entire language.

(Wittgenstein 1993: 185)

We are under the illusion that what is peculiar, profound, essential, in [philosophical] investigation, resides in its trying to grasp the incomparable essence of language. That is, the order existing between the concepts of proposition, word, proof, truth, experience, and so on. This order is a super-order between – so to speak – super-concepts. Whereas, of course, if the words 'language', 'experience', 'word', have a use, it must be as humble a one as that of the words 'table', 'lamp', 'door'.

The idea now absorbs us, that the ideal 'must' be found in reality. Meanwhile we do not as yet see how it occurs there, nor do we understand the nature of this 'must'. We think it must be in reality; for we think we already see it there ... Where does this idea come from? It is like a pair of glasses on our nose through which we see whatever we look at. It never occurs to us to take them off.

We predicate of the thing what lies in the method of representing it. Impressed by the possibility of comparison, we think we are perceiving a state of affairs of the highest generality.

(Wittgenstein 1953: §104)

[Philosophical problems] are, of course, not empirical problems; they are solved, rather, by looking into the workings of our language, and in such a way as to make us recognize those workings; in despite of an urge to misunderstand them. The problems are solved, not by giving new information, but by arranging what we have always known. Philosophy is a battle against the bewitchment of our intelligence by means of language.

(Wittgenstein 1953: §109)

Our investigation is therefore a grammatical one. Such an investigation sheds light on our problem by clearing misunderstandings away. Misunderstandings concerning the use of words, caused, among other things, by certain analogies between forms of expression in different regions of language. – Some of them can be removed by substituting one form of expression for another.

(Wittgenstein 1953: §90)

There is not *a* philosophical method, though there are indeed methods, like different therapies.

(Wittgenstein 1953: §133)

Born in Austria in 1889, Ludwig Wittgenstein (d. 1951) began studying philosophy at Cambridge University in 1911. After a few years serving in the Austrian army during the First World War and a spell teaching elementary school, he began lecturing in philosophy in Cambridge in 1930. In 1939 he was elected to a professorial chair. His lectures attracted a dedicated coterie of students and colleagues, many of whom served to spread Wittgenstein's ideas and method to a wider public – often much to Wittgenstein's dismay. The only major work that he published during his lifetime is the *Tractatus Logico-Philosophicus* (Wittgenstein 1922), the distillation of what is conventionally referred to as the 'early period' in Wittgenstein's philosophical evolution.

In his early writings, Wittgenstein develops an approach to philosophical problems that is based on analysing the symbolic means by which those problems are conceptualized, posed and 'solved'. In other words, in keeping with the logical focus of work by Frege (see Volume I, Chapter 15), Bertrand Russell and others, in his early period Wittgenstein is interested in clarifying philosophical reasoning by means of analysing the instrument, language, by which that reasoning is carried out. To this end, the *Tractatus* proposes a theory of symbolic representation: in other words, a theory of how it is possible, by means of language and other forms of symbolism, to represent the facts, objects and states of affairs that constitute 'the world', i.e. reality. In so doing, the *Tractatus* also explores the limits to the representational powers of symbolic systems. The theory presented in the *Tractatus* came to be known as 'the picture theory' because it presents language and other forms of symbolism on the model of pictorial representation. 'A picture depicts reality by representing a possibility of existence and non-existence of states of affairs' (Wittgenstein 1922: §2.201). There are different forms of pictorial representation, different ways in which a representation may picture a state of affairs and assert its existence. In language, the words making up a proposition – or meaningful sentence – stand in a determinate relationship to each other. Each of the component words stands for an object in the state of affairs depicted. The relationships between the words in the proposition must be isomorphic with – that is, must mirror – the relationships between the objects for which the words stand in the state of affairs depicted. That is, the two structures – that of the proposition and that of the state of affairs – must have a common 'logical form' (Wittgenstein 1922: §2.18). The proposition is true if the state of affairs depicted does indeed obtain. 'A proposition is a picture of reality' (Wittgenstein 1922: §4.01). To understand a proposition is 'to know what is the case if it is true' (Wittgenstein 1922: §4.024). As with Aristotle and the speculative grammarians (see Volume I, Chapter 2, Chapter 6), the mind has a fairly transparent role in the representational relationship between language and the world. According to the *Tractatus*, a thought is a logical picture of a state of affairs, a picture that a proposition expresses in a way 'that can be perceived by the senses' (Wittgenstein 1922: §3.1).

An essential feature of a proposition, according to Wittgenstein's early thinking, is its capacity to convey a meaning that we have never hitherto considered. Propositions use 'old' expressions – words – to communicate 'new' senses (Wittgenstein 1922: §4.03). In other words, linguistic structure is creative: it allows the language-user to construct and to understand meaningful sentences that he or she has not encountered before. This feature of linguistic creativity – or generativity – came to be a crucial feature of the generative theory of language developed by Noam Chomsky (see Chapter 9 below).

Wittgenstein admits that the propositions of actual natural languages – such as English, German, Swahili, Mohawk etc. – do not appear to have pictorial structures mirroring the logical structures of the situations they represent. However, it is crucial to Wittgenstein's early thinking that, under analysis, *every* meaningful utterance – of any language whatsoever – could in principle be shown to have such a structure: that is, to the extent that the utterance is in fact meaningful. Propositions possess accidental as well as essential features (Wittgenstein 1922: §3.34). What is essential in a proposition is that which it requires in order to represent and assert the existence of a particular state of affairs. 'Accidental features are those that result from the particular way in which the proposition . . . is produced' in a given language (Wittgenstein 1922: §3.34). In other words, a proposition will have an accidental structure, which is a superficial property peculiar to the particular language in which it is expressed. But to the extent that it is meaningful, a proposition will also have an underlying structure: one that is common to all propositions which assert the existence of a given state of affairs – regardless of the particular language in which that proposition is expressed. 'Language disguises thought. So much so, that from the outward form of the clothing it is impossible to infer the form of the thought beneath it, because the outward form of the clothing is not designed to reveal the body, but for entirely different purposes' (Wittgenstein 1922: §4.002). All philosophy, therefore, is a 'critique of language' (Wittgenstein 1922: §4.0031): that is, the goal of philosophy is to clarify what philosophical sentences really mean. It does this by identifying their underlying propositional forms and discarding those aspects of the superficial properties of the sentences which are the potentially misleading sources of philosophical problems. 'A proposition states something only in so far as it is a picture' (Wittgenstein 1922: §4.03). 'Philosophy aims at the logical clarification of thoughts. [It] is not a body of doctrine but an activity . . . resulting in the clarification of propositions' (Wittgenstein 1922: §4.112).

The *Tractatus* had a substantial impact on the development of linguistic thought between the world wars. However, it is the lectures and writings of Wittgenstein's 'later period' that made the most distinctive and significant contribution to twentieth-century linguistic thought. Accordingly, the primary focus of this chapter is on the main focus of Wittgenstein's work in the 'later' period: the *Philosophical Investigations*, published in 1953, two years after his death.

Although the posthumously published writings of Wittgenstein's later period have had a major influence on modern linguistic thought, these writings are controversial, enigmatic at times and largely misunderstood. Wittgenstein was trained as a philosopher; naturally, then, he lectured and wrote about the topics that are characteristic of academic philosophical discourse – in particular, about problems concerning the foundations of logic, epistemology, mathematics and psychology. However, his later approach to philosophical problems is not based on the clarification of propositions. In the *Philosophical Investigations* (Wittgenstein 1953) Wittgenstein maintains that philosophical problems are caused by 'prejudices' and 'illusions' that have their source in language: they are the product of what he called 'grammatical confusions'. In other words, Wittgenstein believed philosophical problems to be the legacy of some of the ways that we language-users are inclined to use words when talking and writing – and so also thinking – about particular kinds of topics: the very topics that are the staples of philosophical discourse. Consequently, Wittgenstein's philosophical method is designed to address these problems at their source, employing rhetorical strategies which he termed 'grammatical investigations'.

Even more consequential for Wittgenstein's influence on linguistic thought is the fact that he believed that the most pervasive and damaging of our inclinations in using words are those that emerge *when we reflect on language itself*: that is, when we discuss such issues as what it is for a word or sentence to mean something; what it is to understand a word or sentence or take it to be true; what meanings and concepts are; what it is to intend one meaning rather than another; and so on. These reflexive linguistic inclinations – the ways that we routinely talk about talk – lead to the grammatical prejudices that plague theoretical approaches to language and generate the illusory problems that are the traditional subject matter for academic philosophy (see also Chapter 14 below). 'The problems arising through a misinterpretation of our forms of language have the character of depth. They are deep disquietudes; their roots are as deep in us as the forms of our language and their significance is as great as the importance of our language' (Wittgenstein 1953: §111).

In his later writings, Wittgenstein never proposed a theory of language. Indeed, in spite of the claims of many commentators, Wittgenstein makes no theoretical claims about any of the linguistic topics that his later writings and lectures so often address. On the contrary, he often stated explicitly that it was not his goal – and that it would run counter to his rhetorical intentions – to offer any explanatory theses, whether about language or about other philosophical topics. So, if Wittgenstein made no theoretical claims about language, is there in fact nothing that one can legitimately say about his linguistic thought? The answer to this question would doubtless have to be 'yes' – that is, if linguistic thought were considered to consist only in the assertion of explanatory theses and theoretical claims. But Wittgenstein was a writer who shows us that linguistic thought is not only expressed in assertions and theories. The expression of Wittgenstein's distinctive views about language abounds in his writings. But these ideas are expressed not in theoretical claims but in his method of treating the grammatical confusions and prejudices that he took to be the source of philosophical problems. Where we will find Wittgenstein's thought about language is in the rhetorical strategies that he employs in his 'grammatical investigations' and in his reflexive remarks about the goals of these investigations and their design. Wittgenstein was not a theorist of language; his grammatical investigations have a practical purpose – to bring about particular therapeutic results. This therapy is successful if those to whom it is addressed – his audience, his readers, himself – are no longer inclined to talk and reason in the confused ways that lead to philosophical perplexity. Wittgenstein's writings are full of such reflexive commentary and explanation of what he is doing, why he is trying to do it and how he thinks it should work. We should therefore look at what he says about 'grammatical investigation' *as a rhetorical tool* – specifically, as a set of verbal strategies for treating what are fundamentally verbal problems. It is in his use of these rhetorical tools and in what he says when he reflects on them – their purpose, their design and their use – that we may discern the distinctive form of Wittgenstein's linguistic thought.

Wittgenstein says that his grammatical method is designed to address the sources of our 'bewitchment by means of language'. The major source of grammatical prejudices and illusions is our inclination, when we philosophize, to impose features of the methods we use to *represent phenomena* on the phenomena themselves. For example, we may take *the sky itself* to be red – but simply because we are looking at it through red-tinted glasses.

Or perhaps we take the spatial world itself to be constituted of inches, feet, and yards – because these are the units in the system with which we measure the world. 'We predicate of the thing what lies in the method of representing it' (Wittgenstein 1953: §104). The result of this grammatical confusion is that while we think we are investigating and gaining information about the phenomenon represented, we are in fact merely *tracing on to the phenomenon* some features of the method or model with which we are representing it. Worse, we don't realize that we are seeing things with this built-in prejudice. Rather, we assume that the reason the phenomenon *appears* to have those features is that they are part of *its own nature or essence*. It looks that way because – at some deep level – it really is that way. This prejudicial assumption amounts to treating the method of representation as 'a preconceived idea to which reality *must* correspond' (Wittgenstein 1953: §131). 'It is like a pair of glasses on our nose through which we see whatever we look at. It never occurs to us to take them off' (Wittgenstein 1953: §104).

How is Wittgenstein's rhetorical method intended to address the grammatical confusion of 'predicating of the thing what lies in the method of representation'? This question may best be answered by looking at an illustrative application of Wittgenstein's method in the opening pages of the *Philosophical Investigations*. The book begins by quoting a passage from Augustine's *Confessions* in which the author imagines how he learned language as a child.

> When they [my elders] named some object, and accordingly moved towards something, I saw this and I grasped that the thing was called by the sound they uttered when they meant to point it out . . . Thus, as I heard words repeatedly used in their proper places in various sentences, I gradually learned to understand what objects they signified; and after I had trained my mouth to form these signs, I used them to express my own desires.
>
> (Wittgenstein 1953: §1)

Here we have what Wittgenstein clearly takes to be a fairly common-sense account of *how* language is learned. As he points out, it incorporates an equally common-sense picture of the properties of *what is learned*: that is, a picture of the properties of language, in particular, the properties of words, meanings and sentences and their relation to the objects we use language to speak about. In other words, Augustine's account of how he learned language incorporates a particular way of representing what language is.

> These words, it seems to me, give us a particular picture of the essence of human language. It is this: the individual words in language name objects – sentences are combinations of such names. – In this picture of language we find the roots of the following idea: Every word has a meaning. This meaning is correlated with the word. It is the object for which the word stands.
>
> (Wittgenstein 1953: §1)

Augustine's account represents words as meaning by standing for particular objects; the word's meaning is the object it stands for. This is hardly a bizarre way to talk about words and meanings, and Wittgenstein does not present it as such. On the contrary, it is because this way of representing language *is* so commonsensical – and we, his readers, presumably find it so easy to agree with it – that Wittgenstein uses it in beginning his book. The confusion begins only if we give in to the inclination to go beyond taking at face value this method of representing language – that is, as simply a way of talking about talk. In this initial philosophizing step, we treat this method of representation as a repository of facts about the very nature of talk – that is, about the essential properties of the words and meanings *themselves*. For example, it is a perfectly common thing to do to point at a table and explain (say, to someone learning English) that 'The word "table" stands for THIS→' But when we philosophize, we find ourselves trying to explain how it is that something like a word (mere sounds) can possibly have this remarkable property of *standing for* an object in the world. We do not even notice that we have read off this purported property of words from the characteristics of the way, in some circumstances, we talk about words – that is, from our method of representation. We have prejudicially taken it for granted that meaning and standing for a particular object simply *are properties of the word itself.*

Wittgenstein's initial goal in the opening paragraphs of the *Philosophical Investigations* is simply to give a demonstration of how easily and unwittingly we incorporate taken-for-granted premises ('grammatical prejudices') into the initial steps of philosophical theory-building. Related to our inclination to predicate of phenomena what lies in the method of representing them is the inclination to generalize. Accordingly, in these opening passages Wittgenstein also draws attention to the tendency to extend the method of representing the meanings of concrete nouns to non-nouns.

> Augustine does not speak of there being any difference between kinds of word. If you describe the learning of language in this way you are, I believe, thinking primarily of nouns like 'table', 'chair', 'bread', and of people's names, and only secondarily of the names of certain actions and properties; and of the remaining kinds of word as something that will take care of itself.
>
> (Wittgenstein 1953: §1)

Because we analogically extend this method of representation to words other than concrete nouns, we assume that they must also mean by standing for objects. But what kinds of objects? What objects are we to take words like 'virtue', 'strength', 'believe', 'infinity', 'today', and 'unless' to stand for? Here is a characteristically *philosophical* sort of problem! 'When words in our ordinary language have prima facie analogous grammars we are inclined to try to interpret them analogously: i.e., we try to make the analogy hold throughout' (Wittgenstein 1958: §7).

Having demonstrated by example how easily we take these first steps in constructing a philosophical concept of meaning, Wittgenstein then asks us to consider two imaginary uses of language – what he calls 'language-games'. In the first language-game there is a shopkeeper and also a customer who gives the shopkeeper a slip marked 'five red apples'. The shopkeeper 'opens the drawer marked "apples"; then he looks up the word "red" in a table and finds a colour sample opposite it; then he says the series of cardinal numbers – I assume that he knows them by heart – up to the word "five" and for each number he takes an apple of the same colour as the sample out of the drawer' (Wittgenstein 1953: §1).

Wittgenstein does not yet say why he is asking the reader to imagine this language-game, but one thing is noteworthy: in explaining what the words 'red' and 'five' mean in this language-game, Wittgenstein has not said that they stand for particular objects. He has simply told us what the shopkeeper *does* when handed the written note. For 'red', the shopkeeper looks at a table of colour samples, finds the one marked 'red', and then takes an apple from the drawer matching the colour of that sample. For 'five' he recites a series of memorized numerals – 'one', 'two', 'three', 'four', 'five' – and at the utterance of each numeral he takes one of the appropriately coloured apples out of the drawer. This seems perfectly clear.

At this point, Wittgenstein voices a question motivated by the grammatical confusion at the heart of Augustinian picture of meaning: 'But what is the meaning of the word "five"?' (Wittgenstein 1953: §1). The Augustinian picture portrays 'five', like any word, as having a meaning that is the object for which it stands. But in Wittgenstein's description of language-game 1, no object has been mentioned for 'five' to stand for – and none appears to be needed. Wittgenstein told us how 'five' was used – the shopkeeper simply acts as described: he counts 'one', 'two', 'three', 'four', 'five', taking an apple out of the drawer at the utterance of each numeral. At least for this little language-game, asking for the object meant by 'five' appears to be a *non sequitur* – like learning how the knight moves in chess and then asking 'Yes, but what does the knight mean?'. The analogy we were inclined to make – between how we talk about the meanings of nouns such as 'table' and 'chair' and how we talk about other words such as 'five' and 'red' – seems to have led us up the garden path.

In a second such invented language-game Wittgenstein asks us to imagine a builder communicating with his assistant.

> The language is meant to serve for communication between a builder A and an assistant B. A is building with building-stones: there are blocks, pillars, slabs and beams. B has to pass the stones, and that in the order in which A needs them. For this purpose they use a language consisting of the words 'block', 'pillar', 'slab' 'beam'. A calls them out: – B brings the stone which he has learned to bring at such-and-such a call ... Besides the four words 'block', 'pillar', etc., let [this language-game] contain a series of words used as the shopkeeper ... used the numerals (it can be the series of letters of the alphabet); further, let there be two words, which may as well be 'there' and 'this' (because this roughly indicates

their purpose), that are used in connection with a pointing gesture; and finally a number of colour samples. A gives an order like: 'd—slab—there'. At the same time he shows the assistant a colour sample, and when he says 'there' he points to a place on the building site. From the stock of slabs B takes one for each letter of the alphabet up to 'd', of the same colour as the sample, and brings them to the place indicated by A. – On other occasions A gives the order 'this – there'. At 'this' he points to a building stone. And so on.

(Wittgenstein 1953: §§2 and 8)

In this language-game, as in the one with the shopkeeper and customer, we again learn the uses of the words without being told anything about their standing for particular objects. Clearly, what a competent participant in this game understands about 'there' is simply that he or she should place the appropriate building stone where the builder is pointing. This is not a matter of knowing what the word stands for. Similarly, what he or she knows about the word 'd' is that he or she should recite 'a, b, c, d', picking up one of the appropriate building stones as he or she utters each such 'numeral'. No object is needed for 'd' or any other of these 'numerals' to serve as 'what "d" means'. So, in contradiction to what the Augustinian picture of meaning leads us to assume, in *this* language-game, at least, knowledge of an object that 'd' or 'there' stands for is irrelevant to understanding their function in the game.

One might think that Wittgenstein's intention is merely to reveal that the 'standing-for' method of representation is not suited to the task of explaining numerals, adjectives, demonstratives and other *non-nouns*. But what about nouns such as 'apple', 'slab', 'block', 'pillar' etc.? Wittgenstein asks us to look at the facts of the language-games as he has described them. According to this description, what does a competent participant in these language-games know about these words? For 'apple', he or she knows to pull out the drawer marked 'apples' and to take out as many of the objects contained therein as instructed by the customer's written note. No mention is made of 'apple' standing for one or all of the objects in the drawer: we are simply told what the shopkeeper does. What does the building assistant know who understands what 'slab' means? Again, the description Wittgenstein gives of the language-game includes nothing about 'slab' standing for an object. Knowing how these 'games' are played does not seem to require taking these nouns to stand for any objects.

Wittgenstein responds to the anticipated objection that, while the adults in these language-games may act as described, what Augustine was talking about was how he learned language as a child. Wittgenstein concedes that it is *possible* that children could be taught the meanings of nouns such as 'slab' by ostensive teaching: that is, by their parents uttering the noun while pointing to an appropriate object. And this training *might* even have the effect of a mental image subsequently occurring to them every time they hear the word. But even so, these are not by themselves reasons to assume that that mental image – or the object that it is an image of – is *what 'slab' means* in this game. The description says how the assistant acts if he understands the builder's language and no mention is made, or needs to be made, of a mental image or the object it is the image of. Training *might* have the effect of establishing

> an association between the word and the thing . . . [A] picture of the object comes before the child's mind when it hears the word . . .
> But if ostensive teaching has this effect, – am I to say that it effects an understanding of the word? Don't you understand the call 'Slab!' if you act upon it in such-and-such a way?
> (Wittgenstein 1953: §6)

It is important to see that Wittgenstein's aim is *not* that of arguing against the claim that, as a result of their training, people come to make an association between the noun and some object, perhaps via a mental image of the object. He pointedly does not deny that this is possible. Instead, Wittgenstein's goal is to get us to consider two language-games in which such an association is irrelevant to understanding how the games work. *In these games* one understands a noun (just as any of the other words) if one knows how it is used (Wittgenstein 1953: §6): how to use it in giving instructions and how to respond appropriately to its use. We may speculate that the shopkeeper and the builder do in fact have mental images each time they hear a word. And they may also associate every word with a particular object. But whether they do (or do not) isn't what matters – at least not in these games.

What matters is that they use each word appropriately in giving instructions and respond appropriately to its use. How you learned the word and the legacy of associations and mental imagery that remain with you from that experience are not relevant factors. 'One cannot guess how a word functions. One has to *look at* its use and learn from that. But the difficulty is to remove the prejudice which stands in the way of doing this. It is not a *stupid* prejudice' (Wittgenstein 1953: §340).

Wittgenstein's target in these passages – indeed in the whole of the *Philosophical Investigations* – is our tendency to impose particular methods (or models) of representation when we talk and think about language. The 'standing-for' method of representation instanced in the book's opening paragraph leads to a form of 'grammatical prejudice': we feel that meaning *must* be explained by means of a canonical formula such as 'Word W means (stands for, signifies, designates) X'. This method of representation leads us to assume that standing for something is the essence of word-meaning and hence to raise questions about how words come to stand for things, what it is to stand for something, what sorts of things non-nouns stand for and so on: questions that are characteristic topics of debate in the philosophy of language. In other words, we dogmatically demand that every account of a word's function be given according to a canonical method of representation. 'So we are asking for the expression "this word signifies this" to be made part of the description. In other words the description ought to take the form: "The word ... signifies ..."' (Wittgenstein 1953: §10).

And yet what language-games 1 and 2 have shown us is that, at least for those language-games, the component words are made perfectly clear simply by describing how they are used. This description is complete and informative without being reduced to a canonical reflexive formula.

> Of course, one *can* reduce the description of the use of the word 'slab' to the statement that this word signifies this object
> . . .
>
> But assimilating the descriptions of the uses of words in this way cannot make *the uses themselves* any more like one another. For, as we see, they are absolutely unlike.
>
> (Wittgenstein 1953: §10, emphasis added)

These opening passages therefore have a relatively limited goal. By considering the role of words in language-games 1 and 2, the reader is intended to realize that words *do not have to have* the common function of standing for some object, even though this is what the canonical 'standing-for' method of representation inclines us to assume. So the aim of Wittgenstein's strategy is for the reader, on the strength of this realization, to lose the inclination to impose the standing-for prototype dogmatically in talking about word-meanings. If the reader stops imposing this method of representation in reflexive discourse about words, and therefore stops raising the questions to which that discourse inevitably leads, many traditional philosophical puzzles will simply lose their charm.

> [The] general notion of the meaning of a word surrounds the working of language with a haze which makes clear vision impossible. It disperses the fog to study the phenomena of language in primitive kinds of application in which one can command a clear view of the aim and functioning of the words.
>
> (Wittgenstein 1953: §5)

As is illustrated by this explanation of Wittgenstein's strategy in the opening sections of the book, the discussions of linguistic topics in the *Philosophical Investigations* do not argue to explanatory conclusions. Instead they address grammatical prejudices one by one, using a course of approach suited to root out the rhetorical source of each prejudice. Wittgenstein's goal is of a practical or persuasive nature; it is achieved if the reader no longer has the inclination to make those initial wrong steps that lead to grammatical prejudice – and from there to philosophical puzzlement.

Many of the prejudices addressed in the *Investigations* and in Wittgenstein's other writings concern topics that are central to Western linguistic thought. Some of the most important linguistic topics addressed include:

• the relationship between an utterance and the thought that it expresses
• the function of ostensive definition
• the relationship between a rule, its formulation in words and behaviour following that rule

- the relationship between a stated intention and the act that satisfies it
- the adequacy of communicational understanding
- the relationship between an 'inner' sensation or experience, 'outer' behaviour, and the verbal report of that sensation or experience
- the properties of a proposition (or sentence-meaning)
- the meanings of mental terms
- the relationship between word- or sentence-meaning and the use of that word or sentence
- the integration of language and cultural forms of life
- the status and function of 'common-sense' utterances
- the nature and function of logical propositions.

As in the example of the 'standing-for' prototype, in discussing these topics Wittgenstein's aim is never to give a theoretical 'solution' or explanatory 'answer' to the questions these topics usually raise. Rather, he addresses the confusions that give rise to the questions or to the prejudicial or dogmatic ways in which the topics are theorized. In so doing, the rhetorical method that he employs typically relies on constructing one or more language-games, as in the example illustrated above. These language-games, he often asserts, are intended as objects of comparison. As with language-games 1 and 2, their characteristics – and Wittgenstein's descriptions of them – are intended to throw light on language 'by way not only of similarities, *but also of dissimilarities*' (Wittgenstein 1953: §130, emphasis added).

> For we can avoid ineptness or emptiness in our assertions only by presenting the model as what it is, as an object of comparison – as so to speak, a measuring-rod; not as a preconceived idea to which reality *must* correspond. (The dogmatism into which we fall so easily in doing philosophy.)
>
> (Wittgenstein 1953: §131)

Wittgenstein uses the invented language-game to draw the reader's attention away from habitual and dogmatic ways of representing the issues raised by each topic. The reader is asked to focus instead on the uses of words in that language-game – uses that are in some ways similar (and dissimilar) to those on which discussions of these issues typically focus. Because these language-games are simpler than the whole complex of human language, it is possible to survey the functions of their component words – to get a clear picture of the words' uses – in particular, of how their use is integrated with the participants' actions. (For example: the way that knowing the function of 'apple' or 'red' or 'five' is a matter of knowing what to do in response to an instruction in which they are used.) By constructing a 'perspicuous representation' of each such language-game, Wittgenstein's intention is to induce the reader to make sense of its component patterns and techniques independently of the methods of representation that we are inclined to use when we consider the whole vast patchwork of human language practices.

As Wittgenstein points out, this strategy is similar to that which one might employ with a person who had always seen Figure 6.1 as a duck and who had so far been unable to effect the aspect-shift required to see it as a rabbit. The strategy would be to place images of rabbit heads next to the figure – visual objects of comparison – and ask the person to look back and forth from each such rabbit head to the figure itself. By this means, one might succeed in bringing the person eventually to undergo an aspect-shift and recognize that the figure can be seen *as a rabbit*.

Figure 6.1

Similarly, the goal of Wittgenstein's language-game strategy is to bring his readers to undergo an aspect-shift in how we make sense of the patterns and techniques of word-use on which discussion of a philosophical problem – say, the relationship between an utterance and the thought it expresses – typically focuses.

Hitherto, we have only been able to see (to talk about) these patterns and techniques under one aspect – that imposed by the canonical method of representation. But now we are asked to examine 'objects of comparison': language-games whose techniques and patterns of word-use are in some way similar and in some ways dissimilar to these. The intention again is to effect an aspect-shift: to bring us to the realization that the method by which we have always represented these uses of words – say, according to the 'standing-for' prototype – is not the only possible way of making sense of them. If, by these means, we can come to appreciate that there is at least one other way of making sense of these uses of words, then we will have freed ourselves from the grammatical prejudice that assumes that the canonical method of representation *must* be used and that the reason it must be used is that it is nothing more nor less than a faithful reflection of *the way things really are* – that is, of the essential facts of language.

Because his writings address problems in how we talk about and conceptualize language, many commentators have taken Wittgenstein to be advocating a theory of language, or at least a set of theoretical claims about language. Among these are typically included such purportedly 'Wittgensteinian' claims as the following.

- The meaning of a word is its use.
- Psychological and experiential terms, such as 'intention', 'idea', 'think', and 'pain', do not – cannot – refer to private, mental entities.
- Language use is governed by rules.
- Logic is grounded in social agreement.
- Word-meanings are typically characterized by family resemblances rather than categorial identity.
- There is a semantic asymmetry between first- and third-person psychological statements.
- The meanings of psychological statements, such as 'My foot hurts', depend on criteria in observable behaviour.
- 'I' is not a referring expression.
- Ostensive definition is inherently ambiguous.

A considerable amount of the influence that Wittgenstein is said to have had on twentieth-century linguistic thought actually has its source in these 'Wittgensteinian' commentaries. Indeed, he is claimed to have had a significant influence on various twentieth-century theories of language, including verificationism and anti-realism, integrationism (see Chapter 14 below), ordinary language philosophy (see Chapter 7 below), social interactionism (see Chapter 12 below), discourse analysis (see Chapter 11 below), and even generativism (see Chapter 9 below). Yet Wittgenstein repeatedly insisted that he was not proposing a new theory of language, that he had no explanatory goals and that his only aim was to *give descriptions* that would make the grammatical confusions and prejudices troubling our discourse 'disappear'. Nor did he have any positive claims to make about traditional philosophical problems concerning the foundations of psychology, logic, linguistics, epistemology or mathematics.

On the contrary: to see what Wittgenstein thought about language one must take at face value his rhetorical method. Wittgenstein's discussions of linguistic topics should not be interpreted as a covert form of theorizing. The crucial point is that what he says about language is offered not as a theory but as part of a rhetorical strategy for addressing and dissolving philosophical confusions and their related prejudices. His discourse about these aspects of language is an instrument that he constructs for particular rhetorical purposes. His aim is to teach his audience 'some know-how, not a body of knowledge (facts, theory, doctrine)' (Baker 1998: 29).

Given that Wittgenstein himself repeatedly insisted that he had no positive claims to make, one might conclude that there is therefore no genuinely Wittgensteinian legacy to linguistic thought, but only that of the interpretative contortions of his commentators. But this would be a mistake. The use that Wittgenstein makes of his rhetorical method and the remarks that he makes about its purpose do in fact yield a positive picture of language as a motley of behavioural practices (or 'techniques'; McGinn 1997: 50). These practices integrate the use of words and action within particular situational contexts. To investigate language, one should describe what happens – what people *do* – in these practices and how their words and actions function therein. However, human language is such a complex, indefinite and variable patchwork of such practices that it is not easily surveyed. This in itself can lead us into grammatical confusion. It is therefore better to focus on individual components in that patchwork and attempt to get a clear view of them one by one.

Among our language practices, especially important are those culturally prescribed ways of talking about language itself. Although these reflexive forms of expression are essential in determining what Wittgenstein calls 'grammar', they are also – as we have seen – potential sources of grammatical and philosophical confusion. Their misapplication as methods of representing linguistic facts can lead us into dogmatic and misleading prejudices. Examining the particular confusions and prejudices that Wittgenstein discusses in his writings, it quickly becomes clear that they yield an inventory of the issues that characterize linguistic thought in the Western tradition. In other words, Wittgenstein's legacy to linguistic thought can also be seen as a critical one, providing a diagnostic survey of the problems that have plagued Western linguistic thought from its beginning to the present day, problems whose sources he shows to lie in the misuse of reflexive methods of representation. However, his legacy is hardly confined to the critical, for Wittgenstein's rhetorical strategy amounts to a therapeutic method whose application is intended to make those intellectual confusions and prejudices completely disappear.

Chapter 7

Austin on language as action

In particular, the following morals are among those I wanted to suggest:

(A) The total speech act in the total speech situation is the *only actual* phenomenon which, in the last resort, we are engaged in elucidating.

(B) Stating, describing, &c., are *just two* names among a very great many others for illocutionary acts; they have no unique position.

(C) In particular, they have no unique position over the matter of being related to facts in a unique way called being true or false, because truth and falsity are (except by an artificial abstraction which is always possible for certain purposes) not names for relations, qualities, or what not, but for a dimension of assessment – how the words stand in respect of satisfactoriness to the facts, events, situations, &c., to which they refer.

(D) By the same token, the familiar contrast of 'normative or evaluative' as opposed to the factual is in need, like so many dichotomies, of elimination.

(Austin 1962b: 148)

The idea that language consists primarily in an activity is a recurrent focus of attention in the Western tradition: among its more salient latter-day champions one might mention Wilhelm von Humboldt (see Volume I, Chapter 13), J. R. Firth (see Chapter 5 above), and the later Wittgenstein (see Chapter 6 above). The reason it is merely recurrent, rather than permanent, is obvious enough. Western thought about language is predicated upon literacy (see Chapter 14 below). Writing abstracts from the total 'speech act' (which here stands for the act of utterance in any medium) a product which is offered to the reader as semiotically independent of the circumstances of its production. Authorship of the utterance you are now encountering is, indeed, ascribed to a triumvirate – a literary convention that would make no sense if it could not be safely assumed that an adequate grasp of the communicational interaction in progress is possible without answers to such questions as what the original speech act actually was, who performed it, in what specific context and for what precise purposes. Writing is responsible for propagating the idea that words have an intrinsic and self-sufficient semiotic 'content'; and, since systematic inquiry into language is itself conducted in writing, that inquiry is wedded from the outset to the conviction that this is no mere idea about the object under investigation, but constitutive of its very essence. Hence both the logico-philosophical and grammatico-philological strands in the Western tradition tend to divorce language from its human sponsors, focusing instead on the internal logical or grammatical mechanisms by which it putatively works as a situation-neutral device for encoding and decoding information about an objectively given extra-linguistic world.

From time to time antinomian thinkers have come forward to restore the lost perspective, redirecting attention to language as a complex of behavioural patterns embedded in the social lives of human beings. John Langshaw Austin (1911–60) approached the matter from an interestingly novel angle. To say that he viewed language as a form of activity is true enough, but fails to distinguish him from many others who have characterized language in such terms. Firth, for example, pointed out that to say something is to do something, but his main interest is in the saying. Austin, by contrast, is primarily concerned with what is done – with the ways in which doing something *may take the form of* saying something. The difference between Firth's term 'speech *event*' and Austin's term 'speech *act*' is instructive here (see Chapter 5 above).

In fact, linguistic topics per se are not especially prominent among the philosophical questions that Austin addressed. The essays in *Philosophical Papers* (Austin 1961) that deal specifically with language are outnumbered by those concerned with various other matters, while the courses of lectures posthumously published as *Sense and Sensibilia* (Austin 1962a) and *How to do Things with Words* (Austin 1962b) are on the face of it primarily contributions to, respectively, the philosophy of perception and the philosophy of action.

However, although language does not loom large among his overt philosophical interests, Austin was from first to last a linguistic philosopher. The distinction here is that between a topic or subject, and a method or mode of approach to a topic or subject. Philosophy of language is a subject; linguistic philosophy is a method. To illustrate the method, as used by Austin, we may take the long digression interpolated into *Sense and Sensibilia* on the 'Nature of Reality' (Austin 1962a: 62–77). The quest for criteria for a general distinction between appearance and reality has long preoccupied philosophers, and is clearly relevant to the philosophical study of perception. Hence the interest – indeed, Austin says, the importance – of the issue. Characteristically, he proceeds to tackle it by considering the English word *real*.

Real, he starts by saying, 'is an absolutely *normal* word, with nothing new-fangled or technical or highly specialized about it' (Austin 1962a: 62). It is firmly established in 'the ordinary language we all use every day' and therefore cannot 'be fooled around with *ad lib*' by philosophers who 'think that they can just "assign" any meaning whatever to any word'. Moreover, we must be wary of the philosophical habit of dismissing some of the ordinary uses of words as unimportant. For instance, 'if we are going to talk about "real", we must not dismiss as beneath contempt such humble but familiar expressions as "not real cream"; this may save us from saying, for example, or seeming to say that what is not real cream must be a fleeting product of our cerebral processes' (Austin 1962a: 63–4).

His next point is that *real* is '*not* a normal word at all, but highly exceptional', in that, although not ambiguous, it 'does not have one single, specifiable, always-the-same *meaning*' (Austin 1962a: 64). Comparable in this respect, Austin suggests, is *cricket*, as in *cricket ball, cricket bat, cricket pavilion, cricket weather* etc. *Cricket* here does not qualify the various nouns in these phrases in the way that, say, *yellow* qualifies the nouns in *yellow ball, yellow bat, yellow pavilion*: it does not point to some property or quality that the things so described observably all have, but to an extrinsic connection, different in different cases, with a certain game. Similarly, to call things 'real' is not to identify an attribute ('reality') that they all have in common. In the case of the phrase '(a) real *X*', the meaning of *real* will depend on what, in the context, real excludes. The point of calling cream 'real', for instance, will very often be to specify that it is not artificial.

In contrast, someone who says 'now that's a *real* carving-knife!' is concerned not to deny that it is artificial (what carving-knife is not?) but to assert that, unlike many carving-knives, it is especially apt for its purpose.

A rather different issue arises when *real* is collocated with nouns such as *colour, taste, shape*. Here the difficulty is to provide any answer at all to questions of the form 'What is the real X of this Y?'. What is the real colour of a fish that looks vividly multicoloured at a depth of a thousand feet, but a muddy sort of greyish white when caught and laid out on deck? What is the real taste of saccharine, given that when dissolved in a cup of tea it makes the tea sweet, but tastes bitter when taken neat? What is the real shape of a cat?

> Does its real shape change whenever it moves? If not, in what posture *is* its real shape on display? Furthermore, is its real shape such as to be fairly smooth-outlined, or must it be finely enough serrated to take account of each hair?

Austin continues:

> It is pretty obvious that there is *no* answer to these questions – no rules according to which, no procedure by which, answers are to be determined. Of course, there are plenty of shapes which the cat definitely is not – cylindrical, for instance. But only a desperate man would toy with the idea of ascertaining the cat's real shape 'by elimination'.
>
> (Austin 1962a: 67)

This is all good fun, but what of that supposedly important matter, the Nature of Reality? For the Austinian linguistic philosopher who proposes to deal with such a matter, the first step is to pay close attention to the ordinary usage of the words in which the problem is posed. But not only did Austin never take the next step, or even specify in general terms what that might be, it is often far from clear that the first step itself leads in any philosophically significant direction. The discussion of *real* is a case in point. The problem with which we are ostensibly concerned here is how to establish the distinction between something's seeming to be the case (from what one sees, hears, feels etc.) and its really being the case. Far from solving or dissolving that problem, or even demonstrating how attention to the words concerned yields a useful reformulation of it, Austin's lexicographical deliberations leave it essentially untouched. Indeed, to the extent that, in equating his discussion of *real* with an inquiry into the Nature of Reality (note the capital letters), his tongue is lodged in his cheek, it must in the end be doubtful how far Austin himself believed otherwise. Other philosophers, both contemporaneously and subsequently, have been much less equivocal: the current consensus is that, broadly speaking, Austin's linguistic method is philosophically useless. But in the present context that may be beside the point.

To start with the specific case in hand, the point of the discussion of *real* is that it reveals, not the nature of reality, but something about the relationship between reality and language. What mistake is made by someone who supposes, or misguidedly expects, that any premodifier does or should qualify its noun in such a way that the things so described will have some attribute in common? There is no doubt that very many premodifiers in English do work in this way: *yellow* may well, as Austin suggests, exemplify the 'normal' case. The mistake is to expect that how the language reflects or exhibits the reality in the normal case (i.e., here, by providing a linguistic formula $Y\ X$ for use when X has the perceptible attribute Y) will instantiate a stable or consistent or universal relationship between the piece of linguistic machinery in question and a certain kind of state of affairs in the world. In other words, a language is unreflectingly taken to provide a straightforward mapping of an objectively given reality. The interest of Austin's linguistic method, minimal though it may be as regards the light shed on the specifically philosophical issues the method is apparently intended to deal with, lies in the demonstration he offers that the mapping is not straightforward, and that conceptions of reality are not objectively given.

For instance, it is 'normal', Austin would say, for nouns to name, or designate, or refer to, some corresponding thing. That is why, in 'The meaning of a word', he treats the question 'what is the meaning of *rat*?' as equivalent to 'what is a rat?' (Austin 1961: 58). But preoccupation with the normal case can lead to the absurd belief that *whenever* there is a noun there must be a corresponding thing. In 'Are there *a priori* concepts?' (Austin 1961: 32–54) he rejects the idea that because we may call different sensa by the same name there must be a 'universal' common to all sensa called by that name. 'But why', asks Austin, 'if "one identical" word is used, *must* there be "one identical" object present which it denotes?' (Austin 1961: 38).

A striking example of a piece of linguistic machinery whose role in mapping the world is misunderstood if no account is taken of human contexts and purposes is the word *true*. Philosophers and linguists have expended much effort in attempting to set up a falsely monolithic correspondence between 'truth' on the one hand and 'states of affairs' on the other. Austin comments:

> We say, for example, that a certain statement is exaggerated or vague or bald, a description somewhat rough or misleading or not very good, an account rather general or too concise. In cases like these it is pointless to insist on deciding in simple terms whether the statement is 'true or false'. Is it true or false that Belfast is north of London? That the galaxy is the shape of a fried egg? . . . There are various *degrees and dimensions* of success in making statements: the statements fit the facts always more or less loosely, in different ways on different occasions for different intents and purposes.
>
> (Austin 1961: 129–30)

Furthermore, the 'facts' themselves are not objectively given. Typically, Austin arrives at this point via the consideration that *what*, in such an expression as *I know what I am feeling*, may be misconstrued as equivalent to Latin *quod* rather than *quid*. This confusion fosters the 'uncritical use of the direct object after *know*', and that in turn

> seems to be one thing that leads to the view that (or to talking as though) sensa, that is things, colours, noises, and the rest, speak or are labelled by nature, so that I can literally *say* what (that which) I *see*: it pipes up, or I read it off. It is as if sensa were *literally* to 'announce themselves' or to 'identify themselves', in the way we indicate when we say 'It presently identified itself as a particularly fine white rhinoceros'. But surely this is only a manner of speaking, a reflexive idiom in which the French, for example, indulge more freely than the English: sensa are dumb, and only previous experience enables *us* to identify them.
>
> (Austin 1961: 97)

We have to decide both what the facts are and what statement will fit them (more or less loosely), for particular purposes in particular circumstances. The fact–statement relationship is not provided, ready-made, for our use. The idea that it is – that both language and the world are given, and that the one somehow achieves a mapping of the other without human intervention – encourages the untenable expectation that language will provide in advance the appropriate verbal equipment for use in any contingency:

> If we have made sure it's a goldfinch, and a real goldfinch, and then in the future it does something outrageous (explodes, quotes Mrs Woolf, or what not), we don't say we were wrong to say it was a goldfinch, *we don't know what to say*. Words literally fail us: 'What would you have said?' 'What are we to say now?' 'What would *you* say?'
>
> (Austin 1961: 88)

Language, then, is an activity, something human beings *do* in the various situations and circumstances in which they find themselves. One of the things they do with it is construct a general understanding of the world, as expressed in the statements they make about the world. But making statements is by no means the only thing human beings do by or in speaking; and in *How to do Things with Words* (Austin 1962b) Austin's interest in what it is to do things – as expressed e.g. in 'A plea for excuses', 'Pretending', 'Three ways of spilling ink' (collected in Austin 1961) – combines with his linguistic method to bring about a large-scale contribution to the philosophy of language itself.

One important function of what grammarians identify as declarative (i.e. non-interrogative) sentences in the indicative mood is to permit the making of statements or assertions as to matters of fact. 'I name my goldfish after Roman emperors', 'I give little money to charity', 'I bet on the horses' serve to describe the utterer's behaviour – to give information, true or false, about what the utterer does. But there are other utterances, grammatically and perhaps (as here) even lexically similar to these, which are not, in appropriate contexts, used to make statements at all. Some of Austin's initial examples are: 'I name this ship the *Queen Elizabeth*' (as uttered when smashing the bottle against the stern), 'I give and bequeath my watch to my brother' (as occurring in a will), 'I bet you sixpence it will rain tomorrow'. In these cases, he says: 'it seems clear that to utter the sentences . . . is not to *describe* my doing of what I should be said in so uttering to be doing or to state that I am doing it: it is to do it' (Austin 1962b: 6).

Austin calls such utterances 'performatives'. When, at the appropriate stage of the ceremony, the duly appointed person says 'I name this ship . . .' he or she is not making a statement. In fact, he or she is not primarily *saying* something at all; he or she is performing an action, which in cases of this kind happens to take the form of uttering certain words. This view of the matter is supported, Austin observes, by American legal procedure, according to which a report of what someone says is admissible as evidence (that is, not ruled out as hearsay) if what he or she said was performative in this sense.

If in uttering a performative one is not making a statement, then what one says is not true or false. However, there is a dimension in which performatives may be assessed that in some respects corresponds to the true/false distinction for statements (or 'constatives'): performatives may be 'happy' or 'unhappy'. Austin proceeds to a categorization of the 'infelicities' to which performatives, or apparent or would-be performatives, are liable. Broadly summarizing for present purposes, we may say that infelicities are either 'misfires' or 'abuses'. To avoid a misfire, 'the particular persons and circumstances must be appropriate for the invocation of the particular procedure invoked', and 'the procedure must be executed by all participants both correctly and completely'. Abuse, in contrast, is what may occur when 'the procedure is designed for use by persons having certain thoughts or feelings, or for the inauguration of certain consequential conduct on the part of any participant'. If the performative procedure is to avoid abuse, 'a person participating in and so invoking the procedure must in fact have those thoughts and feelings, and the participants must intend so to conduct themselves, and further, must actually so conduct themselves subsequently' (Austin 1962b: 15). 'I name this ship . . .', for instance, is liable to misfire, while 'I promise . . .' is liable to abuse.

The distinction between the truth or falsity of a constative and the happiness or unhappiness of a performative seems at first sight clear enough. But Austin proceeds to probe it carefully. He observes, fairly trivially, that in the case of 'I promise' abuse may take the form of issuing what we call a 'false promise', but we should not be misled here: if I utter the performative formula 'I promise . . .' when I have no intention of keeping my word, I may be said to have promised falsely, but that does not show that 'I promise . . .' was a false *statement*; on the contrary, I did indeed promise. What it shows is merely that 'false' has other uses, in contexts where assessing the truth or falsity of statements is not in question, as in, for example, 'a false move', 'a false (musical) note'. Less trivially, Austin points out that the idea of a hard and fast distinction between constatives and performatives in terms of 'true/false' versus 'happy/unhappy' begins to lose its appeal once we think about particular utterances in particular contexts. The constative 'the cat is on the mat', we may say, is clearly false if uttered in a situation where we have a cat and a mat, but the cat is curled up on the sofa. But what if we have no cat, or two cats, or several mats? Would we say that the statement is *false*, or rather that the speaker's oral *performance* is infelicitous in some other way? Conversely, take the case where one says, performatively, 'I warn you that the bull is about to charge' when the bull is not in fact about to charge. As the performance of an act of warning, this is somehow problematic, but it is not a misfire or an abuse, as Austin has defined these. Is it not rather that the implied *statement* is false? That is, in actual contexts of utterance, 'considerations of the happiness or unhappiness type may infect statements (or some statements) and considerations of the type of truth and falsity may infect performatives (or some performatives)' (Austin 1962b: 55).

Having taken such steps 'out of the desert of comparative precision' (Austin 1962b: 55), Austin then considers whether performatives have any specific grammatical earmark. The initial examples all had verbs in the first-person singular present indicative active. But, as we have seen, this is clearly not a sufficient criterion of performativeness: non-performative utterances may also have such verbs. Nor is it necessary: the verb in a performative need not be first person ('you must turn right here'), or singular ('we promise . . .'), or present ('you were offside', as uttered by the referee), or indicative ('eat up your spinach') or active ('trespassers will be prosecuted'). Indeed, there need not be a verb at all ('out!', 'guilty!'). So what, if anything, is special or significant about the cases where there is such a verb?

The essence of a performative utterance, Austin now says, is that 'there is something which is *at the moment of uttering being done by the person uttering* . . . the "I" who is doing the action

... come[s] essentially into the picture' (Austin 1962b: 60–1). If the 'I' is not overtly present in the utterance itself, he or she is there in some other way, either in virtue of being the person doing the uttering, or, in the case of written performatives, in the form of his or her signature (without which many written legal acts, for instance, are void). In sum, 'what we should feel tempted to say is that any utterance which is in fact a performative should be reducible, or expandible, or analysable into a form, or reproducible in a form, with a verb in the first person singular present indicative active' (Austin 1962b: 61–2).

So 'guilty' is equivalent to 'I find (pronounce, deem) you to be guilty', 'you are warned that the bull is dangerous' is equivalent to 'I, John Jones, warn you that the bull is dangerous', 'we promise . . .' is equivalent to 'I, in conjunction with the other person(s) referred to by "we", promise . . .'. Performatives in which such a verb appears overtly make explicit what is at least latent in any performative: that the speaker, in uttering these words, is performing an action. One-word utterances such as 'bull' or 'thunder' *could* be warnings, or predictions; but they could be constatives, used to give information that might be true or false. The explicitly performative alternatives 'I warn you that . . .', 'I predict that . . .' eliminate this ambiguity.

However, it is far from clear that the availability of an alternative expression with an explicit verb in the first-person singular present indicative active suffices to distinguish performatives from constatives. For is not such an alternative available when 'constating' too? Just as the *warning* 'there is a bull in the field' may be expanded into 'I warn you that there is a bull in the field', so the *statement* 'there is a bull in the field' may be expanded into 'I state that there is a bull in the field'. In fact, it appears that *any* utterance may be prefixed by 'I *x* (that)', where *x* indicates the kind of speech act in progress. What has emerged from Austin's attempt to isolate performatives as a special class of utterances where to say something is to do something is that to say *anything* is to do something: every utterance is a communicative act of some kind, the nature of which may or may not be overtly specified in the utterance itself. The initial distinction between performatives and constatives, so apparently clear and straightforward, has broken down.

The reason it has broken down is that, having started out (for pedagogical or expository reasons, presumably) by identifying as performatives some of the clearest and most striking cases where to say something is to do something – namely, where the performative utterance functions as a or the operative element in an established ritual or ceremonial procedure ('I name this ship . . .', 'I give and bequeath . . .'), Austin proceeds to conflate performatives in this sense with, or to see them as a special subtype of, the very large class of utterances where to speak is to do something other than state facts (e.g. express a wish, a hope; give an order, a warning; make a plea, an entreaty; etc.). If 'performative' has this much more general sense (and it is clear enough that it was really intended to have this more general sense all along), then the dichotomy of performative and constative is clearly untenable, for in this sense stating a fact is just as much a 'performance' as giving an order, issuing a warning, etc. Given (what appeared to be) the original understanding of 'performative', the quest for a line of demarcation between utterances that do, and utterances that do not, constitute (part of) the performance of an act, was fair enough. Given the broader sense, however, it leads up a blind alley. So Austin makes a new start and proceeds 'to consider from the ground up how many senses there are in which to say something *is* to do something, or *in* saying something we do something, and even *by* saying something we do something' (Austin 1962b: 94).

The act of saying something, in and of itself, Austin proposes to call a 'locutionary act'. The locutionary act is simultaneously a 'phonetic' act, a 'phatic' act, and a 'rhetic' act. The phonetic act is the act of uttering certain noises. The phatic act is the uttering of certain words (i.e. noises of certain types) belonging to a certain vocabulary and conforming to a certain grammar. The rhetic act is the act of using those words 'with a certain more or less definite "sense" and a more or less definite "reference" (which together are equivalent to "meaning")' (Austin 1962b: 93). So, for example, 'Mary said [ðəkʰætɪzɒnðəmæt]' reports Mary's phonetic act, 'Mary said "The cat is on the mat"' reports her phatic act, while 'Mary said that the cat is on the mat' reports her rhetic act. Austin continues:

> To perform a locutionary act is in general, we may say, also and *eo ipso* to perform an *illocutionary* act, as I propose to call it. Thus in performing a locutionary act we shall also be performing such an act as:

asking or answering a question,
giving some information or an assurance or a warning,
announcing a verdict or an intention,
pronouncing sentence,
making an appointment or an appeal or a criticism,
making an identification or giving a description,
and the numerous like.

(Austin 1962b: 98–9)

He then goes on to contrast the locutionary and the illocutionary acts with the *perlocutionary* act. Take, for example, an utterance 'shoot her!'. Here the locutionary act is the act of saying 'shoot her!' meaning by 'shoot' shoot, and referring by 'her' to the female in question. The illocutionary act exploits a superimposed communicative import those words have as uttered in the given situation: in this case it is the act of ordering (or, in different circumstances, perhaps urging or advising) me to shoot her. The perlocutionary act is the purpose or effect of uttering those words in the given situation: in this case it might be the act of compelling me to shoot her. To start from the other end, we might say that (1) he compelled me to shoot her by uttering words which (2) in their context constituted an order, and which (3) bear the meaning 'shoot her', where (1), (2) and (3) correspond to the perlocutionary, illocutionary and locutionary acts respectively.

Austin is chiefly interested in contrasting the illocutionary act with the other two. (This is not surprising, since the illocutionary act is the 'performance' that he has been concerned with from the outset.) All three clearly have something to do with meaning, but there is, he suggests, a tendency to approach the general domain of meaning armed with a simplistic and misleading dichotomy of 'sense' versus 'force' (other pairs of terms would do just as well) that may obscure the distinctiveness of the illocutionary act. The sense of an expression (word, sentence) is that part or aspect of its meaning establishable in the abstract, irrespective of any actual or envisaged context of utterance: it is 'what the words mean'. The force of an expression is what is contributed to its meaning by the circumstances of its use on a particular occasion: it is 'what is meant by using the words'. The locutionary act, by definition, is the act of uttering certain words with a certain context-free sense. The perlocutionary act depends on a certain context-dependent force attached to those words. The illocutionary act cuts across, or is sandwiched between, the terms of this dichotomy. The illocutionary force of an utterance is not part of the meaning the words have simply in virtue of being those words. On the other hand, the illocutionary act is performed *by* or *in* rather than merely *through* using those words. The illocutionary force of an utterance is simultaneously both context-dependent and, in context, inherent in the uttering of the words themselves. To say 'shoot her!' is, in the appropriate context, to issue an order – a fact that could be made explicit by substituting 'I order you to shoot her'. But to say 'shoot her!' is not *eo ipso* to compel me to shoot her, even if I am in fact compelled by your words. (And if I am not, substituting 'I compel you to shoot her' will hardly help matters.) Ordering is something one does by using certain words; compelling is something one may succeed in doing through the use of certain words.

So 'performativeness', which Austin originally identified as a (indeed, the) function of utterances of a certain special kind, eventually re-emerges from a consideration of speech acts in general as a property or attribute of any utterance – i.e. its 'illocutionary force'. He concludes the book with a general typology of illocutionary forces.

What is the legacy? First, the concept 'speech act', at least in the English-speaking world, seems likely to become part of the common cultural stock of notions pertaining to language: to that extent Austin has made a pervasive and lasting contribution. More specifically, speech acts have been the focus of a great deal of technical philosophical discussion: Austin wrote the introduction to a new and not yet completed chapter in the philosophy of language. Within linguistics, he may be seen as presaging the 'subjectivist' semantics associated with Langacker's 'cognitive linguistics' (Langacker 1987, 1991). Consideration of the aspect of his thought invoked in this connection will enable us to pinpoint a crucial lacuna in his vision of language.

One or another version of the thesis that languages are not nomenclatures – that words are not labels attached to, or names standing for, the components of a reality whose analysis into those components is manifest *in rerum natura* – was widely accepted by twentieth-century theorists: Austin by no means stands alone in this regard. Wittgenstein rejects the view that words 'stand for' things at all. Saussure rejects the view that words stand for things that are extra-linguistically given. For Saussure, a language may be seen as providing names for things (concepts), but what those things are is determined holistically by the language itself: there are no independently given things, and what thing a given word names is a matter of the gap left for it by all the other words in the same language. Cognitivist semantics puts flesh on this jejune and abstract Saussurean vision by suggesting *how* a language selects things for which to supply names. A language does this, according to the cognitivist, by reflecting its speakers' cognition – their particular way of construing the world. This is where Austin comes in. Words come to us, says Austin, 'trailing clouds of etymology':

> a word never – well, hardly ever – shakes off its etymology and its formation. In spite of all the changes in and extensions of and additions to its meaning, and indeed rather pervading and governing these, there will still persist the old idea. In an *accident* something befalls: by mistake you take the wrong one: in *error* you stray: when you act *deliberately* you weigh it up ...
>
> Going back into the history of a word ... we come back pretty commonly to pictures or *models* of how things happen or are done ... We take *some very simple action*, like shoving a stone, usually as done by and viewed by oneself, and use *this*, with the features distinguishable in it, as our model in terms of which to talk about other actions and events: and we continue to do so, scarcely realising it, even when these other actions are pretty remote and perhaps much more interesting to us in their own right than the acts originally used in constructing the model ever were, and even when the model is really distorting the facts rather than helping us to observe them.
>
> (Austin 1961: 202–3)

Whatever the value of this view of words as embodying a fossilized understanding of things, Austin fails to reconcile it with his theorizing about speech acts. The total speech act in the total speech situation is the only actual phenomenon we are engaged in elucidating. That is because it is the only actual linguistic phenomenon that occurs. What this consideration calls in question is the notion of illocutionary and perlocutionary acts as a superstructure erected on a *locutionary* act, which is the act of uttering certain words with a certain antecedently given, context-independent, fossilized-understanding-of-things-embodying meaning. In so far as words come to have such a meaning, it can presumably have been conferred on them, on Austin's own account, only as an unintended perlocutionary effect of prior speech acts. At the very least, a word cannot have a 'locutionary meaning' on the first occasion of its utterance; and the first speech act could not have been a locutionary act. There is a dimension missing from Austin's theory of speech acts – an account of how, *through the performance of speech acts themselves*, language as an activity gives rise to the very conception of language and languages that the theory sets out to undermine.

Chapter 8

Skinner on verbal behaviour

The study of speech-sounds without regard to meanings is an abstraction: in actual use, speech-sounds are uttered as signals. We have defined the *meanings* of a linguistic form as the situation in which the speaker utters it and the response which it calls forth in the hearer.

(Bloomfield 1933: 139)

Behaviourism is a form of 'anti-psychology', limited to the study of the objectively observable actions of human beings, without any speculation as to mental processes. Introduced in its modern form by the American John B. Watson (1878–1958), it has clear links with Western empiricism extending back to Aristotle, and more particularly with the tradition of British empiricism that began in the sixteenth century with Francis Bacon (1561–1626). The first twentieth-century linguist to take the behaviourist doctrine up explicitly was Leonard Bloomfield (1887–1949). For modernists such as Bloomfield and Sapir (see Chapter 1 above), the kind of language analysis found for example in the *Oxford English Dictionary* is itself part of the language's cultural heritage, and therefore could not be expected to penetrate the essence of the language from without, in an objective, scientific way. That could be done only by analysing English just as one did with 'primitive' languages – dropping traditional categories in favour of something so pure in its logical rigour as to be above suspicion of cultural non-objectivity. The approach proposed by Saussure, in which no element in a language system is invested with value except through its difference from any other element, seemed to achieve that sort of purity. Behaviourism too offered a methodological purity, the appeal of which was not entirely lost even on Sapir, though in the end his intense interest in the bond between psychology and culture prevented him from adopting it as a master schema in the way Bloomfield did.

There has been much confusion about Bloomfield's position on meaning in language. One reason for the confusion is that in statements like the one at the start of this chapter he emphasizes the need for the study of speech forms to take account of meaning in order to avoid being purely abstract. But then he makes clear that he is using 'meaning' in the peculiarly behaviouristic sense of situation and response. Thus he does give a prominent place to meaning – in the letter, but not in the spirit. So far as the common-sense meaning of linguistic 'meaning' is concerned, Bloomfield wants to avoid it. It implies a pre-behaviouristic notion of the sense of a word residing in the 'mind'. Again, behaviourism is a highly 'positivistic' approach to science that takes only directly observable facts to be real. The mind is not directly observable, at least not objectively. We may feel or sense its existence, but in an entirely subjective way. We have no means of observing anyone else's mind, nor can anyone else observe ours. This lack of objective verification makes any positivistic proof of the mind's existence impossible. Behaviourists therefore preferred to treat the concept of 'mind', like that of God, as a relic of an older, metaphysical way of thinking which had no place in modern, physical, objective science. Bloomfield himself frequently characterized his own way of thinking as 'mechanistic', in contrast to the 'mentalistic' approach which he rejected.

> Adherents of mentalistic psychology believe that they can avoid the difficulty of defining meanings, because they believe that, prior to the utterance of a linguistic form, there occurs within the speaker a non-physical process, a *thought, concept, image, feeling, act of will*, or the like, and that the hearer, likewise, upon receiving the sound-waves, goes through an equivalent or correlated mental process . . . For the mentalist, language is *the expression of ideas, feelings,* or *volitions.*
>
> The mechanist does not accept this solution. He believes that *mental images, feelings,* and the like are merely popular terms for various bodily movements, which, so far as they concern language, can be roughly divided into three types:

(1) large-scale processes which are much the same in different people, and, having some social importance, are represented by conventional speech-forms, such as *I'm hungry* (*angry, frightened, sorry, glad*; *my head aches*, and so on);

(2) obscure and highly variable small-scale muscular contractions and glandular secretions, which differ from person to person and, having no immediate social importance, are not represented by conventional speech-forms;

(3) soundless movements of the vocal organs, taking the place of speech-movements, but not perceptible to other people ('thinking in words').

. . . The mechanist believes that the processes in (2) are private habits left over, as traces, from the vicissitudes of education and other experience; the speaker reports them as *images, feelings*, and so on, and they differ not only for every speaker, but for every occasion of speech. The speaker who says, 'I had the mental image of an apple,' is really saying, 'I was responding to some obscure internal stimuli of a type which was associated at some time in my past with the stimuli of an apple' . . . In sum, then, the 'mental processes' seem to the mechanist to be merely traditional names for bodily processes . . .

. . . The events which the mentalist designates as mental processes and the mechanist classifies otherwise, affect in every case only one person: every one of us responds to them when they occur within him, but has no way of responding to them when they occur in anyone else. The mental processes or internal bodily processes of other people are known to each one of us only from speech-utterances and other observable actions.

(Bloomfield 1933: 142–3)

Today, when 'mechanistic' is used exclusively as a term of abuse for any method which fails to take account of the complexity of wilful human action, it is surprising to see Bloomfield embrace it as a label for his own work. Yet even at the start of the 1930s he was still writing in the palpable wake of Darwin (1809–82). The general cultural mood had become receptive towards evolutionary theory, and a science of language that approached it from strict observation of people as essentially signalling and responding animals, operating within an environment which determined their every action and reaction, corresponded to one interpretation of the evolutionary picture of history as being based on environmental determination of sexual selection. In the spirit of the time such an approach was perceived as more modern and scientific than one which still gave a central role to the mind as the agent of human will or, as in Freud's theory, its shaping force.

The year after the publication of Bloomfield's *Language* (1933), Burrhus Frederic Skinner (1904–90), a failed novelist turned experimental psychologist, launched a similarly spirited but methodologically very different programme for the behaviourist analysis of language.

> Idioms and expressions which seem to explain verbal behavior in term [*sic*] of ideas are so common in our language that it is impossible to avoid them, but they may be little more than moribund figures of speech . . . One unfortunate consequence is the belief that speech has an independent existence apart from the behavior of the speaker . . . It is true that verbal behavior usually produces objective entities. The sound-stream of vocal speech, the words on a page, the signals transmitted on a telephone or telegraph wire – these are records left by verbal behavior. As objective facts, they may all be studied, as they have been from time to time in linguistics, communication engineering, literary criticism, and so on. But although the formal properties of the records of utterances are interesting, we must preserve the distinction between an activity and its traces.
>
> (Skinner 1957: 7)

The Preface to *Verbal Behavior* (Skinner 1957) lays out its long history. Skinner completed a major portion of it in 1934, and taught courses from it at Harvard and Chicago in 1938–9. A Guggenheim Fellowship to complete it in 1941 was interrupted by the war, during which he first gained notoriety for his work using behaviourist principles in training pigeons to guide missiles. A shorter version was presented as the William James Lectures at Harvard in 1947 and circulated in mimeograph, following nationwide publicity for the 'Skinner box', a unit for controlling the environment of infants, which he tried without success to market commercially. The book was finally published a decade later, by which time Skinner, the exponent of 'radical behaviourism', had become the most famous psychologist of his generation. Then in 1959 *Verbal Behavior* was demolished in one of the most famous academic book reviews of the twentieth century.

During the book's long gestation period, Skinner remained surprisingly out of touch with American linguists, despite their shared commitment to behaviourism. Mainstream American linguistics of the 1940s and 1950s was committed to the behaviourist line established by Bloomfield's *Language* (1933), but Bloomfield's students differed among themselves over how seriously to take his anti-mentalism. If one accepted the behaviourist view that, because the mind does not allow objective observation, it cannot be the proper object of a scientific inquiry, then what exactly were the status and location of the language system itself? No one believed more strongly in its real existence than Bloomfield did, but *where* it might exist does not seem to have worried him.

That Skinner was familiar with the work of Bloomfield and his students is clear from his reasonably accurate summary of how they treat the phoneme (Skinner 1957: 15–16). But he differentiates his approach from theirs by suggesting that they are interested in form whereas he is interested in function; they in the practices of whole verbal communities, he in the behaviour of an individual speaker; they in the conditions in which past behaviour has occurred, he in prediction and control of future behaviour. The main difference, and the one that goes farthest to explain the distance he and the linguists kept from one another, is alluded to in the quotation from *Verbal Behavior* above, and stated explicitly in the one which follows.

> In defining verbal behavior as behavior reinforced through the mediation of other persons we do not, and cannot, specify any one form, mode, or medium. Any movement capable of affecting another organism may be verbal. We are likely to single out vocal behavior, not only because it is commonest, but because it has little effect upon the physical environment and hence is almost necessarily verbal.
>
> (Skinner 1957: 14)

For the linguists – even the Bloomfieldians – a great deal rode on 'the belief that speech has an independent existence apart from the behavior of the speaker'. If it does not have that independent existence, then what exactly is the status of linguistics? Linguists would seem to be studying merely the 'traces' of the activity, as Skinner puts it, rather than the essential activity itself. The implication is that linguistics is a sort of counterfeit, compared with the real act of studying language that is the work of the behaviourist psychologist. *Verbal Behavior* sets out to lay the foundation of this study.

> What is needed for present purposes – and what the traditional 'word' occasionally approximates – is a unit of behavior composed of a response of identifiable form functionally related to one or more independent variables . . . Any unit of such behavior is conveniently called 'an operant.'
>
> (Skinner 1957: 20)

The key term in Skinner's system, *operant*, might be thought of as simply a relabelling of the traditional category 'word' – except that, since Skinner does not confine the verbal to the spoken-written-signed, a verbal operant could just as well be a movement of the body. Moreover, he allows for the possibility that certain collocations of words such as *when all is said and done* or *haste makes waste* may be shown to vary as a unit under the control of a variable, in which case they would constitute a single operant. The whole set of operants which appear in a speaker's behaviour make up his or her *verbal repertoire*, which is understood as 'a convenient construct' defining the speaker's potential behaviour.

The keywords of first-generation behaviourism, 'stimulus' and 'response', which figure prominently in Bloomfield's *Language* (1933), occur less frequently than one might expect in *Verbal Behavior*. Skinnerian behaviourism shifts the focus from stimulus and response as external and purely objective facts to their internal effects on the individual – what it is that happens between receiving the stimulus and performing the response that allows the link between them to be explained and, most importantly, predicted. Skinner's term for this process within the individual is *operant conditioning*. The innumerable impressions we receive from the world around us do not automatically constitute 'stimuli' that will contribute to operant conditioning. They do so only when the response they call forth is *reinforced*, rewarded in some way, by the other party or parties taking part in the verbal behaviour. The 'schedule of reinforcement' of a particular operant determines its 'strength' within the individual's verbal repertoire, understood as its probability of emission under specified circumstances. The strength of an operant is measurable by the energy level, speed and repetition of its emission, as well as by a tendency for it to be emitted inappropriately, i.e. with 'inadequate' stimulation. 'The probability that a verbal response of a given form will occur at a given time is the basic datum to be predicted and controlled. It is the "dependent variable" in a functional analysis' (Skinner 1957: 28). Predicting and controlling the occurrence of verbal operants will be achieved by analysing the independent variables, which include conditioning and reinforcement, aversive control (escaping injury), motivation (e.g. satiation and deprivation, and including ageing and the effects of drugs and alcohol), emotion (e.g. joy and frustration, which, not surprisingly, he treats purely in terms of physical reactions). He does not attempt to distinguish rigorously among these categories, so that aversive control is sometimes treated as part of motivation, and deprivation as part of emotion, and he emphasizes that multiple causation is the rule, not the exception.

In subsequent chapters of *Verbal Behavior* (1957), Skinner introduces three further neologisms for the analysis of verbal behaviour: the 'mand', the 'tact' and the 'autoclitic'. The mand is 'the type of verbal operant in which a response of given form is characteristically followed by a given consequense [*sic*] in a verbal community' (Skinner 1957: 35): *Wait!* followed by someone waiting, *Sh-h!* followed by silence, *Candy!* followed by receipt of candy. He notes that what is singular about the mand from the behaviourist point of view is that, whereas other types of verbal operants are associated with behaviour that mainly benefits the listener, the mand tends to work for the benefit of the speaker. It is not obvious how listeners are conditioned to respond to the mand *Candy!*, when they themselves do not receive reinforcement from it in the form of a piece of candy. Therefore the 'total speech episode' must be taken into account, 'all the relevant events in the behavior of both speaker and listener in their proper temporal order' (Skinner 1957: 36). The category of mands includes not only what are traditionally called commands but also requests, prayers or entreaties, questions, advice, warnings, permission, offers and calls.

'Extended mands', including monologues, talking to dolls or animals, wishes and other 'superstitious' or 'magical' mands, are treated in a section highly reminiscent of Ogden and Richards's long chapter on 'Word magic' in *The Meaning of Meaning* (Ogden and Richards 1923) – which, for reasons outlined in Chapter 1 on Sapir, also gives Skinner an indirect link with Whorf (see Chapter 4 above). Indeed, the quotation at the start of the present chapter proposes in Whorfian fashion that 'the belief that speech has an independent existence apart from the behavior of the speaker' is the 'unfortunate consequence' of 'moribund figures of speech'. Hence too the necessity of neologistically remaking our vocabulary for talking about talking.

The tact is defined by Skinner as 'a verbal operant in which a response of a given form is evoked (or at least strengthened) by a particular object or event or property of an object or event' (Skinner 1957: 81–2). It is what is normally referred to as the use of a word to 'talk about' a thing or event, as when, in the presence of a doll, a child says *doll*. Skinner is interested not in the relationship between word and thing but in how the relation between response and controlling stimulus is conditioned within the individual – again, not so obvious given that there is no immediate reward for talking about something one already has in hand. 'Extended tacts' include metaphors, solecisms, naming, guessing and the sort of 'generic extension' that occurs when a speaker calls a new kind of chair a 'chair'.

Metaphor is central to Skinner's whole conception of verbal behaviour, just as it has been for so many theories of language which focus on the problem of meaning (as Skinner does, despite all his attempts to behaviour-babble it away).

> Metaphorical extension is most useful when no other response is available. (Unfortunately, metaphor is also often useful when there is nothing to say. John Horne Tooke pointed this out ...). In a novel situation to which no generic term can be extended, the only effective behavior may be metaphorical. The widespread use of metaphor in literature demonstrates this advantage ... A Dostoyevsky, a Jane Austen, a Stendhal, a Melville, a Tolstoy, a Proust, or a Joyce seem to show a grasp of human behavior which is beyond the methods of science.
> (Skinner 1957: 98)

Throughout the book, most of the data cited by Skinner, apart from unsystematic, anecdotal observations he had noted down over the years, are examples taken from works of literature. Considerable stretches of the book, particularly the later chapters, focus on literature exclusively. Rather than give up his boyhood enthusiasm, the failed novelist tried to integrate it into his behaviourism, where it did not sit comfortably, and likely provided a further irritant to the linguists, who had struggled long and hard to establish their disciplinary independence from literature-centred philology.

Skinner says that the extension of tacts, if carried on without limit, would result in chaos, since every possible stimulus would potentially call forth every possible response. The verbal community counteracts extension by introducing *abstraction*, whereby a particular property of a thing is uniquely authorized to stand for the whole class of those things. 'A proper noun is a tact in which the response is under the control of a specific person or thing. A common noun is a tact in which the response is under the control of a property defining a class of persons or things' (Skinner 1957: 113). Only the latter, in Skinner's terms, is an abstraction.

This section on 'Abstraction' is a point of no return for readers of *Verbal Behavior* (Skinner 1957). Those who may have given Skinner the benefit of the doubt for the first hundred pages can here scarcely ignore the fact that he has identified the tact as the most important class of verbal operants, dwelt at length on its metaphorical and other extensions, declared them a danger – and then sets up in opposition to them a process of 'abstraction' that is not clearly separable from the extensions themselves. He defines it with false distinctions such as the one just quoted between proper and common nouns, which not only describes inaccurately the common usage it purports to report but glosses over its reliance on the ontological gaps between 'control' by persons, things and words. Just when he should confront the problem, Skinner abruptly changes the subject, and introduces several long quotations, including one from I. A. Richards on 'word magic'.

The last of Skinner's key neologistic analytic categories, the autoclitic, is even more heterogeneous than the mand or the tact. It includes expressions containing what are normally called intention, propositional attitudes, assertion and deliberate composition. Negation is always autoclitic, whereas the autoclitic function is cancelled with quotation marks. Thus *I say he's right* contains an autoclitic (an assertion), *I say 'He's right'* does not, and *I don't say 'He's right'* does (a negation). But to complicate matters enormously, Skinner includes all of grammar and syntax under 'autoclitic processes'. The chapter devoted to them climaxes in an extended account of that 'extraordinary book written in the late eighteenth century by John Horne Tooke', *The Diversions of Purley* (see Volume I, Chapter 12), with Skinner adopting Tooke's view that nouns and verbs are the only real words, and all others are 'abbreviations' of complex relations (Skinner 1957: 340). Skinner further agrees with Tooke – with strong echoes of Ogden – that the grammatical distinction between nouns and verbs is arbitrary and unnecessary. He identifies the following passage from Tooke as the one in which 'Perhaps he came closest to the present position' (Skinner 1957: 343).

> The business of the mind, as far as it concerns language, appears to me to be very simple. It extends no further than to receive impressions, that is, to have Sensations or Feelings. What are called its operations, are merely the operations of Language. A consideration of *Ideas*, or of the *Mind*, or of *Things* (relative to the Parts of Speech), will lead us no further than to *Nouns*: i.e., the signs of those impressions, or names of ideas. The other Part of Speech, the *Verb*, must be accounted for from the necessary use of it in communication. It is in fact the communication itself: and therefore well denominated Ρημα‛, *Dictum*. For the verb is *QUOD loquimur*; the Noun, *DE QUO*.
>
> (Tooke 1857)

'What Tooke lacked', according to Skinner, 'was a conception of behavior as such'; nevertheless, here 'Tooke is talking about verbal behavior' (Skinner 1957: 343). It becomes clear that Skinner ultimately believes syntax is unimportant because his basic picture is one of the discrete operant, a single word or set phrase, being produced in response to a discrete stimulus, and functioning in turn as a discrete stimulus for the listener. 'An obscene word', he points out, 'has its effect regardless of its location or grammar' (Skinner 1957: 344).

If this summary of *Verbal Behavior* (Skinner 1957) has seemed disjointed and unsystematic, with no clear sense of how it goes about achieving the goals set at the beginning, then it has succeeded all too well in conveying the nature of the book itself. It was a fragile vessel on which to launch a new theory of

language, and, at least as far as linguistics was concerned, it was
sunk explosively.

> He confidently and repeatedly voices his claim to have demon-
> strated that the contribution of the speaker is quite trivial and
> elementary, and that precise prediction of verbal behavior
> involves only specification of the few external factors that he
> has isolated experimentally with lower organisms . . . Since
> Skinner's work is the most extensive attempt to accommodate
> human behavior involving higher mental faculties within a
> strict behaviorist schema of the type that has attracted many
> linguists and philosophers, as well as psychologists, a detailed
> documentation is of independent interest. The magnitude of
> the failure of this attempt to account for verbal behavior serves
> as a kind of measure of the importance of the factors omitted
> from consideration, and an indication of how little is really
> known about this remarkably complex phenomenon.
>
> (Chomsky 1959: 27–8)

The first sentence quoted here is inaccurate. The only way readers
of *Verbal Behavior* could come away with the sense that the contribution of the speaker is trivial and elementary is if they believe
that to extend the measure of that contribution beyond words
to actions, and beyond isolated speakers to include those with
whom they are interacting, is to deny the strictly vocal speaker
their rightful place at the centre of the linguistic universe. Nor
does Skinner claim any extension from his experiments with
lower animals to human verbal behaviour. As Andresen (1990b:
149b) points out, 'Chomsky's review is 31-pages long. On 13 of
those pages, Chomsky refers to rats or Skinner's bar-pressing
experiments, often more than once per page – although nowhere
in *Verbal Behavior* is there mention of rats.' In the wake of
Chomsky's review, few linguists would bother to read the book
and find out what it was really about.

This is not however to say that Chomsky's fire was entirely
misdirected. When it came to Skinner's analytical system of mands
and tacts and operant conditioning, Chomsky's criticisms were
levelled with deadly accuracy.

> Other examples of 'stimulus control' merely add to the general
> mystification. Thus a proper noun is held to be a response

'under the control of a specific person or thing' . . . I have often used the words *Eisenhower* and *Moscow*, which I presume are proper nouns if anything is, but have never been 'stimulated' by the corresponding objects . . . Elsewhere it is asserted that a stimulus controls a response in the sense that presence of the stimulus increases the probability of the response. But it is obviously untrue that the probability that a speaker will produce a full name is increased when its bearer faces the speaker. Furthermore, how can one's own name be a proper noun in this sense? A multitude of similar questions arise immediately. It appears that the word 'control' here is merely a misleading paraphrase for the traditional 'denote' or 'refer'.

(Chomsky 1959: 32–3)

[I]n each case, if we take his terms in their literal meaning, the description covers almost no aspect of verbal behavior, and if we take them metaphorically, the description offers no improvement over various traditional formulations.

(Chomsky 1959: 54)

Everything Skinner had to say, in other words, was either irrelevant or amounted to old wine in new bottles. Even what Chomsky infers to be Skinner's view of how children learn their native language – another topic Skinner in fact never broached – is treated by Chomsky as merely common sense, bringing us no closer to an understanding of how that learning takes place.

As far as acquisition of language is concerned, it seems clear that reinforcement, casual observation, and natural inquisitiveness (coupled with a strong tendency to imitate) are important factors, as is the remarkable capacity of the child to generalize, hypothesize, and 'process information' in a variety of very special and apparently highly complex ways which we cannot yet describe or begin to understand, and which may be largely innate, or may develop through some sort of learning or through maturation of the nervous system.

(Chomsky 1959: 43)

Over the next decade Chomsky's position would become more firmly polarized to Skinner's, as he moved to the view that children's general, non-linguistic cognitive capacities are actually unconnected to their acquisition of language, and that input from those around them is not an important factor in acquisition, having only the rather trivial function of triggering mechanisms which must be innate (see Chapter 9, Chapter 12 below). Again, *Verbal Behavior* never raises the issue of children's learning of language, nor gives any sort of privileged status to the child language-learner. The fairest inference to draw from Skinner's book is that children's language can be studied in its own terms, to determine the operant conditioning that allows us to predict what a child will utter at a given stage of its development, and that those predictions will change at every stage of a person's life, so there is no 'critical age' at which operant conditioning stops or ceases to be of scientific interest to the behaviourist. It is not necessarily unfair of a reviewer to suggest that the book ought to have articulated a specific theory of child language acquisition. But such was the power of Chomsky's review that many people today believe that Skinner did just that, and that the theory he articulated was untenable.

Surprisingly, the linguistic 'establishment' of Bloomfield's former students did not take Chomsky's review as an attack on their own behaviourist inclinations. On the contrary, they generally relished it as the fending off of an encroachment into their field by a famous and powerful outsider. Chomsky was certainly on their side when he contested Skinner's views that:

- words and collocations of words, rather than phonology, grammar and syntax, are the core of linguistic inquiry
- verbal behaviour extends beyond the vocal, which aligns Skinner with the British pragmatic tradition as well as with semiotics
- linguists study the mere trace of what is real in verbal behaviour.

Regarding the second point, Andresen (1990b: 150) writes that 'With this excoriating review, Chomsky might be said to have programmatically exiled pragmatics from language theory'. The third point meant that Chomsky succeeded in turning around the implication of who was doing the real thing and who was counterfeiting.

Over the following five years, however, the generation gap separating Chomsky and his followers from the students of

Bloomfield would widen immensely, so that the latter would come to be seen as the enemy by Chomsky's students and associates, and would gradually be assimilated to Skinner in the mythology of Chomsky's generative linguistics. This was an ironic turn of events, given that, in hindsight at least, Chomsky actually shared with Skinner, in opposition to the Bloomfieldian linguists, at least two key positions:

- that linguistics should be concerned with explanation and prediction rather than with description;
- that linguistics should shift from the study of the community to the study of the individual.

In the latter case, the way both Skinner and Chomsky construct 'the individual' has proved spurious. Neither is interested in actual individuals. Rather, both are committed to a view of science as generalizable knowledge that requires the 'individual' to be an idealization – in fact, an idealization of a whole community.

Looking back today at the points on which Chomsky saw himself differing with Skinner, it is not obvious which position has prevailed. Computer programmes using parallel distributed processing have shown that even with a rule-based model of linguistic knowledge, acquisition can be accounted for just as effectively without 'innate knowledge' as with, if they are endowed with a general cognitive capacity for extrapolating regularities from the data to which they are exposed and thus 'teaching themselves how to learn'. Even the precise concept of operant 'strength' has been taken over in these models.

Chomsky's strong version of nativism has been pushed from the mainstream by the more interactive view of language acquisition maintained for example by Steven Pinker. Chomskyan generative linguistics has come to the position that grammar and syntax do not exist, and that virtually all the effects attributed to them should actually be located in the lexicon. Corpus linguistics has demonstrated that language is not structured in units of individual words combined in infinitely creative ways but that language is structured by a far greater use of collocations – the opposite of linguistic creativity as Chomsky defined it.

The spectacular growth of pragmatics has returned 'verbal behavior beyond the vocal' to central importance in linguistic study. Skinner's argument about speech being inseparable from action is reminiscent of Firth (see Chapter 5 above), Austin (see Chapter 7 above), Wittgenstein (see Chapter 6 above) and Harris (see Chapter 14 below). In the light not only of these links but of its references to Ogden and Richards's *The Meaning of Meaning* (Ogden and Richards 1923), Horne Tooke's *Diversions of Purley* (see Volume I, Chapter 12) and the work of Bertrand Russell and Alfred North Whitehead, the view might be hazarded that Skinner's *Verbal Behavior* (1957) looks like a one-off in twentieth-century American linguistic thought because it is actually part of a *British* linguistic tradition that happened to be written by an autodidact from Susquehanna, Pennsylvania. But it would be more accurate to say that Skinner's is the sort of case that breaks down the often dubious attribution of nationality to intellectual traditions. Moreover, *Verbal Behavior* did in fact spawn a long and continuous analytic tradition of its own, but one conducted entirely within psychology, not linguistics. Chomsky's review ended an opportunity for bringing together strands of inquiry into language across disciplinary as well as national divides.

Nevertheless, Skinner is worse than the forgotten man of the twentieth-century study of language; he is its archetypal villain and loser. Students of linguistics who have never seen a copy of *Verbal Behavior* can tell you in detail about its denial of any possibility of human linguistic creativity. In reality, the book is mostly about such creativity, especially in its artistic sense as represented in literature, and is an earnest attempt at explaining the mechanisms by which it takes place, while adhering to a scientific stricture that only what can be observed may be reported. It is a book crippled by its determination to take up issues already at the centre of a great pragmatic-semantic tradition without explicitly acknowledging that it was doing so, and to replace the methods of that tradition with the only methodology Skinner knew, an experimental psychological one so totally inapplicable to the matter at hand that Skinner did not even bother to try to apply it. The questions he wanted to answer required observation of actual practice, not as prompted by a lab technician in a white coat but as inscribed in social context. This Skinner knew how to do only through anecdote and literary citation. The result has been that, within linguistics, *Verbal Behavior* has been denied credit even for what time has shown that it got right; while in fields where behaviourism had a more substantial impact, including certain

Chapter 9

Chomsky on language as biology

The central fact to which any significant linguistic theory must address itself is this: a mature speaker can produce a new sentence of his language on the appropriate occasion, and other speakers can understand it immediately, though it is equally new to them. Most of our linguistic experience, both as speakers and hearers, is with new sentences; once we have mastered a language, the class of sentences with which we can operate fluently and without difficulty is so vast that for all practical purposes . . . we can regard it as infinite. Normal mastery of a language involves not only the ability to understand immediately an indefinite number of entirely new sentences, but also the ability to identify deviant sentences and, on occasion, to impose an interpretation on them . . . On the basis of a limited experience of the data of speech, each normal human being has developed for himself a thorough competence in his native language. This competence can be represented, to an as yet undetermined extent, as a system of rules that we can call the *grammar* of his language.

(Chomsky 1964: 7–9)

Noam Chomsky was born in Philadelphia in 1928. As a student at the University of Pennsylvania he studied mathematics, philosophy and linguistics. In the early 1950s he pursued research in linguistics as a junior fellow at Harvard, and since 1955 he has held various posts at the Massachusetts Institute of Technology. From the mid-1960s onwards his influence on academic ideas about language has been unrivalled by any living scholar.

Chomsky's linguistic theorizing is rooted in a study of the principles under which a subset of the possible sequences and branches of philosophy, anthropology and applied linguistics as well as psychology, it has achieved the status of a founding text for a methodology it did not practise, among admirers who seem to have read hardly any more of it than its detractors have done.

combinations of words from the vocabulary of a language may constitute grammatical sentences. As soil in which to embed a radically new theory about language, with trans-disciplinary implications of the utmost significance, the technicalities of syntax may seem unpromising. None the less, syntax has from the outset been Chomsky's primary concern, as is reflected in the title of his first published book, *Syntactic Structures* (1957). His remarkable proposal is that close attention to the details of how words are put together to form sentences – and, especially, to how words are *not* put together to form sentences – can shed light on the organization of the human mental capacity for language. No previous grammarian has seen such far-reaching implications in the fact that certain logically possible syntactic configurations never actually occur as grammatically correct utterances. They never occur, says Chomsky, because, given the limitations of the mental 'language organ', they *cannot* occur.

In *Syntactic Structures* Chomsky views a 'grammar' as 'a device . . . for producing the sentences of the language under analysis' (1957: 11):

> We . . . view grammars as having a tripartite structure. A grammar has a sequence of rules from which phrase structure can be reconstructed and a sequence of morphophonemic rules that convert strings of morphemes into strings of phonemes. Connecting these sequences, there is a sequence of transformational rules that carry strings with phrase structure into new strings to which the morphophonemic rules can apply.
>
> (Chomsky 1957: 107)

Simple active declarative sentences (e.g. English *fish swim*, *lions need meat, the tramps eat the turnips*) are treated as basic and generated by phrase-structure rules alone. A phrase-structure analysis involves a form of parsing into constituents, e.g. like this:

1   S[entence] → N[oun] P[hrase] V[erb] P[hrase]
2   NP → (Det[erminer]) N
3   VP → V (NP)

Parentheses enclose optional constituents. The ultimate constituents (Det, N, V) categorize 'formatives' (i.e. 'minimal syntactically functioning units', which for purposes of this example may be equated with individual words). So:

4   Det → *the* ...
5   N → *fish, lions, meat, tramps, turnips* ...
6   V → *swim, need, eat* ...

Rules (1) to (3) generate (define as well formed) the phrase structures in Figure 9.1, among others. And appropriate application of rules (4) to (6) will show that these are the phrase structures assigned to, respectively, *fish swim, lions eat meat, the tramps eat the turnips*. Sentences related to these in being negative, interrogative, passive etc. versions of them (e.g. *fish don't swim, do lions need meat?, the turnips are eaten by the tramps*) are derived from the output of the phrase-structure rules (i.e. the 'deep structure') by 'transformational' rules that alter that structure in various ways. Finally, the 'morphophonemic' rules are required to clothe in phonetic flesh the syntactic skeleton generated by the phrase-structure and transformational rules.

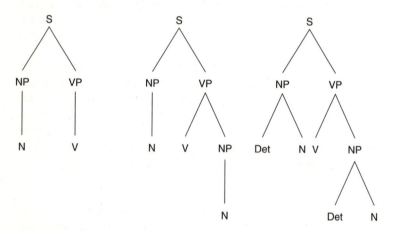

Figure 9.1

In itself the grammatical information offered here is not new, let alone radically new. S→NP VP, for instance, is a reformulation of the ancient wisdom that a sentence has two parts, a subject and a predicate; while any traditional grammar of English will give an account of the passive construction or provide information as to how verbs form their past participles. What is new here has to do with context and purposes, and may begin to emerge if we compare and contrast Chomsky's earliest proposals with those of his distributionalist predecessors.

Distributional linguistics, as explicated e.g. by Chomsky's teacher Z. S. Harris (see Harris 1951), sets out to reveal the permissible patterns of arrangement of linguistic units (in practice, phonemes and morphemes) identified in a corpus of utterances taken for purposes of the analysis as representing the whole language. Chomsky's grammatical 'device' can likewise be seen as a set of distributional statements. Thus, by one of the rules canvassed above, an English noun phrase may consist of a determiner followed by a noun. Assuming that the grammar contains no other rules to the contrary, this excludes the possibility that successive articles and nouns might not form a noun phrase, or that within such a phrase the noun might precede the article.

Perhaps the most significant continuity between Harris's *Methods in Structural Linguistics* (1951) and Chomsky's *Syntactic Structures* (1957) is the exclusion of meaning. Zellig Harris's whole enterprise, in fact, is to show how the phonological and grammatical units of a language can be identified without reference to the meanings of the utterances in which they may be held to occur. In Chomsky's early work, the setting aside of meaning arises from an argument that what makes a particular sequence of words in a language a grammatical sentence has nothing to do with meaningfulness or significance. *Colorless green ideas sleep furiously* and *furiously sleep ideas green colorless* are both nonsensical, but the former is grammatical and the latter is not. Conversely, although there is nothing semantically wrong with *read you a book on modern music?* or *the child seems sleeping* (they are no more difficult to interpret than e.g. *have you a book on modern music?* or *the book seems interesting*), they are ungrammatical in modern standard English. Such examples suggest to Chomsky (1957: 15) that 'any search for a semantically based definition of "grammaticalness" will be futile'.

The most significant discontinuity is Chomsky's inversion of Harris's analytic procedures. Harris starts with a corpus of utterances from which he derives statements as to their component elements and the combinatorial possibilities that hold among them. A Chomskyan grammar, in contrast, sets out the syntactic patterns according to which sentences might be constructed. Harris himself recognized that his methods might be inverted in this way:

The work of analysis leads right up to the statements which enable anyone to synthesize or predict utterances in the language. These statements form a deductive system with axiomatically defined initial elements and with theorems concerning the relations among them. The final theorems would indicate the structure of the utterances of the language in terms of the preceding parts of the system.

(Harris 1951: 372–3)

Chomsky can be seen as having taken up his teacher's challenge to develop a formal system of axioms and deductive rules that would 'synthesize or predict' the well-formed sentences of a natural language.

The underlying reason for this does not emerge at all clearly from *Syntactic Structures*. It is only with his next book (Chomsky 1964, based on a paper delivered to the Ninth International Congress of Linguists in 1962), which opens with the passage excerpted at the head of this chapter, that we begin to see the extent of the revolution ushered in by the seemingly unimportant change from analysing sentences to synthesizing them.

Harrisian distributionalism continues the Bloomfieldian tradition in being a speaker-free linguistics. It treats a language as a closed corpus of data. No aspect of the various human activities that give rise to the data is of any interest; indeed, it is irrelevant to the distributionalist that the decontextualized utterances forming his or her corpus are of human provenance at all. Now if, as Chomsky does, one starts with the abstract patterns in which linguistic units may be arranged, and treats sentences as particular instantiations of those patterns, one comes to see that there are indefinitely many sentences. Thus Chomsky stresses, as Harris does not, the open-endedness of languages. And in doing so he opens up the possibility of restoring a general orientation that Saussure had insisted on, but which recent American linguistics had lost sight of. For the idea of a language as an indefinitely large set of sentences seems to reflect an essential feature of the language-user's experience: the incessant need to produce and understand sentences that have never been encountered before. The conception of a language in play here is capable of leading to a linguistics which would once again be concerned, in one way or another, with human beings (*qua* language-users), and not merely with products abstracted from the linguistic activities of human beings.

The key step towards realizing this potential lay in exploring two analogies. Both analogies focus on the fact that, if a language is envisaged as the subset of the set of possible sequences of words in that language which constitute grammatical sentences, that subset, like the set itself, is infinitely large.

The first analogy is between the information about 'grammaticalness' provided by a generative grammar and the language-user's unconscious knowledge of 'grammaticalness'. A generative grammar specifies a range of abstract syntactic structures, such that any sequence of words which fits one of those structures counts as well formed (grammatical). Any sequence which does not counts as ill formed. The set of structures is finite; the set of word-sequences that conform to them (like the set of word-sequences that fail to conform to them) is infinite. Now mature speakers, says Chomsky, are able to produce and understand indefinitely many grammatical sentences of their language, many or most of which they will never have used or encountered before. Furthermore, they are capable of saying of indefinitely many sequences of words that they do not constitute grammatical sentences of the language. That is, speakers are able to discriminate between well- and ill-formed word-sequences, just as a generative grammar does. How are they able to do this? Chomsky's answer, in effect if not literally, is that they are in (unconscious) possession of a generative grammar. To put it the other way round, a generative grammar models – or, to use Chomsky's own formulation, 'characterizes abstractly' – the speaker's linguistic 'competence'. It does not reflect just the linguist's conscious knowledge of the language he or she is describing but also the speaker-hearer's unconscious knowledge of the language they are using.

One immediate consequence of this move is the readmission of meaning into mainstream American linguistics. The general reason is simply that the exclusion of semantics was tenable only so long as linguistics was restricted to the description of what was taken to be observably, externally 'given'. If what is being described (modelled) is the unobservable, internal linguistic knowledge of the speaker-hearer, that exclusion could be maintained only if one were prepared to argue that knowledge of the meanings of expressions fell outside the domain of 'linguistic knowledge', in the intended sense. On the contrary, some of the abilities to be accounted for by a model of the speaker-hearer's competence, according to Chomsky, are clearly semantic in nature – e.g. the ability to tell that a given sentence is ambiguous, or that two sentences are paraphrases of each other. So a generative grammar came to be seen as requiring a 'semantic component' that specified the 'intrinsic meanings' of sentences (i.e. the meanings sentences have irrespective of the communicational use to which utterances of them may be put on particular occasions).

The second analogy is between the linguist's task of describing a language envisaged as an infinitely large set of sentences, and the child's task in learning ('acquiring') a language as his or her mother tongue. If the set is infinitely large, then the child cannot possibly learn item by item which sequences of words belong to it. It must be a matter of learning a finite set of general principles, or rules, governing the formation of infinitely many word-sequences. The child is envisaged as unconsciously constructing, testing, refining and rejecting hypotheses as to the principles according to which word-sequence X is grammatical and word-sequence Y ungrammatical – activity paralleled on the conscious level by the linguist elaborating a generative grammar.

To take a simple example from the grammar of English, according to what principles are the sentences of (1) below grammatical, whereas those of (2) are ungrammatical?

1   *John is eating*
     John had been eaten
     Does John eat?
     Will John have eaten?
     John may have been eating
     John must not eat
     Mustn't John eat?
     John eats
     John ate
     Will John eat?
     Didn't John eat?
     John will have been being eaten

etc., etc.

2   **John has eating*
     *John been has eaten
     *Eats John?
     *Will have John eaten?

John may been eating
John not must eat
Does John must not eat?
Did eat John?
Did John be eating?
Will John do eat?
Ate not John?
John will have being been eaten

etc., etc.

There may be many ways of stating what the sentences of (1) have in common that makes them different from the non-sentences of (2). One possibility might be a set of rules specifying what kind of item is allowed to come first in a grammatical sequence and, depending on the choice of the first item, what can come second, and so on. ('The first element can be either a subject NP or an auxiliary verb. If the first element is an NP, the second can be either an auxiliary or a lexical verb' etc.) If when sufficiently refined such a set of rules stated the facts correctly, however clumsily, it would be an 'observationally adequate' grammar of the fragment of English in question. But it is obvious enough that the operative principles cannot be understood simply in terms of what is allowed to follow what in a linear sequence. In Chomsky's words, such a grammar would not be descriptively adequate.

A proposal Chomsky once put forward as to the principles that really are operative here is as follows. Underlying structures like those of (1) is a general formula like this:

$$\begin{array}{ccccc} 1 & 2 & 3 & 4 & 5 \end{array}$$
John + (MODAL) + (HAVE en) + (BE ing) + (BE en) + eat

In simple affirmative, declarative sentences, the English verb-complex maximally has five components: a main or lexical verb optionally preceded by up to four auxiliary elements. If all four auxiliaries are present, the first will be one of a small closed set of morphologically defective verbs called 'modals' which have no other function than to serve as auxiliaries, the second will be HAVE, which forms what traditional grammar calls 'perfect tenses' of the verb, the third will be BE, forming progressive or continuous tenses, and the fourth will be BE in its role as exponent of the passive voice. Auxiliary HAVE, and both auxiliary

BEs, require that the next element in the sequence take a particular suffix: progressive BE requires *-ing*; HAVE and passive BE requires *-en* (which stands for the past participle marker, irrespective of its actual form in any particular verb). The leftmost element in the sequence is the finite verb, and except in the case of the modals carries any relevant morphological markings of person (3sg versus non-3sg) and tense (present versus past). Negative sentences are formed by adding the element NOT (or attaching it in the form N'T) immediately after the finite auxiliary (*John must not eat*), and interrogatives by inverting the order of finite auxiliary and subject (*will John eat?*); these two processes may be combined (*mustn't John eat?*). Where there is no auxiliary, then DO must be inserted: the negative and interrogative transformations cannot be applied to lexical verbs. Hence *does John eat?*, *didn't John eat?*, where the dummy auxiliary DO, as the leftmost verbal element, is the finite verb.

So, to take some of the sentences in (1): *John is eating* has the structure:

> 3   5
> John + BE ing + eat

Progressive BE projects *-ing* on to the next verb, and itself takes 3sg present form, giving *John is eating*. *John had been eaten* is:

> 2   4   5
> John + HAVE en + BE en + eat

HAVE projects *-en* on to BE, which itself projects *-en* on to *eat*. As the leftmost item, HAVE is the finite verb, and is marked in this case for past tense. *John eats* is:

> 5
> John + eat

There are no auxiliaries, so *eat* itself is the finite verb, marked for 3sg present. *Will John eat?* is basically

> 1   5
> John + MODAL + eat

Modals project no affix, so *eat* appears in that form. The modal here is *will*, and because the sentence is a question, changes places with the subject *John*. The modal is the finite verb, but as a modal takes no 3sg marking.

All the sentences of (1) conform to these principles and all those of (2) involve violating them in one way or another. Their precise formulation is unimportant here: Chomsky's claim was that some such analysis is required to account for the grammaticality of the sentences of (1) and the ungrammaticality of those of (2); and, moreover, that the English-acquiring child will assimilate the underlying principles and come to produce and understand countless (1) sentences while refraining from producing (2) sentences. In short, this was presented as a fragment of a descriptively adequate grammar of English, which as such models the relevant part of the native speaker's unconscious knowledge or linguistic competence. The claim was that the English-speaker in some sense 'knows' these principles, even if many or most speakers would be hard put to it to articulate them, let alone in the terminology used by linguists.

There is an important disanalogy between the linguist and the language-acquirer, however. In elaborating his or her grammar, the linguist has access to information from many sources not only about the particular language under investigation but about other languages and language in general. The first-language-acquiring infant has none of this. On the face of it, the child has nothing to go on but the data (sometimes called the 'stimulus') constituted by the speech it hears around it. Furthermore, that stimulus is in various ways an inadequate guide to the language being acquired. Firstly, it is impoverished. Not only is it of necessity no more than a finite sample of the infinitely large set of sentences that make up the language, but, more significantly, particular grammatical *types* of sentence may be wholly unrepresented. Secondly, the stimulus is 'degenerate'. The linguistic 'performance' of the speakers the child hears is by no means a faithful reflection of their linguistic competence: normal speech is full of hesitations, anacolutha and other deviations from grammaticality. None the less, so the theory goes, mature native-speaker competence shows that the child has somehow managed to deduce the grammar of his or her language.

But how? Chomsky's answer is that such a feat can be possible only if certain things about the language are known *a priori*. There must be linguistic 'knowledge' available to the child irrespective of the various deficiencies of his or her own linguistic experience. This *a priori* knowledge cannot be knowledge of the grammatical structure of particular languages, since children master whatever language they happen to be exposed to in infancy. What is proposed, therefore, is that certain general abstract principles governing the grammatical structure of all languages are genetically encoded in the brain. Children come into the world already primed to acquire a particular species of the genus 'human language', whose general organizational principles are universal, determined by our common genetic inheritance. The empirically available evidence as to the structure of the language they are acquiring is not all that they have to go on after all. Being inadequate and fragmentary, it could not be. It is supplemented by a system of innately 'known' grammatical universals, which collectively constitute what Chomsky calls the 'initial state' of the 'language faculty'. (For further discussion of Chomky's position on language acquisition, along with contrasting theories, see Chapter 12 below). At a certain level of generality, all languages are cut to a pattern determined by innate mental structures common to all humanity; and Chomsky has explicitly located his thought (see especially Chomsky 1966) in a rationalist tradition in the philosophy of mind that flourished before the rise in the late nineteenth century of 'empiricist' linguistics (see Volume I, Chapter 8).

It is these principles of 'universal grammar' that Chomsky is primarily interested in. The fine detail of the generative grammar of any given language, and the features that distinguish the grammar of one language from that of another, are unimportant (as Chomsky put it at one stage, these merely reflect different settings of the parameters within which the principles of universal grammar operate). What matters is what the grammars have in common.

The English verb, as it happens, is an unpromising area in which to seek universal grammatical principles. In the first place, the extensive use English makes of 'auxiliaries' is idiosyncratic, even by comparison with other Indo-European languages, where their functional role is largely taken by a more elaborate morphology. Second, some of these uses are historically recent developments (the 'modals' are the outcome of the grammatical petrification of what were once ordinary lexical verbs; obligatory DO-support with negatives and interrogatives is only a few generations old). Third, the rules as outlined above are not valid in all particulars for all varieties of contemporary English (there are dialects in which one or two of the sentences of (2) might be acceptable; even in standard English there is variation as to the placement of the negative particle (*didn't he . . . ?* versus *did he not . . . ?*); and what would we want to say about the relation between these rules and the sentence *Have you a book on modern music?*, cited earlier?). Fourthly, the morphology and syntax of the verb being a central *topos* in the European grammatical tradition, much of the information presented in the generative analysis is overtly taught to schoolchildren, albeit not in these terms (*John will have been being eaten*, for instance, exemplifies what traditional grammar would call the future perfect passive progessive of the verb *to eat*). For all these reasons, this area of English grammar tells us almost nothing about the language faculty. In fact, the only principle of any generality illustrated here is 'structure-dependency': a descriptively adequate statement of the rules must make crucial reference to categories of items defined in terms of their grammatical roles or attributes. *Will John eat?* may be 'observationally' the result of taking *John will eat* and, let us say, interchanging the first and second words, but even if 'interchange the first and second words' were generalizable as a rule for forming questions in English beyond the small class of cases where it happens to work, natural languages, says Chomsky, do not have such rules.

A more promising area of grammar in which to look for universal principles involves the workings of reflexive pronouns and other anaphoric expressions. The sentences of (3) seem to establish that *himself* and *each other* in English have a distribution like that of object pronouns:

3   *John was pleased with me*
    John was pleased with himself
    The children were pleased with each other

But there are limits to this parallelism, as can be seen in (4):

4   *John expected that Jane would surprise him*
    John expected that Jane would surprise herself
    John noticed that the children helped each other
    **John expected that Jane would surprise himself*
    **The children noticed that John helped each other*

It looks as though forms such as *himself* and *each other*, unlike ordinary object pronouns, must have an antecedent in the same clause. Hence the ungrammaticality of the starred sentences in (4), even though it is clear enough what they would mean if anyone were to produce them. But, says Chomsky, this restriction (or, at least, the more general principle of which it is a particular manifestation) is no mere peculiarity of a certain variety of contemporary English. No form of English allows such expressions to be anaphoric to an antecedent in a different clause, or ever did. Nor is there any language with comparable expressions that does. Nor do these vagaries of *himself*, *each other* and the like tend to feature on the syllabus of formal English grammar lessons. Nor are speakers likely to produce the starred non-sentences as performance errors. Yet mastery of English includes the unconscious knowledge that *the children noticed that John helped each other* is not a grammatical English sentence. And that can be possible, says Chomsky, only because it violates a principle of universal grammar (in this case, what he once identified as the 'Binding Principle'): the 'language organ' that grows in the mind under the influence of the linguistic environment is simply not equipped to handle such structures, any more than the human digestive system is equipped to deal with grass.

It would be impossible in a short chapter like this to trace all the subsequent developments of Chomsky's model since this early version. But we can at least give a sense of where it stands in the current 'minimalist' programme. Here the sentence *John is eating* is no longer analysed as starting from a 'deep structure' like *John* + BE *ing* + *eat*. Nor do anything like phrase structure rules play a part. Rather, their work is done by information specified for individual words in the mental lexicon. *John is eating* is generated (simplifying so as to focus on the features of the verb *is*) as:

John   [Head-feature: 3S]
is   [Specifier-feature: 3S] [Head-feature: Present]
            [Complement-feature: *+ing*]
eating [Head-feature: *+ing*]

Each of the three words is stored in the mental lexicon fully formed and with the feature specifications shown. The word *is* has a 'specifier-feature' requiring that the word which precedes it have the head-feature third-person singular, and a 'complement feature' allowing it to be followed by a present participle (e.g. *eating*). (It can of course be followed by other things, such as a past participle like *eaten*, an adjective phrase or a noun phrase.) The 'syntax' consists simply of a process of derivation in which the features of words are 'checked' and 'erased' if they match those of the words preceding and following them:

> *John*
> *is* [Head-feature: Present]
> *eating*

Only head-features are allowed to remain unchecked after the derivation, and even these must belong to a certain category called 'semantically interpretable', which includes tense as well as person and number. If this is the case, the derivation 'converges' and the sentence is grammatical. But if any specifier- or complement-feature remains unerased, or any head-feature that is not semantically interpretable, then the derviation 'crashes'. For example, the ungrammatical **John am eating* is initially generated as:

> *John* [Head-feature: 3S]
> *am* [Specifier-feature: 1S] [Head-feature: Present]
> [Complement-feature: +*ing*]
> *eating* [Head-feature: +*ing*]

After derivation, we have:

> *John* [Head-feature: 3S]
> *am* [Specifier-feature: 1S] [Head-feature: Present]
> *eating*

The specifier-feature 1S of *am* has not been checked and erased, and its presence in the derived form is disallowed, making the sentence ungrammatical. (The head-feature 3S of *John* is semantically interpretable, and does not therefore contribute to the ungrammaticality.) This version of the theory is called 'minimalist' because there is so little work left for the syntax to do, basically just feature checking. This is a plus for Chomsky, since the fewer mechanisms that need to be posited as part of the innate language faculty, the less his theory is vulnerable to the charge of simply being linguistic creationism with a modern, technological face.

Investigating the properties of the language organ is a very different enterprise from elaborating generative grammars of languages, and although from the outset Chomsky himself was interested in the latter only in so far as it was thought relevant to the former, various circumstances have conspired to obfuscate this fact.

One such circumstance is Chomsky's use of the term 'a language' itself. At the outset of *Syntactic Structures* he says:

> From now on I will consider a *language* to be a set (finite or infinite) of sentences, each finite in length and constructed out of a finite set of elements. All natural languages in their spoken or written form are languages in this sense, since each natural language has a finite number of phonemes (or letters in its alphabet) and each sentence is representable as a finite sequence of these phonemes (or letters), though there are infinitely many sentences.
>
> (Chomsky 1957: 13)

That is to say, for Chomsky's purposes (here, to introduce and illustrate the idea of a generative grammar), 'a language' is being stipulatively defined as denoting a structure of the appropriate kind; furthermore, a natural language *may be envisaged* as a 'language' in this sense. But this is liable to cause misunderstanding when the underlying psycho-biological agenda is revealed, and first-language-learning is presented as a matter of deducing a generative grammar of a language, for it is far from clear that a language, as thus defined, is what the first-language-learner is acquiring. When we talk about a language, in common parlance, we are usually referring to an open-ended cultural construct subject to multiple dimensions of historical, geographical, social and individual variation, and liable (in many societies) to political monitoring and control. As he makes explicit in later writings, Chomsky is not interested in languages in this real-world sense:

> 'language' is no well-defined concept of linguistic science. In colloquial usage we say that German is one language and Dutch another, but some dialects of German are more similar to Dutch dialects than to other, more remote dialects of

German. We say that Chinese is a language with many dialects, and that French, Italian and Spanish are different languages. But the diversity of the Chinese 'dialects' is roughly comparable to that of the Romance languages. A linguist knowing nothing about political boundaries or institutions would not distinguish 'language' and 'dialect' as we do in normal discourse. Nor would he have any clear alternative concepts to propose, with anything like the same function.

(Chomsky 1980: 217)

Moreover, reflection on the process of learning one's native language might suggest a complex and indefinitely protracted apprenticeship in the business of communicating, by means of recycling and renewing the amorphous and vaguely defined resources of a cultural product of this kind. Chomsky, it turns out, is not interested in 'language acquisition' in this sense. On the contrary, his theory of the language organ is his solution to the 'logical problem' of how acquiring a first language is possible at all, as opposed to the empirical problem of what is actually involved in the real-time process of doing so. Chomsky has consistently pointed out that if progress is to be made with the issues he is concerned with (specifically, uncovering the principles of universal grammar), radical abstraction and idealization of the subject matter of linguistics is necessary:

Linguistic theory is concerned primarily with an ideal speaker-listener, in a completely homogeneous speech-community, who knows its language perfectly and is unaffected by such grammatically irrelevant conditions as memory limitations, distractions, shifts of attention or interest, and errors (random or characteristic) in applying his knowledge of the language in actual performance.

(Chomsky 1965: 3)

While, of course, 'it is understood that speech communities in [this] . . . sense . . . do not exist in the real world. Each individual has acquired a language in the course of complex social interactions with people who vary in the ways in which they speak and interpret what they hear' (Chomsky 1986: 16).

It follows that the enterprise of writing generative grammars of 'whole languages' (whatever they may be) is a non-starter, and

Chomsky himself has never been interested in doing any such thing.

There are at least two factors that may obscure this point. One is that the energy and care Chomsky puts into elaborating exemplifications of the kind of analysis dictated by the syntactic framework he is working with at a given moment may give a misleading idea of how seriously particular frameworks and specific analyses are to be taken. For instance, the early 'transformationalist' treatment of the English verb-complex outlined above offers a satisfyingly neat account of the relevant facts. But, as we have seen, it is quite different from what Chomsky would say about them now, from his latter-day 'minimalist' position that many grammatical phenomena once treated in terms of general syntactic rules are rather properties of particular words and classes of words. (See Lasnik 2000 for a thorough discussion of this area of English syntax in relation to generative grammar.)

The other factor is the rise in Chomsky's wake of a movement or constellation of ideas in linguistics loosely known as 'generativism'. Some generativists have seized on the concept of a generative grammar and, divorcing it from Chomsky's theoretical purposes, have developed and applied it either for its own sake or in areas of language study that have nothing to do with elucidating the structure of the language organ. Not only are there generativists interested in elaborating generative grammars of (what they stipulatively define to be) whole languages, generativism has given rise to an array of competing schools of thought as to the scope of generative-grammatical theory and the organizational structure of generative grammars. Moreover, there are generativist interpretations of historical linguistic change, of sociolinguistic variation, of stylistics and of other matters that are, in Chomsky's eyes, either irrelevant or epiphenomenal.

Ultimately, Chomsky's own linguistics is a branch of biology. He aims to uncover the nature of our biological endowment for language, and the extent to which that endowment determines certain universal features of languages. It is obvious enough that the fact that language is unique to human beings – *if* it is a fact (see Chapter 15 below) – must be correlated with mental, ultimately physical, features that differentiate human beings from other creatures, but the traditional view is that languages themselves, and their structural (grammatical) properties, are the product of free human creativity. Chomsky's unique contribution

lies in asserting that some of the most general structural properties of languages are biologically determined. One such property
seems to be that all languages are organized in terms of units
called 'phrases', which have 'heads', 'arguments' and 'adjuncts'.
Chomsky's claim is that all languages work syntactically in this
way, and no 'language' that did not could be a natural human
language.

In fact, Chomsky's disciplinary affiliation to linguistics, and the
consequent initial presentation of his views as a challenge to
received ideas in that discipline, is something of a red herring: it
is reasonable to predict that the perceived relevance (or threat) of
his thought to linguists' traditional concern with languages as
cultural artefacts (most aspects of which are largely unaffected by
Chomsky's work) will decline in proportion as biological, psychological and philosophical interest in it burgeons.

Chapter 10

Labov on linguistic variation

It is apparent that the immediate meaning of this phonetic feature is 'Vineyarder'. When a man says [rəyt] or [həws], he is unconsciously establishing the fact that he belongs to the island: that he is one of the natives to whom the island really belongs. . . . The problem is, why did this feature develop in such a complicated pattern on the Vineyard, and why is it becoming stronger in the younger age levels? . . .

The answer appears to be that different groups have had to respond to different challenges to their native status . . .

The old-family group of English descent . . . are struggling to maintain their independent position in the face of a long-range decline in the economy and the steady encroachment of the summer people. The member of the tradition-oriented community naturally looks to past generations for his values . . . The great figures of the past are continually referred to, and those who have died only a few years ago have already assumed heroic stature . . .

The sudden increase in centralization began among the Chilmark fishermen, the most close-knit group on the island, the most independent, the group which is most stubbornly opposed to the incursions of the summer people . . . Centralized speech forms are . . . a part of the dramatized island character which the Chilmarker assumes, in which he imitates a similar but weaker tendency in the older generation.

For younger members of the English descent group . . . the old-timers and the up-islanders in particular serve as a reference group. They recognize that the Chilmark fishermen are independent, skillful with many kinds of tools and equipment, quick-spoken, courageous and physically strong. Most importantly, they carry with them the ever-present conviction that the island belongs to them. If someone intends to stay on the island, this model will be ever-present to his mind. If he intends to leave, he will adopt a mainland reference group, and the influence of the old-timers will be considerably less. The differential effect in the degree of centralization used is a direct result of this opposition of values. . . .

In summary, we can then say that the meaning of centralization, judging from the context in which it occurs, is *positive orientation towards Martha's Vineyard*. If we now overlook age level, occupation, ethnic group, geography, and study the relationship of centralization to this one independent variable, we can confirm . . . this conclusion.

(Labov 1963: 307–8)

Martha's Vineyard is a small island off the coast of Massachusetts. Among many features of English pronunciation peculiar to the island is a tendency to centralize the first element of the diphthongs /ai/ and /au/. In the case of the former, the centralization represents the conservative retention of a pronunciation historically widespread in the dialects of New England; in the latter we see a recent development within the island community itself. In dealing with such a state of affairs, traditional dialectology might well confine itself to some such bare statement as the foregoing, coupled with a geographical mapping of the feature under investigation. William Labov (b. 1927) goes much further. By careful correlation of its incidence with such variables as age, sex, social status, attitude to the island, Labov makes a reasonable claim to have *explained* it. (But see Cameron 1990.) This is quantitative sociolinguistics.

Labovian quantitative sociolinguistics arises out of an interest in genuinely empirical fieldwork in linguistics. The first sentence of his study of Martha's Vineyard – his first published article – points out that it 'concerns the *direct observation* of a sound change in the context of the community life from which it stems' (Labov 1963: 273; emphasis added).

From detailed empirical work of this kind there soon arose a general theoretical challenge to currently received ideas in linguistics:

We will argue that the generative model for the description of language as a homogeneous object is itself needlessly unrealistic and represents a backward step from structural theories capable of accommodating the facts of orderly heterogeneity. It seems to us quite pointless to construct a theory of change which accepts as its input unnecessarily idealized and counterfactual descriptions of language states. Long before predictive theories of language change can be attempted, it will be necessary to learn to see language – whether from a diachronic or synchronic vantage – as an object possessing orderly heterogeneity . . .

The facts of heterogeneity have not so far jibed well with the structural approach to language . . . For the more linguists became impressed with the existence of structure in language, and the more they bolstered this observation with deductive arguments about the functional advantages of structure, the more mysterious became the transition of a language from state to state. After all, if a language has to be structured in order to function efficiently, how do people continue to talk while the language changes, that is, while it passes through periods of lessened systematicity? Alternatively, if overriding pressures do force a language to change, and if communication is less efficent in the interim (as would deductively follow from the theory), why have such inefficiencies not been observed in practice?

This, it seems to us, is the fundamental question with which a theory of language change must cope. The solution, we will argue, lies in the direction of breaking down the identification of structuredness with homogeneity. The key to a rational conception of language change – indeed, of language itself – is the possibility of describing orderly differentiation in a language serving a community. We will argue that native-like command of heterogeneous structures is not a matter of multi-dialectalism or 'mere' performance, but is part of unilingual linguistic competence. One of the corollaries of our approach is that in a language serving a complex (i.e. real) community, it is absence of structured homogeneity that would be dysfunctional.

(Weinreich, Labov and Herzog 1968: 100–1)

By the 1960s Chomsky's neo-Saussurean postulate of a homogeneous speech community was widely accepted as a useful idealization on which to base linguistic theorizing, and intuitive acceptability judgements (often provided by the linguist personally) were believed to reveal the virtual structures of language, which could then be described in terms of uniform, categorical rules. Variation was declared to be theoretically unimportant and was interpreted either as 'dialect mixture', i.e. interference from other, separate linguistic systems, or as 'free variation', i.e. optional and independent of linguistic structure. Questioning the rigid Saussurean dichotomy of synchrony and diachrony, the dialectologist Uriel Weinreich (1926–67), Marvin Herzog (b. 1930) (who had worked with Weinreich on the dialectology of Yiddish) and Weinreich's student Labov argued that, in order to reconcile theories of synchronic structure with theories of linguistic change, linguists would have to recognize heterogeneity as an inherent property of linguistic rules and systems. That is, while it is possible to study completed changes as categorical replacements which change homogeneous systems, the study of the actual process of linguistic change cannot afford to neglect the facts of linguistic variation, since in order to ensure continuing communication within the speech community the new forms and structures must at some stage have coexisted with the old forms and structures. During processes of change linguistic variability typically acquires social significance, and, by taking into account the social context in which language occurs, variable linguistic phenomena can be dealt with without the simplification and idealization inherent in Chomsky's notion of a homogeneous speech community.

Much of the empirical evidence cited in their paper in support of this position comes from Labov's graduate research: his MA dissertation (the Martha's Vineyard study) and his doctoral thesis *The Social Stratification of English in New York City* (Labov 1966). Unlike Chomsky, whose primary data are intuitive grammaticality judgements, or Sapir and Bloomfield, who relied on information elicited from single informants, Labov argued that linguistic theory must be based on, and account for, naturally occurring speech:

When I first entered linguistics as a student, in 1961, it was my intention to gather data from the secular world. The early projects that I constructed were 'essays in experimental linguistics', carried out in ordinary social settings. My aim was to avoid the inevitable obscurity of texts, the self-consciousness of formal elicitations, and the self-deception of introspection. A decade of work outside the university as an industrial chemist had convinced me that the everyday world was stubborn but consistently so, baffling at the outset but rewarding in the long run for those who held to its rational character. A simple review of the literature might have convinced me that such empirical principles had no place in linguistics: there were many ideological barriers to the study of language in everyday life . . . To come to grips with *language*, we must look as closely and directly at the data of everyday speech as possible, and characterize its relationship to our grammatical theories as accurately as we can, amending and adjusting the theory so that it fits the object in view . . .

I do not believe that we need at this point a new 'theory of language'; rather we need a new way of doing linguistics that will yield decisive solutions. By enlarging our view of language, we encounter the possibility of being right: of finding answers that are supported by an unlimited number of reproducible measurements.

(Labov 1972a: xiii, 201, 259)

Labov approached the question of what constitutes linguistic evidence in some detail in a small publication entitled *What is a Linguistic Fact?* (Labov 1975), and critically examined the reliability of introspective data. Although there are large areas of consensus in grammaticality judgements (i.e. what Chomsky called 'clear cases' (Chomsky 1957: 14)), intuitive judgements are often unstable across informants. Furthermore, the linguist's own intuitions are liable to be contaminated by the 'experimenter effect', i.e. preconceived theoretical ideas have been shown to affect the linguist's judgements. The most damaging evidence, however, comes from the observation of actual linguistic behaviour, and Labov cites the use of positive *anymore* (meaning 'nowadays') as an example. In Philadelphia Labov found speakers who disapproved of sentences such as *John is smoking a lot anymore*, but were found to use positive *anymore* freely in their own speech. Although Labov emphasizes that naturally occurring speech constitutes the primary data for linguistic theory, he does not deny the importance of introspective judgements and believes it possible to reconcile the two. Linguistics is defined as a 'joint enterprise' whose facts are both external (accessible through the observation of language use within the speech community) and internal (accessible through the introspective judgements of individual speakers). Considering the case of positive *anymore*, Labov describes the complementary use of observation and introspection as follows:

> If we return to the case of positive *anymore*, we can readily see that introspective judgments are weak enough. We ultimately reached the stage where our informants' introspections told us nothing more about the state of the rule in the Philadelphia dialect. But note that we could not have reached that stage by observation alone. The first stage was to collect observations of the use of positive *anymore* in Philadelphia: that initiated the inquiry. The second stage was a study of introspective judgments, which showed us that Philadelphia contrasted sharply with the North and Coastal South by having at least 50% positive reactions to this rule. The third stage was to raise that percentage to 85–90% by more refined tests of semantic interpretation. The fourth test was extended observation, which showed that a remarkable number of the residual cases eventually betrayed their knowledge of the rule through spontaneous use. The several hundred examples of positive *anymore* observed in spontaneous speech could never have brought us to this conclusion alone, without the systematic sampling of introspective judgments.
>
> This seems a clear demonstration of the way data from observation, experiment and introspection can jointly be brought to bear on a linguistic problem of some subtlety.
>
> (Labov 1975: 57)

Labov's way of doing linguistics included interviews with large samples of speakers from different social groups, and aimed at eliciting a wide range of contextual styles from each individual. This objective was made feasible by the general diffusion and availability of portable tape-recorders from the early 1960s, which allowed for the recording of substantial examples of spontaneous speech and the careful examination of, especially, phonological variation. To capture the individual's full linguistic repertoire, Labov divided the interview into four 'styles': (1) general conversation (including sequences of both casual and careful speech), (2) the reading of a short passage, (3) the reading of word lists including examples of the sounds under investigation and (4) the reading of minimal pairs involving these sounds. Labov repeatedly emphasized the importance of eliciting casual speech (in part (1) of the interview). Casual speech (the 'vernacular' in Labov's usage) is the kind of language used when talking to friends and family members in informal situations. According to Labov, the vernacular is of central importance for understanding linguistic change, since it is more regular in structure than formal styles, which often show erratic influence from prestige dialects. Formal speech styles, he says, are usually learned only in adolescence and early adulthood when the speaker comes into regular contact with the educational system where linguistic prestige norms are propagated and enforced. Labov has used a variety of techniques to ensure that examples of casual speech occur in the interview. The most famous technique has come to be known as 'the danger of death question': 'Have you ever been in a situation where you were in serious danger of being killed, where you thought to yourself, *this is it*?' The danger of death question serves to divert the informant's attention from monitoring his or her own language use, and has been useful for breaking up stretches of formal style in the conversation part of the interview; this is clearly visible in one of Labov's New York City interview transcripts (casual style in italics; the informant is an eighteen-year-old Irish-Italian man):

INFORMANT: The school I go to is – uh – Food and Maritime. That's – uh – maritime training. And I was up in the masthead, and the wind started blowing. I had a rope secured round me to keep me from falling. *But the rope parted* [hh] *an' I was jus' hangin' there by my fingernails* [hhh]. *I never prayed to God so fast* [hh] *and so* [hh] *hard in my life. But I came out all right.*

INTERVIEWER: What happened?

INFORMANT: *Well the guys came up an' 'ey got me.*

INTERVIEWER: How long were you up there?

INFORMANT: *About ten minutes* [hhh].

INTERVIEWER: Jees! I can see you're still sweatin' thinkin' about it.

INFORMANT: *Yeh* [hhh]. *I came down. I cou'n' hold a pencil*

in my han' [hhh]. *I cou'n touch nuttin'. I was shakin' like
a* [hhh] *leaf.* Sometimes I get scared t'inkin' about it. But
– uh – well it's training.

(Labov 1972c: 114)

Faced with the danger of death question the informant laughs
nervously (indicated in the transcript by [hh] and [hhh]), increases
his speech rate and pitch range, and makes use of a number of
non-prestige variants: *-ing* shifts from [ɪŋ] to [ɪn], the fricatives
[θ] and [ð] to [t] and [d]; the number of consonant-cluster simpli-
fications increases and the informant produces a non-standard
double negative. These are characteristics of casual New York
City speech absent from his more formal conversational style.

The interview extract comes from Labov's Ph.D. dissertation
investigating the patterns of language use in New York City. The
study drew on an earlier sociological survey of the Lower East
Side of New York and was based on interviews with 122 speakers.
Among other characteristics of the New York dialect Labov
studied the presence or absence of consonantal constriction of *r*
in post-vocalic, pre-consonantal and word-final position. Historically New York City became non-rhotic in the early 1800s, when
southern British prestige patterns were adopted in the cities of the
East Coast, and dialectological studies from the 1930s show the
existence of an *r*-less New York dialect. Since the 1950s, however,
use of post-vocalic *r* has been on the increase, leading to a 'mixed'
system characterized by variable frequencies of pronunciation
of *r*. Thus in New York City a word such as *guard* will be
pronounced variably as [ga:d] or [ga:rd]. Conventionally this variation has been discussed under the label 'free variation', i.e. as a
random phenomenon.

In order to study the structures of linguistic heterogeneity in
more detail, Labov introduced the construct of the 'linguistic variable'. Briefly, a linguistic variable is a loosely defined linguistic
set consisting of two or more identifiable variants whose basic
meaning is identical. Thus in New York City the linguistic variable *r* has two variants, [r] and [ø]. The observation that dialects
can be distinguished by such qualitative phonological (as well as
lexical or grammatical) alternating forms is a well-established principle of traditional dialectology. However, Labov questioned the
categorical view underlying most dialectological work and argued
that patterns of alternation are best described in terms of relative

frequencies. These frequencies can then be correlated with linguistic factors (such as word-class membership or phonemic environment) and non-linguistic group characteristics such as age, sex or social class. Following the terminology introduced in Weinreich, Labov and Herzog (1968), Labov described his method of investigating language use and change under the heading 'the embedding problem':

> The *embedding* problem is to find the continuous matrix of social and linguistic behavior in which the linguistic change is carried. The principal route to the solution is through the discovery of correlations between elements of the linguistic system, and between those elements and the nonlinguistic system of social behavior. The correlation is established by strong proof of concomitant variation: that is, by showing that a small change in the independent variable is regularly accompanied by a change in the linguistic variable in a predictable direction.
>
> (Labov 1972a: 162)

Labov found that with regard to the pronunciation of Lower East Side post-vocalic *r*, use of *r* was most common at the top of the social ladder (a group he classified in accordance with previous sociological work as the 'upper middle class') and least common among members of the lowest status group, which suggests that post-vocalic *r* functions as a marker of social prestige in New York. Individuals in the middle of the social hierarchy used lower frequencies of *r* than those belonging to the upper middle class, but higher frequencies than those of the lower or working classes. This observation confirmed the results of a simple but ingenious pilot study which Labov had carried out in three New York City department stores. The three shops were sharply stratified with regard to the socio-economic background of their customers, and Labov hypothesized that shop assistants would tend to approximate to the behaviour (social and linguistic) of their respective customers. In the pilot study Labov would first find out which articles were sold in a given store on the fourth floor, and then ask employees for directions to find these articles; thus *fourth floor*, containing two possible instances of post-vocalic *r*, would spontaneously occur in the shop assistant's response. The pilot study showed that use of *r* co-varied with the social standing of the store and emphaticness, i.e. the higher the social standing and the more emphatic the utterance, the higher the frequency of post-vocalic *r*. Similarly, in the larger New York City study, use of *r* was found to increase monotonically with formality: *r* was pronounced most frequently in the interview sections (3) and (4) (reading lists and minimal pairs) and least in casual speech. This stylistic 'slope' was the same for all four social classes or status groups which Labov distinguished on the basis of a combination of different social indicators (occupation, education and income) on a nine-point scale (0–1 = lower class, 2–4 = working class, 5–6 = lower middle class, 7–8 = upper middle class, 9 = upper class). However, there was one important exception to the regular pattern: lower-middle-class speakers produced a higher percentage of prestige forms (i.e. pronunciation of *r*) than upper-middle-class speakers in the formal styles (3) and (4), a behaviour Labov termed 'hypercorrection'. The hypercorrection of the lower middle class can lead to an acceleration of the generally slow process of linguistic change: 'Instead of a gradual, generation-by-generation spread of a feature from the highest-ranking group to the lowest-ranking group, we have here a means by which the process can be brought to an entirely different tempo' (Labov 1972a: 141).

Labov's discussion of the 'hypercorrect' behaviour of the lower middle class forms part of his critique of the traditional dogma of the unobservability of linguistic change. Bloomfield (1887–1949), for example, had postulated that linguistic change is a slow and imperceptible process and thus removed the study of linguistic change from empirical research (see also Martinet 1955, Hockett 1958). As a result historical linguists have concentrated on the description of completed changes and have approached the question of the transition from variant A to variant B mainly through hypothetical thought experiments. Labov's empirical work, however, has shown that the process of linguistic change is indicated in synchronic data by shifting frequencies between social groups. Most important in this respect are differences in the speech of two successive generations, and the distribution of linguistic variants across age levels has been interpreted as indicating change in 'apparent time'. Generational changes were observed both on Martha's Vineyard and in New York. With regard to the pronunciation of *r* Labov found that young speakers belonging to the highest social group used a much higher percentage of *r* than all other groups. In order to assess whether the observed pattern reflects a 'change in progress' or merely a pattern of regular and repeated age-grading, it is, however, necessary to compare the recorded frequencies with some contrasting point in 'real time', i.e. to observe the speech community at two discrete points in time. In 1986 Joy Fowler repeated Labov's department store study and showed that the overall use of *r* had increased in New York during the past twenty-five years; change in real time had taken place in the New York speech community.

To investigate the perceptual correlates of sociolinguistic vari-ation, Labov used subjective reaction tests based on Wallace Lambert's matched-guise experiments. The test design consists of tape-recordings of several versions of the same text, differing only in pronunciation. The speakers on the tape are usually actors who imitate the different accents for these purposes. Listeners (in this case members of the New York speech community) are then asked to judge the recorded speakers in terms of their suitability for occupations such as 'television personality', 'receptionist', 'sales girl' or 'factory worker', occupations differentiated by the degree to which they demand certain linguistic skills, in particular knowl-edge of the prestige dialect. Labov found that different social classes agreed in their evaluation of prestige variants, such as post-vocalic *r*, which was perceived as prestigious even by those who rarely used it in their own speech. Labov therefore formu-lated the following 'axiom of sociolinguistic structure': 'The correlate of regular stratification of a sociolinguistic variable in behavior is uniform agreement in subjective reactions towards that variable' (Labov 1972a: 249).

In other words, a speech community is a group of speakers who share the same evaluation ('homogeneity of interpretation') of the linguistic variants that differentiate the speakers socially ('hetero-geneity of production'). To explain the seemingly paradoxical fact that working-class speakers in New York acknowledge social pres-tige norms such as the pronunciation of post-vocalic *r* but none the less maintain a high frequency of non-prestigious variants in their own speech, Labov introduced the concept of 'covert pres-tige'. That is, although certain variants are evaluated negatively in the speech community, working-class speakers (or other non-dominant groups) continue to use these forms to express their adherence to an alternative set of social norms or values attributing positive connotations to modes of behaviour associated with a non-dominant (typically non-middle-class) social identity. On Martha's

Vineyard, for example, as we have seen, a centralized variant of the diphthong in lexical items such as *right, pride, wife* was used by those who identified strongly with the island's distinct identity and who resisted the direction of social change on the island.

In order to formally describe the systematic interaction of language-internal and language-external constraints within the then 'standard model' of generative grammar, Labov developed the notion of 'variable rules' in the context of his work on African American Vernacular English (AAVE). AAVE (formerly called Negro Black English or Black English Vernacular, BEV) is a variety used as the general vernacular by black youth in the urban ghettos of American cities and by black adults in relaxed conversation with family and friends. AAVE is characterized by a number of salient grammatical features, such as loss of the copula (*he beautiful*) and loss of *-s* in the third-person singular (*she write*), and its tense-aspect system differs from that of standard English. AAVE also shows a marked pattern of word-final consonant cluster simplification: word-final *-t* and *-d* may be deleted after a consonantal segment if the following word does not begin with a vowel (i.e. *firs' thing* or *las' month* but not *las' October* or *firs' of all*). However, since no speaker simplifies these consonant clusters in all cases, the process is usually described as an optional phonological rule, i.e. the application of the rule is at the speaker's discretion:

$$-t/-d \rightarrow \emptyset \ / \ [\text{+cons}] \ \_\_\_\_ \ \#\# \ [\text{-syll}] \quad \text{(optional)}$$

However, in this form the rule does not capture Labov's empirical observation that, although the nature of the following segment affects the likelihood of rule application, it does not constitute a categorical constraint: 'the second consonant is absent *more often* when the following word begins with a consonant than with a vowel' (Labov 1972a: 217; emphasis added). The rule as given also excludes cases of cluster simplification involving inflectional morphemes (e.g. *he rol'* for *he rolled*), which are possible in AAVE. However, deletion of the past-tense marker is less frequent than deletion within monomorphemic clusters. Labov suggested the use of angled brackets to describe frequency variability (which, unlike optionality, is structured and non-random), and used Greek letters to indicate formally relations of more or less, thus giving:

$$-t/-d \rightarrow <\emptyset> / \ [+cons]^\beta <-\# > \underline{\qquad} \#\#^\alpha <-syll>$$

In this form the rule specifies that in AAVE the grammatical constraint is more powerful in restricting the application of the rule than the phonological constraint, and thus makes predictions about the probability or likelihood of the occurrence of particular forms. Social factors can also be incorporated into variable rules, as in New York where the feature [+ working class] has a constraining effect on the realization of *r*. Variable rules formally stating the probabilistic patterns of variability are not merely descriptions of performance or production but are, according to Labov, an important aspect of linguistic competence. That is, the probability of the application of a rule is part of its structural description (and thus the speaker's competence), while the actual frequencies of rule application are part of performance.

> The ability of human beings to accept, preserve and interpret rules with variable constraints is clearly an important aspect of their linguistic competence or *langue*. But no one is aware of this competence, and there are no intuitive judgements accessible to reveal it to us. Instead, naïve perception of our own and others' behaviour is usually categorical, and only careful study of language in use will demonstrate the existence of this capacity to operate with variable rules
>
> (Labov 1972a: 226).

Labov's work on AAVE not only led to the interpretation of linguistic variability in terms of probability theory but also served to refute the 'deficit hypothesis' that had informed US education policies in the 1960s. Associated with the work of the British sociologist Basil Bernstein, the deficit hypothesis has it that the communicative strategies used by middle-class parents support the development of abstract thought and logic, while the working-class environment was said to lead to restricted verbal skills and highly context-dependent discourse strategies. In an extension of the theory of linguistic relativism (see Chapter 1, Chapter 4 above) Bernstein interpreted the high rate of school failure among working-class children as a direct result of their deficient verbal skills. In the United States, Bernstein's deficit theory had been taken to new heights by educationalists who maintained that the verbal skills of black children not only were deficient when compared with those of children from middle-class families but constituted a 'basically non-logical mode of expressive behavior', a random series of 'badly connected words or phrases', a mere accumulation of errors (Breitner *et al.* 1966). Labov's linguistic analysis of AAVE, however, showed clearly that AAVE was as structurally complex and rule-governed as standard American English and thus not in itself an obstacle to the acquisition of logical and abstract thought. This position was eloquently formulated in 'The logic of non-standard English' (Labov 1972b, first published in 1969), a passionate plea for the recognition of AAVE as a linguistic system in its own right.

> There is no reason to believe that any nonstandard vernacular is in itself an obstacle to learning. The chief problem is ignorance of language on the part of all concerned. Our job as linguists is to remedy this ignorance ... Teachers are now being told to ignore the language of black children as unworthy of attention and every natural utterance of the child as evidence of his mental inferiority. As linguists we are unanimous in condemning this view as bad observation, bad theory, and bad practice.
>
> (Labov 1972b: 240)

Labov argued that deficit theorists had failed to collect examples of natural speech that would show the complex communicative and narrative skills of black youths in urban ghettos. Instead, they obtained their evidence from formal interviews conducted by white middle-class researchers. Reading failure and educational underperformance are, according to Labov, not the result of linguistic deficiency, but rather reflect alienation from white middle-class culture and educational institutions.

Labov has argued in his work that, if one accepts the 'facts of heterogeneity' as part of linguistic reality, language cannot be seen as 'autonomous in any serious sense' (Labov 1972a: 181), since social stratification and linguistic variation regularly interact in the course of language history. Despite his emphasis on the social aspects of language, Labov initially rejected the label 'sociolinguistics' for his research programme:

> This type of research has sometimes been labelled 'sociolinguistics', although it is a somewhat misleading use of an oddly redundant term. Language is a form of social behavior: statements to this effect can be found in any introductory text. Children raised in isolation do not use language; it is used

by human beings in a social context, communicating their
needs, ideas and emotions to one another . . . In what way, then,
can 'sociolinguistics' be considered as something apart from
'linguistics'?

(Labov 1972a: 183)

Although generally regarded as foundational for the development of quantitative sociolinguistics, Labov's work has not
escaped criticism. Critics have questioned his status-based notion
of social class, the exclusion of the linguistic behaviour of the
'upper class' or elite from the discussion of prestige norms and
his emphasis on quantitative analysis. His compromise with
contemporary mainstream linguistic theory – his interpretation of
variable rules as statements about linguistic competence – has been
questioned very sharply, e.g:

To describe the occurrences of utterances of speakers/groups
in terms of probabilistic laws (which are said to be variable
rules in a model of grammar) is one thing, but to project such
rules on the competence of individual speakers of a language
and then to suppose that speakers or their mental capabilities
are in any way constrained by them is, in my opinion, methodologically inadmissible.

(Romaine 1981: 105–6)

In other words, the relationship between an individual speaker's
linguistic behaviour and mental processes, on the one hand, and
statistical statements about the macro-level or aggregate linguistic
behaviour of the speech community, on the other, is far from clear.

There is also a fundamental problem with the notion 'speech
community' itself, for it is arguably an idealization no less ten-
dentious than Chomsky's 'ideal speaker-listener' (see Chapter 9
above, Chapter 14 below). In an age of increasing international
mobility, when more and more people see themselves as citizens
of the world, to what extent is it useful to postulate speech communities in Labov's sense?

Despite such criticisms, the sociolinguistic methods pioneered
by Labov have since been applied (with some additional refine-
ments) in communities as diverse as those of Norwich, Belfast,
Montreal, Paris, Berlin, Buenos Aires, Tunis, Sydney, Copenhagen
and Tehran.

Chapter 11

Goffman on the communicating self

The study of face-to-face interaction in natural settings doesn't yet have an adequate name ... The subject matter, however, can be identified. It is that class of events which occurs during co-presence and by virtue of co-presence. The ultimate behavioral materials are the glances, gestures, positionings, and verbal statements that people continuously feed into the situation, whether intended or not.

(Goffman 1967:1)

During direct personal contacts ... unique informational conditions prevail ... The human tendency to use signs and symbols means that evidence of social worth and of mutual evaluations will be conveyed by very minor things, and these things will be witnessed, as will the fact that they have been witnessed. An unguarded glance, a momentary change in tone of voice, an ecological position taken or not taken, can drench a talk with judgmental significance. Therefore, just as there is no occasion of talk in which improper impressions could not intentionally or unintentionally arise, so there is no occasion of talk so trivial as not to require each participant to show serious concern with the way he handles himself and the others present ...

In any society, whenever the physical possibility of spoken interaction arises, it seems that a system of practices, conventions, and procedural rules comes into play which functions as a means of guiding and organizing the flow of messages ...

The conventions regarding the structure of occasions of talk represent an effective solution to the problem of organizing a flow of spoken messages. In attempting to discover how it is that these conventions are maintained in force as guides to action, one finds evidence to suggest a functional relationship between the structure of the self and the structure of spoken interaction.

(Goffman 1955: 225–7)

From his first published article in 1951 until he died in 1982, Erving Goffman wrote some of the twentieth century's most influential texts on how people communicate with each other in face-to-face interaction. Born in Canada in 1922, Goffman began teaching sociology at the University of California, Berkeley, and then later at the University of Pennsylvania. He was the founding pioneer of the academic study of conversational interaction (a topic which he simply called 'talk'). Since that time, the field that Goffman first envisaged and whose interest he first propounded has grown steadily to become one of the most active in Western language theory.

Why was Goffman – a sociologist – interested in spoken communication, a subject which few would think of as falling within the sociologist's traditional concerns? The answer is that, like many theorists in the Western tradition, Goffman was convinced that the interest and importance of studying language is very much greater than that of merely gaining knowledge about the specific characteristics of language itself. Since the origins of Western linguistic thought, theorists have argued that by studying language one may learn about such non-linguistic subjects as the human mind, God's intentions, human origins and development, metaphysical essences, ethnic histories, and the differences between humans and animals. In the same vein, Goffman claimed that many of the traditional 'macro' concerns of sociologists – social hierarchy, structure, power, change etc. – were best studied in their 'micro' realizations in face-to-face interactions between individual social agents; and most of such interactions are *verbal* interactions. He argued that in many cases these larger social realities are created, maintained and accorded their significance and power via the forge of face-to-face communicational interaction. Furthermore, even in the case of those social realities which do not have their source in the 'micro', interactional domain, Goffman believed that, nevertheless, it is in this face-to-face domain where the features and powers of social reality are put into operation. So it is there where social reality may best be observed and studied.

Goffman's thinking was firmly rooted in the Western tradition of linguistic thought. Accordingly, it may help us to understand his theory of face-to-face communication if we begin by comparing its foundational questions and assumptions to those underlying John Locke's linguistic discussions in the *Essay concerning human understanding* (see Volume I, Chapter 10). Like Locke, Goffman conceived of verbal communication as a form of telementation: that is, as a means of conveying to hearers the speaker's mental content – thoughts, feelings, attitudes, ideas etc. (Goffman 1981: 80). And both Goffman and Locke maintain that speakers and hearers usually *assume* that communication 'works': that is, that they understand what they say to each other (Goffman 1981: 10). However, while the only vehicles of communication that Locke gives attention to are speech and writing, Goffman extends this list to include hand and facial gestures, postural alignments, eye gaze, intonation and 'paralinguistic' features such as filled and silent pauses, feedback responses, laughter, exclamatory interjections (such as 'Ouch!'), and other common, although non-verbal, communicational devices.

Although Locke and Goffman share a common conception of the general telementational purpose of communication, they also share a common scepticism regarding the powers of words to achieve that purpose. Locke spoke of the 'imperfection' of language as a communicational vehicle (see Volume I, Chapter 10) and Goffman of its 'residual ambiguity' as an obstacle to mutual understanding. 'If speaker and hearers were to file a report on what they assumed to be the full meaning of an extended utterance, these glosses would differ, at least in detail. Indeed, one routinely presumes on a mutual understanding that doesn't quite exist' (Goffman 1981: 10). Yet, for his part, Locke also maintained, somewhat paradoxically, that on the whole, in ordinary conversation communicators do understand each other well enough (Locke 1690: 479). But, if language has all the imperfections that Locke attributes to it, how is it that its use in conversation typically gets the communicational job done? Locke never raises this question, let alone answers it. On the other hand, Goffman's studies of 'talk' may be seen as a lifelong attempt to answer this question. For Goffman starts from the assumption that – in spite of the residual ambiguities of their messages – communicators *are* typically able to reach a 'working agreement' of understanding, an agreement which is sufficient for the 'practical purposes' of ordinary communication (Goffman 1981: 10). His writings on face-to-face communication explore how this working agreement is achieved. 'Given the possibility and the expectation that effective transmission will occur during talk, we can ask what conditions or arrangements would facilitate this and find some obvious answers' (Goffman 1981: 12). During the more than thirty years that Goffman studied and wrote about talk, he constructed, piece by piece, a theory of communicational interaction as organized by two fundamental kinds of requirements: system constraints and ritual constraints. He believed that it is because communicators obey these constraints – and expect that they will each obey them – that talk is an 'orderly' or structured sort of behaviour in which a working agreement of understanding is a regular occurrence.

System constraints organize talk into the familiar patterns of dialogue, with one speaker speaking at a time, speakers taking turns to occupy the floor, and with each turn produced as a relevant response to the prior turn. Because conversationalists expect that system constraints will be obeyed – and because they assume that their co-conversationalists also expect this – the constraints are, on the whole, adhered to. Equally important, conversationalists rely on those expectations when interpreting what each other says. The result is that the elliptical, ambiguous and frequently non-literal character of talk is much less of a threat to communicational understanding than the Lockean sceptic might expect. Consider, for instance, Shelley's response in the following exchange.

1   Alan: 'Do you want to go to Chez Anatole tonight?'
2   Shelley: 'Well, which bank do you think we should rob first?'
3   Alan: (Sighs) 'I suppose so. Order in pizza again then?'
4   Shelley: 'Oh, not again – why don't we just have a salad tonight?'

Although Shelley's response in (2) is elliptical, ambiguous, and non-literal, Alan would doubtless have little difficulty understanding it. Goffman's theory of the system constraints of talk is intended to explain *why* this is. Still, one might take the position that explaining the success of such a mundane conversational exchange does not require a sophisticated theoretical apparatus – in other words, that all that Alan requires to understand what Shelley says is common sense. But Goffman makes it clear that the superficially trivial appearance of ordinary conversational exchanges should not blind the analyst to their accomplished character – in particular, to the cognitive 'work' involved in coming to a shared interpretation. To see this, it is worth considering some of the possible interpretations which, in principle, could be given to Shelley's remark in (2).

- She could be practising one of her lines in a play
- She could be bringing up another topic
- She could be singing a line from a new song she heard
- She might have misheard Alan's question, or not have heard it at all
- Her remark might be addressed to an earlier part of their conversation.

In other words, taken on its own the sentence that Shelley produces in (2) is highly ambiguous, and, if talk were usually so ambiguous, then Lockean worries about communicational understanding would be justified. And yet, we count on ordinary talk to be communicationally sufficient, and that expectation is not typically defeated. The reason talk usually results in mutual understanding, according to Goffman, is that hearers do not even consider the range of *possible* meanings that an utterance like Shelley's *could* have. But why not? How do hearers spontaneously determine which possible meaning is the one intended by their interlocutor?

Goffman takes the answer to these questions to lie in the taken-for-granted system constraints underlying talk. These constraints would lead Alan to assume that Shelley's utterance in (2) is intended as – and is intended to be interpreted as – a relevant response to his initial question (1), in spite of the superficially ambiguous character of her utterance. Note that there is nothing in Shelley's remark that explicitly indicates that it is a relevant reply to (1). Nevertheless, all things being equal, Alan would indeed assume that her remark in (2) is intended as a reply to (1). To put this in more general terms, system constraints lead conversationalists to assume that participants' contributions to an ongoing conversation are intended as – and are intended to be interpreted as – contributions to the development of a sequential chain in which each turn is a relevant response to that which preceded it. For this reason, Alan assumes that Shelley's remark in (2) is intended as a reply to his question.

However, merely assuming that the response is relevant to the question he had asked is not enough for Alan to determine precisely what the content of Shelley's remark in (2) is intended to be. More needs to be 'spelled out' if Alan is to understand that the intended interpretation of Shelley's reply is something like

> If we do as you suggest and dine at Chez Anatole tonight, our meal will cost more than the funds we have available. So, we would have to obtain more funds. One obvious way of doing that would be to rob a bank. But since that is something we would never do, then my answer to your question is that we had better decide not go to Chez Anatole tonight.

So, given Alan's assumption that what Shelley says is a relevant reply to his question in (1), he still has the task of working his way 'back' to the particular meaning Shelley intended him to understand. To do this he must rely on another component of the system constraints governing talk: that which Goffman and others have called 'presupposition' (see also Grice 1989): 'A presupposition (or assumption, or implication, or background expectation) can be defined very broadly as a state of affairs we take for granted in pursuing a course of action' (Goffman 1983: 1). In one of the last papers he wrote, 'Felicity's condition' (Goffman 1983), Goffman argues that in conversation presuppositions help hearers narrow down the possible meanings generated by an inherently ambiguous sentence and so come closer to the actual meaning intended by the speaker in uttering that sentence. Hearers derive these presuppositions from earlier parts of the conversation, from their knowledge of the speaker and his or her background, from features of the situational context and from the type (or 'frame': see below) of communicational encounter in which the talk is occurring.

> Given (two speakers) lodged in face-to-face talk ... their cumulative discourse to that point, their jointly perceivable surroundings, and the knowledge each knows or assumes the other has brought to the encounter, can all provide understandings that are presupposed in the phasing of a next utterance and without which the relevant meaning of the utterance might not be easily discoverable.
>
> (Goffman 1983: 28)

Moreover, Goffman argues that speakers are (subconsciously) aware that hearers will rely on presuppositions in their effort to understand what is said. In turn, speakers are said to be aware that it is their responsibility – the responsibility which Goffman termed 'Felicity's condition' – to construct their contributions to an ongoing conversation in such a way that their hearers *can* work out the intended meaning by drawing on available presuppositions. 'Whatever else, our activity must be addressed to the other's mind, that is, to the other's capacity to read our words and actions for evidence of our feelings, thoughts, and intent. This confines what we say and do, but it also allows us to bring to bear all of the world to which the other can catch allusions' (Goffman 1983: 51).

In other words, in constructing their contributions to an ongoing conversation, speakers make use of more materials, in addition to those provided by the structural and lexical resources of their language. They do not simply utter the sentence by which their language encodes the meaning that they wish to convey. Rather, they construct each utterance drawing *both* on the resources of their language and on the presuppositions that they take to be available to their hearers in the current situation: presuppositions concerning background knowledge, situational features, the progress of the exchange so far, shared perspectives and preju- dices, and so on. The result is an utterance whose interpretation depends on the twin resources of language and presupposition. Goffman's approach to communicational understanding thereby brings into central focus a domain of interpretational resources that had been ignored in previous attempts to explain communi- cation as a matter of knowing and using a common language.

For example, in the exchange presented above, Alan will have to draw on presuppositions to interpret Shelley's remark in (2). So, we may imagine that, because of what he knows about their joint finances, about Shelley's concerns about those finances, about her law-abiding character and about her sarcastic sense of humour, Alan determines that she is *not* seriously suggesting that they rob a bank. He further determines that her sarcastically suggesting that they do so is intended instead to bring him to understand not only that she rejects his proposal but also the reason why she is rejecting it. Moreover, not only does Alan take it for granted that he is intended to draw on these (and other) presuppositions in order to interpret Shelley's remark but Shelley herself assumes that he will do so and has constructed her remark accordingly.

Related to presupposition is another communicational resource – the frame – which Goffman saw as important in explaining how communicators are able to understand each other in spite of the superficially ambiguous characteristics of their utterances. A frame is an interpretational schema that provides for speaker and hearers' identification of a particular stretch of talk as an instance of a given type of (communicational) event. It is the frame which explains their mutual recognition that what is 'going on' at a given conversational moment is, say, 'telling a joke' (or 'making a complaint' or 'giving directions' or 'telling a story' or 'making a suggestion' or 'explaining what happened' or 'teasing' etc.). If speaker and hearer agree on the interpretational frame for a current state of talk, then the range of possible meanings which they will attribute to a given utterance is accordingly restricted, thereby increasing the chance that they will understand that utterance in the same way. Analogously, the significance of playing a given card depends on the game we are playing – bridge, hearts, gin rummy, crazy eights etc. We interpret the card's current significance because we see it within the interpretational frame of a particular card game. If we did not both agree on the applicable frame – that is, on what game we were playing – nor, then, would we agree on the significance of playing, say, an eight of clubs. Similarly, if speaker and hearer are not both aware that they are in a 'teasing' frame, a given remark may well be misunderstood by one of them and taken as an insult. 'I assume that definitions of a situation are built up in accordance with principles of organization which govern events – at least social ones – and our subjective involvement in them; frame is the word I use' (Goffman 1974: 10–11).

To illustrate how important is the hearer's reliance on frames in interpreting an utterance, we may switch our illustrative focus to Shelley's task in interpreting Alan's opening remark in (1). This remark takes on a different meaning if we imagine it to have been produced, and so interpreted, within different frames. This can be illustrated by the different responses that Shelley might have given in (2), according to the different frames she took to be operative.

1   Alan: 'Do you want to go to Chez Anatole tonight?'
2a Shelley: 'No, that wasn't the title, but it was something like that.'
    FRAME: They have been trying to think of the title of a movie they once saw.

2b Shelley: 'Look, it's no good changing the subject. We have to deal with this problem immediately.'
    FRAME: They're having an argument.
2c Shelley: 'That's fine, Alan. A few more times and you'll have that question intonation right.'
    FRAME: She is a teacher helping him improve his English conversation.
2d Shelley: 'Wake up, dear. You're talking in your sleep again.'
    FRAME: It is the middle of the night and they are both asleep.
2e Shelley: 'Go find someone else to try your moves on, will you? I'm not interested.'
    FRAME: She is sitting alone in a bar; he walks up . . .
2f Shelley: 'No, dear, I really don't want to practise your lines any more tonight.'
    FRAME: They have been practising his lines for a play.

Another assumption shared by Goffman and Locke is that, from the point of view of its communicational efficacy, the ambiguous character of language is further complicated by the privacy of meaning. If what a speaker means by his or her utterance – as well as what the hearer(s) takes it to mean – could be open to public inspection, the utterance's inherent ambiguity would not pose such a challenge to mutual understanding. But, as Locke emphasized, meaning and understanding are mentally 'private'. In this case, how is it possible for a conversation to proceed smoothly – as it typically does – if speakers are always in doubt whether what they say is correctly understood by their hearers and if hearers always doubt whether they understand exactly what the speaker means? And if they are *not* always in doubt – as would seem to be the case – then what is the basis of their confidence? Given that meaning is private, what enables speakers and hearers to determine that they understand each other?

Again, whereas Locke proposes no solution to this dilemma, Goffman does. His answer is that the system constraints of talk oblige hearers to give public indications of how they understand a speaker's utterance. In particular, a hearer manifests his or her understanding of a speaker's remark by the characteristics of his or her response to that remark. And those same constraints oblige the speaker in his or her next turn to display acceptance or rejection of the hearer's displayed understanding. Consider, for instance, the continuation of the exchange presented above:

3   Alan: (Sighs) 'I suppose so. Order in pizza again then?'

This remark manifests Alan's understanding

- that Shelley's remark in (2) is a relevant reply to his question about going to the expensive restaurant;
- that (2) amounts to a rejection of the suggestion implied in his question;
- that the reason Shelley rejects his suggestion in (2) is that the restaurant in question is too expensive;
- and that she wants them to find a less expensive way to dine that evening.

Furthermore, because of the system constraints governing talk, Shelley's next remark in (4) is obliged to display her acceptance – or possibly rejection – of the understanding of (2) that Alan had displayed in (3). This is her opportunity to confirm or correct Alan's interpretation of her prior turn. So, we might imagine her responding in (4) with something like

4   'Oh, I don't know about pizza again – why don't we just have a salad tonight?'

Among other things, this remark manifests her ratification of the understanding of (2) that Alan had displayed in (3). For if she had said in (4) something like

4a   'Don't be silly. I only mean that we should also see if they have any job openings left'.

she would be manifesting her rejection of the understanding of (2) that Alan had displayed in (3). Goffman terms the rejection of a displayed understanding and initiation of corrective sequence a 'remedial exchange', a process by means of which publicly ratified mutual understanding may be re-established.

In sum, an important consequence of the system constraints organizing talk is what subsequent conversation analysts have termed 'the sequential architecture of intersubjectivity' (Heritage 1984). Goffman puts it this way:

Given a speaker's need to know whether his message has been received, and if so, whether or not it has been passably understood, and given a recipient's need to show that he has

received the message and correctly – given these very fundamental requirements of talk as a communication system – we
have the essential rationale ... for the organization of talk
into two-part exchanges.

(Goffman 1981: 12)

The structure of talk as a system of two-part exchanges is an organizational resource that allows conversationalists to determine
whether what they say is being correctly understood by their
hearers and whether the meaning they attribute to a speaker's utterance is what the speaker intends. And, with remedial exchanges
it gives them the means of repairing any misunderstandings
detected. System constraints organize conversation in a way that
facilitates not only the arrival at a common understanding but also
the mutual recognition of that common understanding.

Thus far we have seen that Goffman's account of the structure
of talk addresses the kinds of sceptical doubts that Goffman, like
Locke, had raised about language as a vehicle of understanding.
However, Goffman also indicates another kind of danger which
threatens verbal communication, a danger concerning the self-
images of those participating in a conversation.

[W]hen a person volunteers a statement or message, however
trivial or commonplace, he commits himself and those he
addresses, and in a sense places everyone present in jeopardy.
By saying something, the speaker opens himself up to the
possibility that the intended recipients will affront him by not
listening or will think him forward, foolish, or offensive in
what he has said. And should he meet with such a reception,
he will find himself committed to the necessity of taking face-
saving action against them ...

Thus when one person volunteers a message, thereby
contributing what might easily be a threat to the ritual equilibrium, someone else present is obliged to show that the
message has been received and that its content is acceptable
to all concerned.

(Goffman 1955: 227–8)

Goffman's point is that we should not assume that two people
engaged in talk are concerned only with the task of conveying their
cognitive content, or thoughts, to each other. A communicational

exchange is much more than a vehicle for the expression and understanding of thoughts. It is also a form of personal interaction – an encounter between two (or more) selves. Moreover, communicators place great value on the public self-images – what Goffman calls their 'face' – that they display in their interactions, to some extent even more value than they place on the accurate exchange of meanings. However, every interaction inevitably presents dangers to the maintenance of one's face. The resources by which these dangers can be – and usually, if not always, are – avoided are what Goffman calls 'ritual constraints'.

> [The communicator's actions] are directed not merely to system constraints; ... an additional set apply, namely, constraints regarding how each individual ought to handle himself with respect to each of the others, so that he not discredit his own tacit claim to good character or the tacit claim of the others that they are persons of social worth whose various forms of territoriality are to be respected.
>
> (Goffman 1981: 16)

The participants in a conversation typically attend to the construction, presentation and maintenance of their face (public self-image), and this attention serves to structure talk no less than does their attention to the achievement of mutual understanding. Moreover, there is a kind of trade-off in face-work: in return for the right of each participant to present and protect his or her own face, they must help their co-participants do the same for their faces. Attention to the other's face also contributes to the structural properties of talk. Communicators engage in interaction as players in 'a ritual game' (Goffman 1955: 225). It is in this ritual character of talk that concepts such as deference, demeanour, politeness, diplomacy, considerateness, honour, dignity, self-respect, tact etc. have their source. Much of Goffman's work is devoted to the analysis of the ways in which these concepts contribute to the construction of particular occasions of talk. The result is that Goffman's theory of talk is a theory not only of conversational structure but also of the structure of the communicating self (Goffman 1955: 227). For Goffman, the self is constructed in communicational practices, which are in turn governed by the system and ritual constraints which were his analytical focus. 'Universal human nature is not a very human thing. By acquiring it, the person becomes a kind of construct, built up not from inner psychic propensities but from moral rules that are impressed upon him from without' (Goffman 1955: 231). Because of the connections that he draws between talk and self, Goffman's work has attracted as much interest from psychologists and psychiatrists as it has from linguists and sociologists.

Goffman characterizes face as the 'positive social value' that a communicator claims for himself or herself – 'an image of self delineated in terms of approved social attributes' (Goffman 1955: 213).

> [A] person's attachment to a particular face, coupled with the ease with which disconfirming information can be conveyed by himself and others, provides one reason why he finds that participation in any contact with others is a commitment. A person will also have feelings about the face sustained for the other participants, and while these feelings may differ in quantity and direction from those he has for his own face, they constitute an involvement in the face of others that is as immediate and spontaneous as the involvement he has in his own face.
>
> (Goffman 1955: 213)

In other words, Goffman is not suggesting that communicators are always or even often consciously aware of the considerations of face. Face-work is a matter of 'habitual and standardized practices', for the observance of which we hold each other morally responsible; however, they can be brought to conscious awareness during an 'incident': that is, a conversational event 'whose effective symbolic implications threaten face' (Goffman 1955: 216)

To illustrate, imagine the following exchange:

5   Alan: 'I thought that concert we went to last night was fantastic.'
6   Shelley: 'I thought it was awful.'

Shelley's response threatens Alan's face. In particular, her response challenges the public self-image that Alan is assumed to want – and to expect – to be maintained in social interactions: the image of someone who is enjoyable to be with, whose taste and judgement in music are worthy of consideration and respect, and who deserves to be spoken to in terms that manifest this consideration and respect. It is not the fact that Shelley disagrees with Alan's appraisal of the concert that threatens Alan's face but rather the fact that she does so baldly, without any of the mitigating expressions or hedges that would reflect her acknowledgement of the continuing obligation to support Alan's claim to a positive public self-image. The ritual constraints on talk lead us instead to expect Shelley to hedge her reply: to express her disagreement in a way that is structured so as not to threaten Alan's face, perhaps mitigating her negative judgement of the concert with something like the following:

6'   Shelley: 'Well, it was lovely being together; but didn't you think the music was a bit rough?'

Whereas the judgement expressed in (6') would probably be accepted without comment by Alan, the way it is expressed in (6) might well initiate an 'incident' with concurrent damage to the ritual equilibrium of Alan and Shelley's interaction. Alan would have 'hurt feelings'; he would feel, and would probably act, 'snubbed', 'offended' etc. Accordingly, one could say that ritual constraints concern the management of 'feelings' in talk – the source of which lies in the presentation of the self in the everyday social world. In Goffman's theory of talk, if we are to understand the nature of communicational practices, we need to look more closely at the management of these 'feelings'. For they contribute no less to the structuring of a communicational exchange than do matters concerning the expression and understanding of thoughts and ideas.

In general, then, a person determines how he ought to conduct himself during an occasion of talk by testing the potentially symbolic meaning of his acts against the self-images that are being sustained. In doing this, however, he incidentally subjects his behavior to the expressive order that prevails and contributes to the orderly flow of messages. His aim is to save face; his effect is to save the situation. From the point of view of saving face, then, it is a good thing that spoken interaction has the conventional organization given it; from the point of view of sustaining an orderly flow of spoken messages, it is a good thing that the self has the ritual structure given it.

(Goffman 1955: 228)

Goffman argued throughout his career that to understand how talk works we have to appreciate the obstacles facing its production in the social world. There are obstacles presented by the ambiguous, non-literal and elliptical nature of talk. But Goffman also drew attention to many other obstacles which threaten the accomplishment of a successful communicational interchange, including those whose source lies in the fact that communication is an interaction between selves. If we are to understand the kind of mechanism that talk is, we have to understand the different kinds of challenges it is designed to overcome.

Goffman's method consisted in identifying these obstacles and then proposing hypotheses regarding the kinds of constraints and rules which communicators might be using in order to overcome them. Behind his proposals was always the assumption that, typically, they *are* overcome. This method leaves Goffman open to at least two kinds of criticism, both of which have been addressed to his work (see Drew and Wootton 1988). The first claims that his obstacles are red herrings, and that therefore the constraints hypothesized to overcome them are needless. The second accepts the obstacles, but replies that the analyst ought to use empirical methods to study what speakers and hearers actually do to overcome them, instead of postulating constraints and rules that they *might* be using. In other words, the second criticism asks: are these hypotheses true? That is, even if we grant that these constraints *could* work and that the 'problems' they are designed to resolve are real problems for the interactants, are they ones that communicating individuals are actually following? Universally? Goffman has been criticized for failing to address these questions – for assuming that, if his hypotheses solve the problem on paper, then they must actually be 'in operation' in the day-to-day reality of ordinary talk. Later conversation analysts have modified Goffman's methods and his claims about specific rules and principles governing conversational interaction. However, Goffman's merit was to draw language theorists' attention to the varied richness of 'talk' as an investigatory domain, while signalling the relevance of its study to sociology, anthropology, linguistics and psychology. His thinking is still a driving force in the study of conversational interaction today.

> Given that you have something that you want to utter to a particular other, how do you go about getting into the circumstances that will allow you appropriately to do so? ... Here, clearly, philosophy and linguistics must give way to sociology.
>
> (Goffman 1983: 32)

Chapter 12

Bruner on the child's passport into language

Infants learning language are not academic grammarians infer-
ring rules abstractly and independently of use . . . Whatever else
language is, it is a systematic way of communicating to others,
of affecting their and our own behavior, of sharing attention,
and of constituting realities to which we then adhere just as we
adhere to the 'facts' of nature. Let us not be dazzled by the
grammarian's questions. Pragmatic ones are just as dazzling
and just as mysterious. How indeed do we ever learn to get
things done with words?

(Bruner 1983: 119–20)

Language is a specialized and conventionalized extension of
cooperative action. To understand it properly, its acquisition
must be viewed as a transformation of modes of assuring cooperation that are prior to language, prior both phylogenetically
and ontogenetically.

(Bruner 1975: 2)

What may be innate about language acquisition is not linguistic
innateness, but some special features of human action and
human attention that permit language to be decoded by the uses
to which it is put.

(Bruner 1975: 2)

Within three or four years from birth, every child learns a
language. They are not given grammar lessons. They are not
given any explicit instruction. They yet know little about the
world and its ways. However, in spite of all this, *what* they learn
– a language such as English, Swahili, Japanese or Pitjantjatjara

– is an extremely complex object of learning, so complex that well-educated adults can spend years taking formal classes from professional instructors and still not get as far in learning a new language as a three-year-old child gets in learning its first language. Why? Why are children so good at doing something that seems to baffle even the most well-educated adults? How do children learn language?

In the latter half of the twentieth century, these questions became central to intellectual inquiry into language. Many linguists, philosophers, psychologists and anthropologists came to believe that no theoretical account of the central properties of language was acceptable unless it could also explain how children were able to learn language so swiftly and effortlessly. In the last three decades of the century it was the opposition between the answers provided by the psychologist Jerome Bruner (b. 1915) and those advocated by the linguist Noam Chomsky (see Chapter 9 above) that determined the general outlines of this debate.

Before he began writing on language acquisition, Jerome Bruner was already well known as one of the founders of cognitive psychology. Having helped to wean academic psychology away from the methodological puritanism of behaviourism (see Chapter 8 above), he then turned in the early 1970s to the formulation of a new approach to the puzzle of how children learn – and what they learn – in learning language. The result of his efforts was the birth of what, at the turn of the century, has arguably become the most widely influential theory of language acquisition. However, in so doing Bruner had to contend with a powerful school of thought emanating from Chomsky's generative linguistics. Much of Western thought about language in the latter half of the twentieth century can be seen as a response, positive or negative, to the theories of Chomsky – and thought about language development is no exception. Bruner's cognitive interactionist approach to language acquisition is perhaps one of the most explicit illustrations of this general tendency, as nearly all of his writings on language acquisition can be read as one half of a thirty-year dialogue with Chomsky. Therefore, in order to explain Bruner's evolving views on how children learn language, it will help to begin with a summary of Chomsky's arguments for linguistic nativism.

Since at least the middle of the 1960s Chomsky has argued that the adult's knowledge of language is far too complex to have been acquired from experience. As we saw in Chapter 9, Chomsky's generative theory represents linguistic knowledge as the internalization of a complex computational system: a generative grammar. Naturally, as children grow, they undergo no explicit instruction in the mechanics of this formal system, and yet any normal child acquires language effortlessly within the first three to five years of life. This would seem to suggest that the child acquires knowlege of its parents' language from observational experience: listening and watching what the adults around it do with language and then imitating that itself. But Chomsky argues that such a means of learning language would be a complete failure, and so it cannot be what children actually do. For the linguistic information that a child might glean from observational experience is far too inadequate for the child to derive the complex rules and formal structures that constitute the grammar of its parents' language (see Chapter 9 above). All the same, in spite of the inadequate and 'impoverished' nature of the evidence it can glean from experience, the child not only acquires a grammar in a few short years, without effort or conscious attention, but the grammar that it acquires is substantially the *same* grammar as that acquired by all the other children in the speech community. And this is in spite of the fact that the other children's experiences of language will have been as diverse and idiosyncratic as all individual experience presumably is. '[T]he basic problem is that our [linguistic] knowledge is richly articulated and shared with others from the same speech community, whereas the experiential data available are much too impoverished to determine it' (Chomsky 1986: 55).

Chomsky refers to the child's pre-linguistic state – that is, before it has begun to acquire its parents' language – as the 'initial state'. The 'steady state' is that which the child arrives at when it has come to know the language fully.

> The transition from the initial state to the steady state takes place in a determinate fashion, with no conscious attention or choice. The transition is essentially uniform for individuals in a given speech community despite diverse experience. The state attained is highly articulated and very rich, providing a specific interpretation for a vast array of sentences lacking close models in our experience.
>
> (Chomsky 1986: 51)

The logic of Chomsky's argument is simple and clear:

1   The children in a speech community all come to know the same complex, computational system (grammar) in a few short years.
2   They do so without any explicit instruction, conscious attention, or effort.
3   The only experiential evidence they have to help them in this daunting task is grossly inadequate.
4   Therefore, they must have some other source to draw on in formulating this knowledge.

Propositions (2) and (3) tell us that the premise (1) could not possibly occur on the basis of experiental learning. Chomsky's nativist conclusion is therefore (4): children *must* have advance (innate) knowledge on which they draw in acquiring the grammar of their language. For, if they did not, they could not possibly succeed in acquiring that grammar – and yet the premise (1) takes it *as given* that they do.

Chomsky concludes that children must come into the world equipped with a genetically determined faculty of mind: the 'language faculty'. Universal Grammar (UG) is a theory of the properties of this faculty that make it possible for children to advance from the 'initial state' of the language faculty to the 'steady state': that is, to learn the language of their community effortlessly and quickly, and with only a minimal input from experience. The innate knowledge incorporated in the language faculty serves the child as a language acquisition device, or LAD.

> UG (universal grammar) may be regarded as a characterization of the genetically determined language faculty. One may think of this faculty as a 'language acquisition device', an innate component of the human mind that yields a particular language through interaction with presented experience, a device that converts experience into a system of knowledge attained: knowledge of one or another language . . .
>
> How is knowledge of language acquired? . . . The answer to this question is given by a specification of UG along with an account of the ways in which its principles interact with experience to yield a particular language; UG is a theory of the 'initial state' of the language faculty, prior to any linguistic experience.
>
> (Chomsky 1986: 3–4)

Not only does Chomsky's nativist approach to language acquisition treat the child's experience of language as of only minimal
importance (its sole function is in determining whether the particular language acquired is Swahili, Burmese, Mohawk, English,
Twi etc.); it also treats the process of linguistic development –
moving from the 'initial' to the 'steady' state – as separate and
independent from any of the other characteristics of the child's
cognitive development. This reflects a fundamental principle in
Chomsky's generative theory of language, one which he shares
with Saussure (see Volume I, Chapter 16) and which, in spite of
oft-repeated claims to the contrary, distinguishes generative theory
from the universal grammar of the Port-Royal grammarians (see
Volume I, Chapter 8). This is the *principle of linguistic autonomy*: the properties and principles of linguistic knowledge are
autonomous – separate and distinct from any of the other cognitive or non-cognitive properties of the mind. The language faculty,
both initially and in its eventual steady state, is an autonomous
module, independent of any other mental faculty. Furthermore,
because the language faculty is autonomous, 'Universal Grammar',
Chomsky's theory of the language faculty, must similarly rest on
principles and methods that are independent of the theoretical
investigation of other properties of the mind; and the study of
language acquisition must be independent from the study of other
aspects of cognitive development. It is therefore hardly surprising
that, as one of the founders of cognitive psychology, Jerome
Bruner found these characteristics of Chomsky's approach to
language acquisition particularly hard to accept.

In his first few papers on language acquisition, published in the
1970s, Bruner took issue both with Chomsky's position on the
role of experience in language acquisition and with the claimed
autonomy of language – and of language acquisition – from other
cognitive processes. Unlike Chomsky, whose nativist position was
primarily the product of theoretical reasoning rather than of
concrete, observational studies of childhood development, Bruner
applied the empirical methods of developmental psychology in
investigating how and why children learn language. For over ten
years, he and his students observed and recorded children interacting with their caregiver, both in the laboratory and in their own
homes. The first – and most influential – conclusion that he formed
from these investigations was that the child's developmental
environment is far more helpful to the task of acquiring language

than Chomsky had supposed. The linguistic system may indeed be complex and finely articulated, but the child's experience of language is not one of input 'data' from which a formal computational programme must be derived. On the contrary, the child learns language by using it. At first this sounds paradoxical, but Bruner's point is that the child is communicating with its mother (or other caregiver) long before it learns its first words and that there is an essential continuity between many of the features of this pre-linguistic communication and those of later communication with the words and sentences of language. The child's learning of language may thus be said to begin with the development of pre-linguistic means of communicating – manual and facial gestures, eye gaze, vocalizations such as crying, fretting etc. The child makes use of these communicative tools as it participates in co-operative, meaningful interactions with its mother. Its mastery of these pre-linguistic communicative tools becomes the foundation from which the child slowly develops more and more genuinely linguistic means of communication: words, phrases, grammar.

> What the child learns about communication before language helps him crack the linguistic code. For communication is converted into speech through a series of procedural advances that are achieved in highly familiar, well-learned contexts that have already undergone conventionalization at the hands of the infant and his mother.
>
> (Bruner 1977: 274)

> Language acquisition occurs in the context of an 'action dialogue' in which joint undertakings are being regulated by infant and adult. The joint enterprise sets the deictic limits that govern joint reference, determines the need for a referential taxonomy, establishes the need for signalling intent, and eventually provides a context for the development of explicit predication.
>
> (Bruner 1977: 287)

Bruner argued that, by first learning how to participate competently in the routinized, often playful and game-like interactions that constitute much of a child's early social experience, the child learns 'in advance' many of the symbolic and structural properties that are characteristic of language. Bruner referred to these interactions between child and mother as 'joint action formats', 'cooperative routines', 'joint attention formats', or simply 'formats'. These dialogue-like formats 'scaffold' the child's developing communicational skills, helping it to participate competently and productively in the scaled-down communicational exchanges of childhood – *before* it has developed the purely linguistic skills to participate in real dialogues. Supported by this socio-environmental scaffold, the child is assisted in 'cracking the linguistic code' of its parents' language. 'A format is a little microcosm, a task, in which mother and child share an intention to get something done with words. At the start, what the child cannot manage in the format, his mother does for him. Once he can, she requires him to do it thereafter' (Bruner 1984: 171).

Bruner describes various formats in which mother and child jointly attend a co-operative task, such as playing 'peek-a-boo', 'reading' a picture book, getting dressed, bathing or playing with toys. They are a means of 'entering language and culture simultaneously', and Bruner compares them to Wittgenstein's 'language-games' (see Chapter 6 above). Like language-games, formats are simple, game-like, microcosmic versions of the everyday means by which competent members of a culture co-operate in integrating their vocalizations and actions for the purpose of achieving some shared goal. But the formats of childhood are not always so purposive. Some formats may have a particular purpose, such as bathing or dressing, but many formats are perfomed simply to amuse the child, or to occupy it, or just for fun. But, from the present perspective, the most important point about formats – and one that is mentioned also by Wittgenstein regarding language-games – is that formats serve as the nursery for language or cultural development. Formats are crucially adaptable to the child's developing skills – indeed this adaptability is exploited by the mother as she encourages the child, step by step, to try more sophisticated communicational means of participating in their interactions.

For illustration, we might look more closely at one of the formats studied by Bruner: 'book-reading'. The child and mother jointly attend the pages in an open book, with the mother indicating and naming familiar pictures. At an early stage the child may not contribute vocally to the interaction, perhaps only reaching out to turn the pages. Later, it will start to respond to the mother's prompting 'Oh, look! What's that?', perhaps producing an idiosyncratic, non-standard yet increasingly regular vocalization such as [gi]. This will be produced in the appropriate slot in the format – after the mother's prompt – and would typically be followed by the mother's acknowledgement: something like 'That's right! It's a moo-cow'. As the child develops, it will start producing more standard versions of the relevant 'labels'. Such a format is a predictable and routinized series of exchanges in which mother and child each have their assigned roles. It incorporates gestures (e.g. pointing), vocalizations, objects and their joint attentional focus. Mother and child take turns in advancing the action. Because of its simplicity and predictability, the child can more easily understand what is going on and so participate competently and productively. As its skill develops, its contributions can become more and more linguistically sophisticated.

> What a strikingly stable routine it was. Each step of the way, the mother incorporated whatever competencies the child had already developed – to be clued by pointing, to appreciate that sounds 'stood for' things and events, etc. The mother remained the constant throughout. Thereby she was his scaffold – calling his attention, making a query, providing an answering label if he lacked one, and confirming his offer of one, whatever it might be. As he gained competence, she would raise her criterion. Almost any vocalization the child might offer at the start would be accepted. But each time the child came closer to the standard form, she would hold out for it. What was changing was, of course, what the mother *expected* in response – and that, of course, was 'fine-tuned' by her 'theory' of the child's capacities. When he switched from babbling to offering shorter vocalizations as 'labels' (still quite non-standard), she would no longer accept babbles but insist on the shorter 'names'. Then finally, sure that her son knew the standard label, she would shift to delivering her 'What's that?' with a falling intonation on the second word and a special smile to distinguish a rhetorical from a nonrhetorical question. And so it went.
>
> (Bruner 1984: 171–2)

Because formats like these are simple ('microcosmic'), they are easy for the child to learn and to participate in from a very early stage. Furthermore, because of the self-contained, game-like character of formats, they draw the child's attention to the properties of the 'tools' with which the format is being played: the gestures, vocalizations and actions which are the format's symbolic 'counters'. And because the use of these communicational tools is constrained by conventional, sequentially determined 'privileges of occurrence' (such as turn-taking rules), the child becomes familiar with what are also properties of language. No less important, the game-like character of formats invites the child to explore and creatively extend its patterns.

> It is with the buffering of action from its consequences that the child begins to elaborate his signalling in action situations, trying out variations, searching for varied order of combining acts and signals. And it is at this point that the mother's constant interpretations of the child's intended meanings become so crucial in confirming the child's hypotheses.
>
> (Bruner 1975: 11)

In these early papers on language acquisition, Bruner claims that in learning how to participate in joint action formats the child is learning how to operate with certain of the concepts and relationships that underlie the grammars of all human languages. His studies focus on case relationships and topic-comment structure, but he suggests that even more of the universal properties of grammar have precursors in the action patterns of pre-linguistic formats. In other words, the child's developing skill in negotiating the structural and conceptual requirements of formatted interactions is seen as assisting the child to come to grips with many of the same structural and conceptual tools with which linguistic grammars are constructed. The child's 'mastery of procedures for joint action provides the precursor for the child's grasp of initial grammatical forms' (Bruner 1977: 274). Naturally then, the child's acquisition of grammar becomes a less daunting, code-cracking task than it is pictured to be by Chomsky. The child has no need of innate grammatical knowledge, for, without any conscious effort or explicit instruction, it acquires the core features of grammatical knowledge by means of its scaffolded participation in early joint action formats – the interactional episodes which characterize much of its pre-linguistic experience. In other words, the child's early experience is nothing like as impoverished, degenerate and unhelpful to the task of learning linguistic structure as Chomsky has assumed.

In 'The ontogenesis of speech acts' (Bruner 1975), Bruner advocates what he calls the 'strong claim', that is, the claim that

> The child comes to recognize the grammatical rules for forming and comprehending sentences by virtue of their correspondence to the conceptual framework that is constructed for the regulation of joint action and joint attention. This [is] tantamount to saying that grammar originates as a set of rules abstracted from jointly regulated activity which has become codified in the culture of a linguistic community . . . a concept of agent-action-object-recipient at the prelinguistic level aids the child in grasping the linguistic meaning of appropriately ordered utterances involving such case categories as agentive, action object, indirect object, and so forth . . . The claim is that the child is grasping initially the requirements of joint action at a prelinguistic level, learning to differentiate these into components, learning to recognize the function of utterances placed into these serially ordered structures, until finally he comes to substitute elements of a standard lexicon in place of the non-standard ones. The process is, of course, made possible by the presence of an interpreting adult who operates not so much as a corrector or reinforcer but rather as a provider, an expander and idealizer of utterances while interacting with the child. It is not imitation that is going on, but an extension of rules learned in action to the semiotic sphere.
>
> (Bruner 1975: 17–18)

As an example of this process, Bruner discusses what he calls the 'Give and Take' format, involving, say, a toy (the Object) being exchanged (the Action) between one person (the Agent) and another (the Recipient). This format evolves in tandem with the child's developing competence. When the child is still only three months old, much of the responsibility to maintain the interaction falls on the mother. She uses attentional devices – such as 'Oh look at this!' or 'Do you want this?' – to construct the 'offering' stage of the format. Initially, the mother's offering is usually 'limited to a single object . . . being concluded, more often than not, by mother shoving the object into [the child's] fist-shaped hand' (Bruner 1977: 283).

As [the child] approaches the age of six months, the offering phase has considerably diminished in emphasis when compared with the three-month-old. Likewise, many of the attentional devices characteristic of the early period have become abbreviated with the focus residing on [the child's] reach toward the proffered object ... The offering phase thus becomes considerably more condensed – [the mother's] demonstrative 'Look!' as she proffers an object is generally sufficient to capture [the child's] attention and to activate his secondary circular reaction, for [the child] immediately reaches out for the object ... By 12 months the task structure of Give and Take has become quite evident and, increasingly, the child dominates the game. Not only is Give and Take played for considerably longer periods, but [the child] assumes the initiative much more than before – both in offering and showing the objects in his possession to the adults present and in completing the Give. [The child's] earlier hesitancy and checking are superseded by routinized and confident turns. Strikingly ... the task itself, for example exchange for the sake of exchange, gains paramount importance ... Give and Take has become a game involving reciprocal roles and a game with exteriority and constraint ... Such rule-bound sequences as we find in Give and Take provide a solid basis for language to enter the routine and, eventually, for language to become the 'carrier' of the action.

(Bruner 1977: 284–7)

In Bruner's later work on language acquisition, he backed away from this 'strong claim' that the action patterns of formatted interactions serve as developmental precursors for the child's acquisition of the verbal patterns of language. The view that the child had no need of an innate language acquisition device came to seem too dogmatically anti-nativist, and he sought a middle ground. In particular, he retracted the claim that, in structured action formats, children have all they need to learn the grammatical forms and rules of their parents' language. Grammar, he now conceded, is too complex and too arbitrary to be learned merely as a development of the action structures. In his autobiography, he says that his earlier view, that amounted to the claim that communicational function creates grammatical form, was 'a mistake'. Instead, grammar constitutes 'its own problem space'

(Bruner 1984: 169). In the introduction to his *Child's Talk* he is even more explicit: 'The child could not achieve these prodigies of language acquisition without, at the same time, possessing a unique and predisposing set of language-learning capabilities – something akin to what Noam Chomsky has called a Language Acquisition Device, LAD' (Bruner 1983: 18).

However, this did not mean that Bruner dismissed any role for formats or other features of early mother–child communication in explaining how children learn language. On the contrary, formats have a central place in the interactional environment which is a necessary support for the child's linguistic development. In addition to LAD, language acquisition requires what Bruner came to call a language acquisition support system (LASS).

> Formatting, fine-tuned responsiveness, modes of embedding language in action and interaction – all these . . . comprise the Language Acquisition Support System, the LASS that makes possible the operation of a Chomsky-like LAD . . . Parents and more 'expert' speakers . . . help the genetic program to find expression in actual language use . . . the need to use language fully as an instrument for participating in a complex culture (just as the infant uses it to enter the simple culture of his surround) is what provides the engine for language acquisition. The 'genetic' program for language is only half the story. The support system is the other half.
>
> (Bruner 1984: 173)

While Bruner's ideas on language acquisition continued to be very influential in the last decades of the twentieth century, many of those influenced by him have not been willing to accept his concession to Chomsky's grammatical nativism. Perhaps the most important of these is the American developmental psychologist Michael Tomasello who, in the 1990s, published a series of groundbreaking books and articles which further develop the line of reasoning begun in Bruner's earlier work. But Tomasello rejects Bruner's later acknowledgement of the force of the nativist argument for innate features of grammatical knowledge. At the same time, Tomasello also disagrees with the generativist view that linguistic knowledge is 'autonomous', independent of other cognitive abilities, and that the acquisition of grammar therefore occurs in 'its own problem space'. According to Tomasello's cognitivist perspective, there is nothing 'uniquely linguistic' about language or language acquisition. 'Language is a form of cognition; it is cognition packaged for the purposes of interpersonal communication' (Tomasello 1999: 150). Therefore, the child's acquisition of language requires no domain-specific, autonomous linguistic ability. In learning language the child draws on the same cognitive processes and abilities as in acquiring other complex socio-cultural skills.

Tomasello claims that the crucial insight supporting a cognitivist account of language acquisition is already there in Bruner's early work on formats, games and joint attention. Bruner's analysis of the scaffolding function of formats showed that the child does not encounter language as a formal, opaque, meaningless verbal 'input'. If so, the child would not learn it: for instance, a child will not learn language simply by listening to a radio. Language, as the child's object of learning, must be encountered in use – that is, as it is used for communicational purposes. Moreover, it must be being used in ways that the child can make sense of – *before* it has the knowledge to understand its linguistic components. The paradigmatic example of such a scenario is, as Bruner discovered, the joint attentional format. The simple, regular and predictable nature of the formatted interaction makes it possible for the child to make sense of what is going on, to understand the functions that items of language have in the interaction, and eventually to use those items in a functionally apposite way itself (what Tomasello calls 'role-reversal imitation'). And, in turn, Tomasello argues, this development relies on the child's ability to recognize the intentions that the other person in the format has in acting as they do. 'These joint attentional behaviors are . . . all reflections of infants' dawning understanding of other persons as intentional agents' (Tomasello 1999: 69).

For example, consider what a child must be able to do in order to make sense of a move in the 'Give and Take' game. The mother vocalizes and extends her hand holding a toy. This is neither random nor meaningless behaviour: she is intending to offer the toy to the child. In order to learn how the mother's 'Do you want this?' functions – what it means – in this simple game, the child needs to understand this intention, so that it can grasp how her vocalization relates to that intention, that is, as its expression. Tomasello contrasts the human child's ability to recognize communicative intentions with its lack in the non-human animal. The claim is that if, for instance, you hold out a cracker to a parrot and say 'Do you want this?', the parrot will simply see the cracker and take it from your hand. It will not grasp the intention expressed in your behaviour, that is, to offer the cracker to it. This is fine as far as it goes: it is probably sufficient for the parrot to learn to respond appropriately when you say 'Do you want this?' – it looks for an expected cracker in your hand. It may even come to produce that vocalization itself. But it is not sufficient for the parrot to learn what you mean by 'Do you want this?', so that in turn, by means of role-reversal imitation, it can use that same utterance *with the same communicative intention* as you use it: that is, use it to mean what you mean by it. It is because children, but not parrots, are able – given sufficient contextual scaffolding – to grasp some of the communicative intentions behind an adult's behaviour that it is children and not parrots that are able to acquire the meaningful symbols of human language (Tomasello 1999: 103–5; for an opposing view see Chapter 15 below).

> Making sense of things in social interactions . . . relies both on children's ability to understand the game and on their ability to understand the adult's communicative intentions within the game. Children express their understanding of the game by various signs of anticipation, and even active inter-vention, as a particular round unfolds. They express their understanding of what the adult is trying to do in the game most clearly when they take on the adult's role . . . what other researchers have dubbed role-reversal imitation (to distinguish it from straightforward imitation in which the child duplicates the adult's behavior on one and the same entity with no reversal, e.g., they both kick the same ball). Scaife and Bruner (1975) investigated the ability of young infants to enter into joint visual attention with adults by following their line of regard to outside entities. The emergence of skills of joint attention in the months prior to the onset of language demon-strated that one-year-old infants have all the social cognitive skills they need for discerning adult communicative intentions in the context of language learning formats.
>
> (Tomasello 2001: 35–6)

Tomasello's general point is that feats of cultural learning – learning a verbal 'counter' in a formatted game, learning a word or learning a grammatical construction – depend on the ability that human children have to grasp, by means of contextual support, an adult's intention in using those verbal items. The child does not merely learn to *produce* the same word or construction, as a parrot might do; it learns to produce it meaningfully – that is, to use it when the child itself wants to express that meaning. As Bruner had advocated, language is not an abstract, computational system to be learned and used *as such*; it is a means of expressing and communicating meanings – and this essential property must also be part of how it is acquired. Those aspects of the child's social environment to which Bruner drew attention – the features of the language acquisition support system – assist the child in this task. But from a very early age (Tomasello puts this at nine to twelve months), the child must also be able to recognize other humans as intentional agents. Indeed this seems also to be Bruner's point in *Child's Talk* when he argues that children must have an innate 'intent to refer':

> the 'intent to refer' is unlearned and . . . so too is the recognition of that intent in others. Some basis for referential intersubjectivity must exist before language proper appears. Logically, there would be no conceivable way for two human beings to achieve shared reference were there no initial disposition for it . . . It is a primitive that 'other minds' are treated as if they were like our own minds . . . How could the infant 'know' to follow the line of regard of another to search for a joint visual focus save by knowing it in advance?
>
> (Bruner 1983: 122–3)

Tomasello feels that Bruner's concession to the argument for an innate LAD is the product of an inappropriate view of grammar itself. Grammatical constructions, Tomasello argues, are not the output of abstract computational formulae, as generative grammar takes them to be. Grammatical constructions, like words, are symbolic devices for expressing meanings. So, given the words *giraffes*, *eat*, and *leaves* – each with its own individual meaning – the grammatical construction SUBJECT–VERB–OBJECT adds a second layer of intentional meaning to the set of words it is imposed on: i.e. indicating that the first is the agent of the action indicated by the verb and the last the recipient of that action. Tomasello argues that children learn grammatical constructions using the same cognitive processes as they do learning individual words. The child grasps that, in putting the words together in that way, the mother's intention was to indicate that the first word performed the action of the second word on the third. Then, by means of role-reversal imitation, the child uses that construction when it has that same intention to express. Eventually, the child must generalize such constructions into higher-order patterns, but the cognitive process of learning remains the same – context helps the child to grasp the adult's intention in using a particular word or construction and then, through role-reversal imitation, the child comes to use that word or construction when it has that intention. Learning grammar is like learning words, the cognitive and social foundations of which Bruner had already outlined.

> Fundamentally, the way the child learns a concrete linguistic construction . . . is the same way she learns words: she must understand which aspects of the joint attentional scene the adult intends for her to attend to when using this linguistic construction, and then culturally (imitatively) learn that construction for that communicative function.
>
> (Tomasello 1999: 143)

> The essence of this analysis, then, is to redefine syntax in terms of linguistic constructions – of various levels of complexity and abstractness, but always with meaningful communicative functions – and then to apply Bruner's more general acquisition theory to syntax as well. The child is thus learning linguistic structures on several levels of complexity simultaneously (morphemes, words, phrases, constructions) all in basically the same way.
>
> (Tomasello 2001: 45)

The Brunerian, cognitive interactionist account of how children learn language relies on two major assumptions, one of which is supported by empirical studies, while the other is a hypothesis motivated by the (transcendental) argument that, if it were not true, things could not be the way they manifestly appear to be: that is, children could not learn language as easily as they do. The first assumption is that, contrary to Chomsky's 'poverty of experience' argument, the child's acquisition of language is 'scaffolded' by its experience of the nurturing social contexts of childhood. Children do not learn language as isolated individuals; they learn it in supportive cultural contexts that provide *necessary*, if inadvertent assistance to language learning. The second assumption was suggested early on by Bruner but then came to occupy centre-stage in the writings of Tomasello and others (e.g. Trevarthan 1979). This is the claim that, even as very young children, we human beings 'are involved in refining and perfecting our species-unique gift of sharing attention and achieving a workable intersubjectivity' (Bruner 2000: 27). Human beings, unlike chimpanzees and other non-human animals, are claimed to be innately intersubjective; consequently, they recognize other humans *as humans* – even their mothers and fathers! – and as the same kind of intentional agents that they themselves are. This is the endowment required for the child to learn language, as long as it is brought up in the appropriately nurturing socio-cultural environment. Language is therefore the product of general cognitive abilities put to communicational use. An autonomous, genetically programmed mental faculty for acquiring language not only is evolutionarily implausible, it is simply not necessary.

Human children are not innately equipped with a universal grammar applicable to all of the languages of the world equally. They are adapted to enter into joint attentional interactions with adults and to understand adult intentions and attention – and eventually to adopt adult roles in these interactions, including their use of particular linguistic conventions.

(Tomasello 2001: 36)

Chapter 13

Derrida on the linguistic sign and writing

[T]here is no linguistic sign before writing.

(Derrida 1967a: 14)

[F]or modern linguistics, if the signifier is a trace, the signified is a meaning thinkable in principle within the full presence of an intuitive consciousness. The signified face, to the extent that it is still originarily distinguished from the signifying face, is not considered a trace; by rights, it has no need of the signifier to be what it is. It is at the depth of this affirmation that the problem of relationships between linguistics and semantics must be posed . . . [T]he trace affects the totality of the sign in both its faces. That the signified is originarily and essentially . . . trace, that it is *always already in the position of the signifier*, is the apparently innocent proposition within which the metaphysics of the logos, of presence and consciousness, must reflect upon writing as its death and its resource.

(Derrida 1967a: 73)

The beginnings of the intellectual movement known as structuralism have been outlined in Chapter 2. With the enormous success of his book *Tristes tropiques* in 1955, the structural ethnologist Lévi-Strauss (b. 1908) burst on to a French intellectual scene that had been dominated since the end of the Second World War by the Marxist existentialism of Jean-Paul Sartre (1905–80). But Sartre, in the face of mounting evidence of repression in Stalin's USSR, refused to distance himself from Soviet policies. When he did not join in the widespread condemnation of the invasion of Hungary in 1956, existentialism as a philosophy committed to human freedom was discredited in the eyes of many. Structuralism had the good fortune to be on offer as a new approach that was politically neutral.

After linguistics and ethnology, the field that felt the impact of structuralism most directly was literary studies. Roland Barthes (1915–80) caused uproar in 1963 when he brought structuralist principles to bear on his analysis of the classical French playwright Racine. Culler (1975: 98) locates the core of Barthes's structuralism in the fact that he is 'no longer willing to make the author as individual subject the source of the structures he discovers in the works', instead 'Reading individual tragedies as moments of a system' and with an interest in 'the common structures that may be derived from them and that serve as the functional oppositions and the rules of combination of the system'.

Already by this time a schism had broken open within French structuralism over the question of methodological determinism, whether the 'structures', 'oppositions' and 'rules' alluded to by Culler could be taken as fixed and absolute and thus provide a determinate criterion of analysis. The journal *Tel Quel* was launched in 1960 amid the heady atmosphere of the *nouveau roman* and New Wave cinema in France, by a group of younger writers for whom the appeal of structuralism was its rejection of dogmatic certainties, whether philosophical or methodological. (Barthes eventually came over to this view as well.) One of the writers for *Tel Quel* was Jacques Derrida, born in Algeria in 1930 and educated in France from the age of nineteen. Derrida's principal philosophical formation was in the tradition of phenomenology, a central question for which is whether and how it is possible to get an understanding of reality that is independent of the language in which the understanding is cast. Is there, in other words, a consciousness of things in themselves, which transcends language? Ever since Kant, those committed to belief in such a transcendental consciousness and reality have struggled to lay down a path towards reaching it. What Saussure's theory appeared to suggest was that linguistics does not suffer from the phenomenological 'disease' of not being able to separate its object of study – language itself – from the language in which the understanding of that object is cast. Saussure, after all, could speak straightforwardly of a 'signified' that was unproblematically distinct from its 'signifier' and only arbitrarily connected to it.

> The linguistic sign unites, not a thing and a name, but a concept and a sound-image. The latter is not the material sound, a purely physical thing, but the psychological imprint of the sound, the impression that it makes on our senses. The sound-image is sensory, and if I happen to call it 'material,' it is only in that sense, and by way of opposing it to the other term of the association, the concept, which is generally more abstract ... I propose to retain the word *sign* [*signe*] to designate the whole and to replace *concept* and *sound-image* respectively by *signified* [*signifié*] and *signifier* [*signifiant*] ... The bond between the signifier and the signified is arbitrary.
>
> (Saussure 1916: 66–7)

Perhaps, then, the structuralism that was based on Saussure's concept of the linguistic sign offered the way out of the philosophical dilemma.

But in *De la grammatologie* (Derrida 1967a), one of the three books he published in 1967, Derrida undertook a careful examination of Saussure's theory of the linguistic sign, using a novel philosophical strategy he called 'deconstruction'. Its goal is to locate the key conceptual oppositions upon which a work is based, and invert them.

> In a traditional philosophical opposition we have not a peaceful coexistence of facing terms but a violent hierarchy. One of the terms dominates the other (axiologically, logically, etc.), occupies the commanding position. To deconstruct the opposition is above all, at a particular moment, to reverse the hierarchy.
>
> (Derrida 1972: 41)

This is precisely what Derrida is doing with the opposition of signifier and signified in the quotation at the head of this chapter. In Saussure's presentation of them, it appears as though they are equal in status, for instance when he compares them to the two sides of a sheet of paper. But Derrida's close reading of Saussure shows that in fact the two are treated on anything but equal terms. To start with, the signifier is a 'sound-*image*' – not actual sounds, but a sort of trace left by them in the mind. To be its equivalent, the signified 'concept' would have to be imagined as a trace left in the mind by actual things in the world. But Saussure explicitly denies that this is so. The signified is not directly connected to things, but is as a concept *the primary reality* where language is concerned. In this sense, the signified 'occupies the commanding position' over the signifier in a hierarchy of real presence, though this is disguised by Saussure's referring to the concept as 'more abstract'.

Having revealed the covert hierarchy, the deconstructionist's task is to invert it, or more precisely to show how it inverts itself within the logic of the text. For strictly speaking, deconstruction is not something an analyst does to texts, but something texts do, and that the analyst uncovers. In Saussure's system, the signified attains its 'value' – what we normally call 'meaning' – from its place in the whole system of signifieds, just as the signifier attains its value from its place in the whole system of signifiers (see Chapter 2 above). Thus, as Derrida points out in the opening quotation, 'The signified . . . is not considered a trace; by rights, it has no need of the signifier to be what it is'. Yet this directly contradicts Saussure's own view that meaning does not exist outside language, and comes into existence only when sound is imposed upon the stream of thought.

> Psychologically our thought – apart from its expression in words – is only a shapeless and indistinct mass. Philosophers and linguists have always agreed in recognizing that without the help of signs we would be unable to make a clear-cut, consistent distinction between two ideas. Without language, thought is a vague, uncharted nebula. There are no pre-existing ideas, and nothing is distinct before the appearance of language.
>
> (Saussure 1916: 111–12)

The meaning of English *sheep* or French *mouton* is cited by Saussure as an example of seemingly equivalent words that in fact have very different values in their respective systems, since, although used to designate the same animal, the signified of *sheep* does not include the concept of the meat of the animal (*mutton*), while the French *mouton* does. These signifieds are not imagined by Saussure as existing prior to the formation of the whole sign, including the signifier. Thus, as Derrida writes, 'the signified is . . . *always already in the position of the signifier*'. While one part of Saussure's argument implies that the signified has a more immediate psychological reality than the signifier, another part of his argument implies that it does not.

This however is only one strand of a complex web of contradictions, the most important of which for Derrida is Saussure's insistence that the signifier is essentially spoken rather than written. Derrida shows how Saussure characterizes spoken language as real, present and internal, and written language as a mere image, representative and external. He describes at length what he calls the 'dangers' of writing, the greatest of which is its power to fool people into thinking that it constitutes the original and real form of the language, with speech as its partial and degraded representation, rather than the other way round.

> But the tyranny of writing goes even further. By imposing itself upon the masses, spelling influences and modifies language. This happens only in highly literary languages where written texts play an important role. Then visual images lead to wrong [*vicieuses*] pronunciations; such mistakes are really pathological.
>
> (Saussure 1916: 53–4 [31], bracketed references to Baskin's translation)

> For Saussure, to give in to the 'prestige of the written form' is . . . to give in to *passion*. It is passion – and I weigh my word – that Saussure analyzes and criticizes here, as a moralist and a psychologist of a very old tradition. As one knows, passion is tyrannical and enslaving. 'Philological criticism is still deficient on one point: it follows the written language slavishly and neglects the living language' (Saussure 1916: 14 [1–2]). 'The tyranny of writing,' Saussure says elsewhere (Saussure 1916: 53 [31]). That tyranny is at bottom the mastery of the body over the soul, and passion is a passivity and sickness of the soul, the moral perversion is *pathological*. The reciprocal effect of writing on speech is 'wrong [*vicieuse*]', Saussure says, 'such mistakes are really pathological' (Saussure 1916: 53 [31]). The inversion of the natural relationships would thus have engendered the perverse cult of the letter-image: sin of idolatry, 'superstition of the letter' Saussure says in the *Anagrams*.
>
> (Derrida 1967a: 38)

Derrida explains that he is not disagreeing with Saussure: 'I think Saussure's reasons are good. I do not question, *on the level on which he says it*, the truth of *what Saussure says* in such a tone' (Derrida 1967a: 39). What he does question is why 'a project of *general* linguistics, concerning the *internal system in general of language in general*', should define the limits of its field by excluding writing 'as *exteriority in general*'. As for the 'tone', he wonders why Saussure's rhetoric implies such *violence* of writing against speech, its tyranny, imposition, pathology and so on. This is connected to the earlier quotation from Derrida about a traditional philosophical opposition being 'not a peaceful coexistence of facing terms but a violent hierarchy'.

In this case, the hierarchy is plainly one that privileges speech over writing, on the grounds that what is spoken is more 'real' because it takes place in the face-to-face presence of the person being addressed, whereas writing occurs in the *absence* of the addressee. But here we have two further contradictions with other cardinal postulates of Saussure's theory of language. According to Saussure, everything in the language system derives its value not from its intrinsic content but from its difference from every other element in the system. Value, in other words, is a matter not of presence (intrinsic content) but of *absence*. For Saussure, the value of the phoneme /p/ is purely its difference from all the other phonemes in the language, which is as much as to say that /p/ functions through the absence of all those other phonemes. Secondly, in his characterization of the signifier, Saussure insists that it consists not of sound but of a sort of mental imprint left by sound. Thus he excludes from the linguistic sign the very thing, the phonic, that is the basis for his insisting on the greater reality of spoken than of written language. Moreover, he castigates writing as being a representation, a mere trace of spoken language, yet what distinguishes the signifier from the spoken sound or word is *this same characteristic*. The signifier too is a representation, a trace, standing in a relation to the spoken sound or word very similar to that of writing. Being a trace is made by Saussure into an argument for the *lesser* reality of the written versus the spoken, but for the *greater* reality of the mental signifier versus the spoken. Indeed, the latter hierarchization is extended into a privileging of *langue*, the social-mental language system, over *parole*, actual speech by individuals. Again, 'real presence' inheres not in the observable face-to-face encounter, but may be said to be 'deferred' to something more virtual.

Up to this point we have been using words such as 'difference', 'trace' and 'writing' in more or less their usual sense, but in Derrida's work they take on strikingly new and idiosyncratic meanings. In some cases Derrida makes this obvious, as when he uses the spelling *différance*, with an *a*, instead of (and in addition to) *différence*. Although not previously attested, there is nothing un-French about *différance*: it is a perfectly logical formation from the verb *différer*, using the gerundive ending *-ance*, making it equivalent to the English *differing*. But *différer* means not only 'to differ' but also 'to defer', and *différance* therefore means *simultaneously* 'differing' and 'deferring'. Derrida's use of the term *différance* therefore embodies at least four important aspects of his theory of language:

1   As noted at the end of the previous paragraph, the 'difference' that is the operating principle of Saussurean structuralism is also a 'deferral' from the immediately present to the virtual.
2   The signified of *différance* is inherently unstable, shifting from 'differing' to 'deferring' and back again like the perception of the duck or rabbit in Wittgenstein's drawing (see Chapter 6 above), so that its 'real' identity is not fixed in the way the Saussurean sign implies it must be, but is permanently deferred through a difference, not from other elements in the system, but internal to itself.
3   The words *différence* and *différance* are homophonous, identical to the ear, so that the difference (and differance) between them is purely graphic – undermining Saussure's insistence on the purely representative and subsidiary nature of writing.
4   Derrida's subtle alteration to the word, achieved in a way that denies it fixed meaning outside a context that is endlessly changeable and interpretable, undermines Saussure's insistence that *langue* is so socially controlled as to enforce meanings determinate at any given point in time and impervious to change by an individual.

It is interesting that this minimal orthographic alteration produces a word far more charged with theoretical import than one of Derrida's more outright neologisms, such as 'deconstruction'. But in all such cases he has used the word, and then abandoned it, in a way true to his theoretical principles.

> Derrida has consistently avoided giving a full 'definition' of deconstruction lest it become a fixed entity susceptible of onto-logical definition of the type 'S is P' ... Rather than sticking with any one master term, he uses various neologisms, which only gain their meaning from inscription within his own lexical chain. In this way, he practices what he preaches, as he both demonstrates and states the way a term becomes significant in a context, although that context is always open-ended; meaning is therefore differential (context dependent) and deferred (other contexts are always to come).
>
> (Ben-Naftali 1999: 654)

Perhaps the most theoretically loaded terms in Derrida's work of the 1960s are ones whose signifiers he did not alter, even ortho-graphically, such as *writing* and *trace*. In the deconstructionist spirit of reversing hierarchies, he argues, contrary to the common wisdom that speech precedes writing both historically and onto-logically, that *writing precedes speech*, if we take 'writing' in the broad sense of any form or manifestation of language that is not immediately present to the ear, but 'inscribed' in some sense, including in the mind. That lack of 'real presence' is after all the primary criterion Saussure cites in his disparagement of writing. As we have seen Derrida show, however, it is true as well of *langue*, the language system in which linguistic signs are 'deferred' into a virtual social-mental realm of existence. Since *langue* precedes speech and determines what it can be, speech itself is *always already writing*.

> Now we must think that writing is at the same time more exte-rior to speech, not being its 'image' or its 'symbol,' and more interior to speech, which is already in itself a writing. Even before it is linked to incision, engraving, drawing, or the letter, to a signifier referring in general to a signifer signified by it, the concept of the *graphie* [unit of a possible graphic system] implies the framework of the *instituted trace*, as the possi-bility common to all systems of communication.
>
> (Derrida 1967a: 46)

Derrida sometimes uses the term *arche-writing* for this concept of a writing that stands prior to the written–spoken distinction, and so characterizes all language. He proposes 'grammatology' as the science that will take (arche-)writing as its field of study.

As for *trace*, it is so inscrutable and elusive that even books and articles attempting to clarify Derrida's thought for students and the general educated reading public shy away from reducing it to a definition. Spivak, his translator, agonizing over the translation of the word, remarks:

> Derrida, then, gives the name 'trace' to the part played by the radically other within the structure of difference that is the sign. (I stick to 'trace' in my translation, because it 'looks the same' as Derrida's word; the reader must remind himself of at least the track, even the spoor, contained within the French word.) In spite of itself, Saussurean linguistics recognizes the structure of the sign to be a trace-structure.
>
> (Derrida 1967a, Translator's Preface: xvii)

The point of the last sentence is that, since the Saussurean sign is so conceived that the signifier and the signified each derives its value not from what is present in itself but from all the others like itself that are absent, their 'trace' is always present in the sign. It is in this sense that Saussurean linguistics 'recognizes the structure of the sign to be a trace-structure'. But this is 'in spite of itself' because Saussure fails to see, or conceals or denies that in historical terms there is a chicken-and-egg paradox here. What is absent (the trace) comes into existence through its difference from what is present; yet what is present can come into existence only after being imagined in its totality with its trace. It is thus 'that the trace affects the totality of the sign in both its faces. That the signified is originarily and essentially . . . trace, that it is *always already in the position of the signifier*' (see quotation at the head of this chapter). This is the point at which Derrida's logic becomes impossible for many people to follow, either because they cannot understand what he is saying or because they see his metaphysics of the trace as a step beyond reason.

Our point of entry to this discussion was the phenomenological problem of separating understanding and reality from language, and the structuralist hope that Saussure's signifier–signified distinction might provide a way out. Derrida's deconstruction of that distinction reveals however that it is ultimately not a distinction at all. Since one of its terms is 'always already in the position of' its opposite, the two are finally indistinguishable from one another. The opposition that is the very cornerstone of structuralism crumbles under Derrida's analysis, which is why his work is credited with (or blamed for) initiating the 'post-structuralist' era.

No philosopher in the late twentieth century provoked the excesses of both praise and wrath heaped upon Derrida. He himself has found it ironic and intriguing – and grist for his mill – that the most immoderate, impassioned and in some cases frankly irrational attacks against him have been mounted in the name of rationality. Deconstruction is perceived by many people as destruction, laying waste to traditional canons of knowledge and even to the very values upon which civilization is based. Such perceptions are largely misguided: no one has done more during the last thirty years to *promote* the wide, careful, critical reading of traditional philosophical texts than Derrida, and that was always his stated intention. The targets of his deconstructions have included no lesser figures than Plato, Rousseau, Nietzsche, Freud, Lévi-Strauss and his own contemporary rival Michel Foucault (1926–84). As we saw with his comments about not disagreeing with Saussure, Derrida presents deconstruction not as undermining the texts to which it is applied but as strengthening them by unfolding the inevitable and necessary tensions (often revealed in contradiction) from which they derive their power. At the same time, it cannot be denied that his exposing of core contradictions in the greatest Western thinkers, supported by close textual evidence, has had an iconoclastic effect, which some people consider healthy, others dangerous.

The other elements of Derrida's system to have prompted widespread near-hysteria are those having to do with the 'free play of the signifier', including his use of deviant spellings, neologisms, shifting senses and puns. He is sometimes blamed for having provoked a crisis of meaning in the late twentieth century by having disconnected the signifier from the signified. In this case he is certainly being crucified for sins he merely inherited from the phenomenological tradition going back at least to Nietzsche, and in part too from Saussure, whose disconnecting of signifieds from things in the world was surely the most 'radical' move within the whole tradition of structuralist and post-structuralist theory.

If Derrida has become a prime target, it is partly because of his insistence on practising rhetorically what he preaches methodologically: using words in ways carefully calculated to undermine determinacy of meaning, and to embody other aspects of his theory as in the examples discussed above. This practice reached its peak in his extraordinary 1974 book *Glas* (Derrida 1974). The title refuses, naturally, to be reduced to a single meaning, but on one level – the 'theoretical center' of the book according to Leavey (1986: 111) – it alludes to

> [the] discussion of onomatopoeia in Saussure. Saussure claimed that the signifier is arbitrary or unmotivated in its relation to the signified. By way of example, Saussure mentioned 'words like French *fouet* "whip" or *glas* "knell".' The argument was that *fouet* or *glas*, often cited as examples of motivated or onomatopoeic terms, hence exceptions to the rule of arbitrariness, are not in fact authentic onomatopoeias (he refutes these potential counter-examples). 'Glas,' Saussure noted, derives etymologically from the Latin *classicum*. '"The quality of their present sounds, or rather the quality that is attributed to them, is a fortuitous result of phonetic evolution"' (Derrida 1974: 9Ibi [106bi]).
>
> Derrida replies that Saussure takes too much for granted when he assumes that he knows what 'authentic onomatopoeias' are, as if one could refer to a 'pure origin,' trusting in this instance to etymology to distinguish what does and does not belong to the 'linguistic system'. Derrida suggests, rather, that '"words" [the organic elements of a linguistic system] can become onomatopoeic, through the grafting of function, in whole or in part, by decomposition or recomposition, detachment or reattachment. But onomatopoeias can become words, and since the process of being "drawn" [into or outside of the system] has always already begun, which is neither an accident nor something outside the system, the judges . . . no longer know what belongs to what and to whom' (Derrida 1974: 93bi [107bi]). The 'luck' of this particular example, selected by Saussure, is that there is a striking or sounding quality in every word, hence that the fate of this particular example opens onto much larger issues, is generalizable to include a rereading of the entire question of motivation in language, and hence of the concept of mimesis,

reconsidering the relation of language to reality. Saussure's mistake, after concluding that there were no authentic onomatopocias at all, was to avoid also concluding that there are then no authentically arbitrary elements either.

(Leavey 1986: 111, bracketed references
to Spivak's translation)

So far so good – this is an example of Derridean deconstruction at its most straightforward and convincing. But *Glas* (Derrida 1974) is written in two parallel columns in which various things are happening simultaneously, such as the following riff on the initial sounds of *glas*, connecting it with, among many other things, a 'gloss'; two brand names for infant milk formula; and *aigle* 'eagle', homophonous with the French pronunciation of the name of Hegel, who appears here as the 'impassive Teutonic philosopher':

That {gl} has no identity, sex, gender, makes no sense, is neither a definite whole or a part detached from a whole

gl remain(s) gl

falls (to the tomb) as must a pebble in the water – is not taking it even for an archigloss (since it is only a gloss morsel, but not yet a gloss, and therefore, an element detached from any gloss, much more than, and something other than, the *Urlaut*), for consonants without vowels, 'sounding' syllables, nonvocalizable letters, on some drive base of phonation, a voiceless voice stifling a sob [*sanglot*] . . . or a clot of milk in the throat, the tickled laughter or the glairy vomit of a baby glutton, the imperial flight of a raptor

'. . . So the gls of the eagle are at once or alternately the aerian elevation of the concept, absolute knowledge that carries you off *and* the weight of the signifier that crushes you or sinks itself into you . . .

that swoops down at one go on your nape, the gluing, frozen [*glacé*], pissing cold name of an impassive Teutonic philosopher, with a notorious stammer, sometimes liquid and sometimes gutturo-tetanic, a swollen or cooing goiter, all that rings [*cloche*] in the tympanic channel or fossa, the spit or plaster on the soft palate, the orgasm of the glottis or the uvula, the clitoral glue, the cloaca of the abortion, the gasp of sperm, the rhythmed hiatus of an occlusion, the saccadanced spasm of an eructojaculation, the syncopated valve of tongue and lips, or a nail that falls in the silence of the milky say [*la voix lactée*] (I note, in parentheses, that, from the outset of this reading, I have not ceased to think, as if it were my principal object, about the milk trademarks Gloria and Gallia for the new-born, about everything that can happen to the porridge, to the mush of nurslings who are gluttinous, stuffed, or weaned from a cleft breast [*sein*], and now everything catches, is fixed, and falls in galalith).

(Derrida 1974: 119b–21b [137b–9b])

(The French word for 'breast', *sein*, gets linked with German *Sein* 'Being', the word at the very heart – or breast – of phenomenology.) For some, this is Derrida at his most breathtakingly original and unflinchingly consistent, breaking down oppositions between signifiers and signifieds within and across languages, and thus *performing* the very onomatopoeia that he has raised to the dominant position in his deconstruction of the arbitrariness of the linguistic sign. For others, this is Derrida at his most infuriating, a charlatan who masks his intellectual emptiness behind a display of meaningless verbal fireworks. Derrida insists that he 'is never wilfully opaque' (Johnson 1997: 3), and that he is only doing his duty as he sees it, by analysing ideas and texts (and, increasingly since the 1980s, political situations) with all the philosophical rigour he can muster.

One thing at least is clear. It was Derrida above all who put paid to the belief that a structuralism derived from linguistics provided the universal method for analysing every manifestation of human culture in a way that bypasses the phenomenological problem of having to transcend the world we inhabit in order to gain any truly objective understanding of it. Moreover, he forced a radical rethinking of the relationship of written to spoken language among theoreticians, particularly of literature, though many linguists (other than those of critical or anthropological bent) continue to be quite impervious to Derrida's arguments. And it is probably (though unprovably) the case that his deconstructive method has had a widespread influence even among people who are unfamiliar with his work, by shaping the intellectual and cultural *Zeitgeist* in a way that favours the seeking out of underlying hierarchies and contradictions in order to overturn and cancel them.

Of Grammatology (Derrida 1967a) and *Glas* (Derrida 1974) are often described as effectuating a devastating critique of Saussure, but that is to misunderstand both their intention and their import as shown by a close reading of Derrida. For his Achilles' heel is the fact that the objects of his deconstructions are never the texts as such but his own particular (and idiosyncratic) readings of them, which often involve the spinning out of interpretation to an unsustainable degree. This was first pointed out by Barbara Johnson (Johnson 1977), in her deconstruction of Derrida's discussion of the structuralist psychoanalyst Jacques Lacan's analysis of Edgar Allen Poe. Derrida shows how Lacan's argument depends critically on his omission of certain writings by Poe that tend to unsettle Lacan's account. But Johnson, turning the tables on Derrida, shows how he in turn has omitted crucial parts of Lacan's account, in which Lacan takes up some of the very issues Derrida's analysis implies that he has neglected to see (see also Hobson 1998: 173). The Saussure of *Of Grammatology* (Derrida 1967a) has to hold all and only the implications Derrida imputes to him, including, for example, that the signifier and signified have an opposite ontological status in terms of 'real presence' for the mind. The real Saussure, long dead, could not voice a different interpretation – unlike John Searle, for example, who has adamantly refused to accept the implications Derrida read into his work. Perhaps unsurprisingly, what his reply to Derrida called forth was not a simple counter-reply but an entire book, *Limited Inc.* (Derrida 1977), spinning the web of interpretation and implication out ever further.

'Derrida's Saussure' is inevitably a straw man. On one level this is true of all textual interpretation, but the fact that Derrida spins out such *powerful* implications, before setting about to deconstruct them, and rarely if ever considers *alternative* intepretations of the texts he is reading – a failure difficult to reconcile with his position on textual 'openness' – makes him especially susceptible to the charge.

That Derrida's writings are brilliant, always in the worst and often in the best sense of the word, is undeniable. There remains a great deal to sort out in his determinedly unsystematic system of thought, which Hobson (1998) has argued needs to be read via connections that are made across the texts, forming 'circuits of argument'. It may then become possible for more theoreticians of language to confront in a meaningful way the deconstructions of some of the key categories and oppositions on which they continue to rely. The fundamental difficulty will always be, however, that Derrida's ideas elude pinning down as a matter of principle. As soon as we think we have captured one, Derrida himself is there to set it free by recasting it as its own opposite. Even the possibility of deconstruction is one he has reacted against in the spirit of the *Tel Quel* group's rejection of an overly determinate structuralist methodology.

> I would say that deconstruction loses nothing from admitting that it is impossible; also that those who would rush to delight in that admission lose nothing from having to wait. For a deconstructive operation *possibility* would rather be a danger, the danger of becoming an available set of rule-governed procedures, methods, accessible practices. The interest of deconstruction, of such force and desire as it may have, is a certain experience of the impossible ... Deconstruction is inventive or it is nothing at all; it does not settle for methodological procedures, it opens up a passageway, it marches ahead and marks a trail; its writing is not only performative, it produces rules – other conventions – for new performativities and never installs itself in the theoretical assurance of a simple opposition between performative and constative. Its *process* involves an affirmation, this latter being linked to the coming [*venir*] in event, advent, invention.
>
> (Derrida 1987)

We shall probably be well into the twenty-first century, with Derrida safely in his grave, before we are in a position to decide with any confidence whether his work has represented a new beginning for the understanding of language, or the end of the possibility of any such understanding. Or, if Derrida is right, both the beginning and end, and neither the beginning nor the end, and the trace of the opposition between beginning and end that is always already there before the beginning of the beginning can even be thought.

Chapter 14

Harris on linguistics without languages

An integrationalist redefinition of linguistics can dispense with at least the following theoretical assumptions: (i) that the linguistic sign is arbitrary; (ii) that the linguistic sign is linear; (iii) that words have meanings; (iv) that grammar has rules; and (v) that there are languages. This last point, despite its paradoxical appearance, follows from the first four. In effect, to dispense with the first four assumptions is, precisely, to say that linguistics does not need to postulate the existence of languages as part of its theoretical apparatus. What is called in question, in other words, is whether the concept of 'a language', as defined by orthodox modern linguistics, corresponds to any determinate or determinable object of analysis at all, whether social or individual, whether institutional or psychological. If there is no such object, it is difficult to evade the conclusion that modern linguistics has been based upon a myth.

(Harris 1990: 45)

For J. R. Firth (see Chapter 5 above), analysing the meaning of speech events is the ultimate task of linguistics. And the meaning of a speech event is a function of its context. Not only does a Firthian analysis proceed by establishing the context-determined 'meanings' to be attached to linguistic units at the various descriptive levels (phonology, syntax etc.), but the overall semiotic significance of a speech event is to be sought by examining the 'context of situation' in which it is embedded. How far is this enterprise compatible with what Firth himself acknowledges to be the traditional business of linguistics – namely, describing languages – given that languages are abstractions or systems of abstractions from speech events? Firth never squarely confronts this question. If Roy Harris (b. 1931), who held the Chair of General Linguistics at Oxford for ten years from 1978, is sometimes located in a distinctively British tradition of linguistic thought inaugurated by Firth, it is because, adopting what might be seen as a broadly Firthian position on meaning as a function of context, he offers challenging responses to this and other questions implicit or latent or left as puzzling conundrums in Firth's own work.

If linguistics can afford to dispense with the 'assumption' that there are languages, then, clearly, the Firthian dilemma disappears. If there are no languages, it can hardly be the business of linguistics to describe them. But what reasons might there be for taking this line?

To say that there are no languages is not to say that anyone who talks about entities called English or French or Swahili must *eo ipso* be talking nonsense. It is to claim that the world does not contain the 'determinate or determinable' objects that 'orthodox modern linguistics' calls languages and takes itself to be describing. Specifically, the enterprise of synchronic linguistic description rests on the idea that a language, *au fond*, is what Harris calls a 'fixed code' – a determinately identifiable set of meaningful linguistic units. In so far as the description of languages purports to be founded on an empirical inquiry into facts pertaining to speech, the ultimate justification for this idea is the alleged possibility of analysing the stream of speech in terms of the units it instantiates.

It was Saussure (1857–1913) who first spelt out a specific procedure ('contrastive segmentation') for conducting such analysis. For Saussure, a stretch of speech embodies a linear sequence of linguistic signs – that is, a concatenation of discrete, arbitrary combinations of a form with a meaning. As Harris points out (Harris 1981: 95–7), there are difficulties even with Saussure's own brief demonstration of contrastive segmentation, in connection with what one must suppose was a carefully chosen example of his own devising. But whether or not one accepts Saussure's particular procedure, or the specific concept of the linguistic sign on which it is based, the possibility of performing some such analysis is in principle the basis on which the units descriptive linguists subject to grammatical and semantic analysis are identified, even if in practice they are usually taken for granted.

But we do not have to probe the foundational procedure in order to see that there are in any case grave problems with the concept of a language on which the language-describing business rests. For it clearly runs counter to a commonsense view derivable from everyday linguistic experience, which can be summed up by saying that, if English, French and Swahili are languages, then languages are not fixed codes, or conversely, if languages are fixed codes, then English, French and Swahili are not languages. Not only are we well aware, contemplating such languages 'externally', that they have no precise boundaries and are subject to complex patterns of variation in time, in place, and from individual to individual, but also we would find it impossible, by dint of no matter how careful an examination of our 'internal' engagement with them as speakers, to identify a consistent or determinate set of form–meaning pairings that might constitute 'the language' concerned for us personally.

Now 'orthodox' linguists would not dissent from this common-sense view. Chomsky, for example, explicitly endorses it (see Chapter 9 above). But what follows from endorsing it, for the orthodox linguist, is not that descriptive linguistics is impossible, but merely that languages (English, French, Swahili) are not and cannot be what descriptive linguistics describes, precisely because languages are an amorphous flux.

So what then does it describe? The orthodox move is to suppose that the factors making for the amorphous flux are irrelevant contingencies arising from the circumstances in which an underlying fixed code is used. This supposition takes different forms in different theories. In Saussure's view, the fixed code exists in the 'collective mind' of a linguistic community. In Chomsky's version the fixed code is the mental property of the 'ideal speaker-listener', who lives in a 'completely homogeneous speech community' and who 'knows its language perfectly'. So, one way or another, an idealized state of linguistic affairs amenable to the techniques of synchronic descriptive analysis is abstracted from the chaotic reality.

But Harris denies the legitimacy of this move:

> Although the objections mentioned so far already seem suffi-
> cient in themselves to call in question the validity of orthodox
> linguistics, nevertheless they are sometimes dismissed by
> defenders of the orthodox doctrine as irrelevant, on the ground
> that no one, from Saussure onwards, had ever seriously sup-
> posed that the conditions laid down in the fixed-code account

of speech communication were those which normally obtain in real-life speech situations. The fixed code and the homogeneous speech community, it is claimed, are merely theoretical idealizations, which it is necessary for linguistics to adopt, just as other sciences adopt for theoretical purposes idealizations which do not correspond to the observable facts. Thus, for example, geometry postulates such idealizations as perfectly parallel lines and points with no dimensions; but these are not to be found in the world of visible, measurable objects. Nevertheless, it would be a mistake to protest on this ground that the theoretical foundations of geometry are inadequate or unsound. Analogously, it is held, idealizations of the kind represented by the fixed code are not only theoretically legitimate but theoretically essential in linguistics; and those who object to them simply fail to understand the role of idealization in scientific inquiry.

Unfortunately, this defence of the orthodox doctrine is based on a false comparison. Broadly speaking, two different types of intellectual idealization may be distinguished. In the exact sciences, and also in applied sciences such as architecture and economics, idealizations play an important role in processes of calculation. Any such idealization which was in practice found to be misleading or ineffectual when put to the test by being used as a basis for calculation would very soon be abandoned. In the humanities, by contrast, idealization plays an entirely different role. The ideal monarch, the ideal state, and the ideal mother are abstractions not set up in order to be used as a basis for calculation, but as prescriptive stereotypes on which to focus the discussion of controversial issues concerning how human beings should conduct themselves and how human affairs should be managed. But the ideal speech community, the ideal language, and the ideal speaker-hearer turn out to be neither one thing nor the other. They are neither abstractions to which items and processes in the real world may be regarded as approximating for purposes of calculation; nor are they models held up for purposes of exemplification or emulation. In fact they are, more mundanely, steps in a process of explanation; and as such subject to all the usual criticisms which explanatory moves may incur (including, for instance, that they fail to explain what they purport to explain).

(Harris 1990: 36–7)

Whether or not it is defensible in terms of an account of the nature and role of idealization in science, it is worth posing the question: why this particular idealization anyway? From what point of view does the fixed-code conception of languages suggest itself as 'ideal' (in any sense)? What makes it even plausible, let alone attractive, to conceive of languages as essentially fixed codes, or approximately fixed codes, or what would be fixed codes but for the interference of extraneous factors?

Here we encounter a conflicting strand in the (Western) commonsense view of languages. For is not the idea of a fixed code simply the theoretical articulation of a notion about languages which is, and perhaps has to be, taken for granted? We know that languages can be and are subject to systematic synchronic description, because we are familiar with the results of such description as enshrined in dictionaries and grammar books. In fact, for some purposes (for instance, learning a foreign language by traditional methods), a language can be *defined* as the conjoint contents of a dictionary and a grammar. The dictionary displays the lexical repertoire of a language as a determinate inventory of form–meaning pairings (words), which can be combined into larger units according to the rules given in the grammar. Can we not learn a language by assimilating the information given in such texts, and, having learned it, put it to use in communicating with native speakers? Indeed, how is linguistic communication possible at all, in one's own or any other language, unless interlocutors have at least a large measure of shared knowledge of a fixed code? The compilation of dictionaries and grammar books may involve cutting and smoothing the raw data of speech, abstracting away from variation, personal idiosyncrasies etc., but some such processes must surely be involved in language-use itself if a language is to be workable as a means of communication. The corresponding idealization in linguistic theory simply reflects this fact.

Thus presented, the choice between a linguistics of languages and a linguistics without languages seems to be a matter of following the promptings of linguistic common sense in one of two very different directions. In Harris's perspective, the problem with the 'linguistics of languages' route is that, although its starting-point is an understanding of language and how it works that seems self-evidently valid, it cannot in principle *explain* that understanding, how it arises, or how it comes to be in conflict with other, radically incompatible but no less self-evident, observations about language and linguistic phenomena. To take that route, in Harris's view, would be to settle for an academic endorsement and glorification of certain 'folk' attitudes to language, theoretically grounded in nothing more than a dubious appeal to the need for 'idealization' in science. In contrast, Harris proposes 'a quite different foundation for linguistic theory, as well as for the interpretation of our everyday linguistic experience, which at the same time offers an explanation of – and thus transcends – the orthodoxy it rejects. The orthodoxy, on the other hand, offers no comparable transcendence of the integrational view' (Harris 1997: 230).

What is this 'integrational view' that promises so much? Harris presents it thus:

> Integrational linguistics may be defined in terms of the acceptance of three principles which differ from those widely accepted by linguists belonging to one or other of the orthodox modern schools. These three principles are: (i) the integrational character of the linguistic sign, (ii) the indeterminacy of linguistic form, and (iii) the indeterminacy of linguistic meaning.
>
> Principle (i) implies that linguistic signs are not autonomous objects of any kind, either social or psychological, but are contextualised products of the integration of various activities by individuals in particular communication situations. The continuous creation of linguistic signs to meet the exigencies of communication constitutes the first-order linguistic process which is the primary object of study in integrational linguistics. Principles (ii) and (iii) together imply that languages are not fixed codes but second-order social constructs of an intrinsically open-ended, incomplete and variable nature. They are consequently not amenable to the standard bi-planar analyses imposed by orthodox linguistics.
>
> The definition proposed is derived from two basic axioms of integrational semiology. The integrational approach is not restricted to those communicational activities traditionally designated by the term *language*, and *a fortiori* not to those traditionally designated by the term *speech*. The two semiological axioms are:
>
> *Axiom 1.* What constitutes a sign is not given independently of the situation in which it occurs or of its material manifestation in that situation.

Axiom 2. The value of a sign is a function of the integrational proficiency which its identification and interpretation presuppose.

These two axioms apply to all signs in interpersonal communication, and more generally in the human environment; for they also apply to natural phenomena to which human beings assign a semiological value (as, for example, in medicine and meteorology).

(Harris 1993a: 321–2)

In effect, Harris's proposal is that we take seriously Saussure's idea that linguistics should be part of semiology – 'a science which studies the role of signs as part of social life' (Saussure 1916: 33). This means, first, that the study of language is, or should be, intrinsically bound up with the general study of communication by means of signs, whether linguistic or non-linguistic. And that in turn means that linguistics must be theoretically subordinate to semiology, in that theorizing about language must have its source in, and be made to flow from, a viable account of what a sign is and how it works.

For Harris, a sign is neither any kind of thing (object, event, phenomenon) in itself nor any abstraction from a thing held to be permanently latent in it. A temptation to think of a sign as a thing perhaps derives from a common use of the word 'sign' to refer to material objects of various kinds. So a flat metal disc of characteristic size and design bearing certain arabic numerals and attached to a pole planted by the roadside may be called a speed-limit sign. And in this usage it may count as a 'sign' from the moment of manufacture until long after it has been uprooted and consigned to a rubbish tip. But this usage is of no interest to the semiologist, who is concerned with the object only in so far as it functions semiotically, *as* a sign. And it can function as a sign only when *in situ*, i.e. when located in the appropriate topographical context.

Thus far Harris's view is reminiscent of Firth's – topographical contextualization in the case of the road sign might be seen as somewhat analogous to the linguistic contextualization Firth discusses under the heading 'collocation' (see Chapter 5 above). But for Harris, although contextualization in this sense is necessary for any sign, 'context' involves a great deal more:

> *context* is commonly used, and not only by linguists, to desig-
> nate the immediate verbal environment, the words preceding
> and/or following some other word or words: thus, for example,
> in *a big man* and *a big mistake*, the word *big* is said to
> appear in two different 'contexts' ... From an integrational
> point of view, this is a quite inadequate notion of what a
> context is.
>
> (Harris 2000: 84)

Even when located in an appropriate environment, an object functions semiotically only in so far as someone *makes* it do so. The
signhood of the speed-limit sign is not immanent in it. However
impeccably positioned, it is not a sign when nobody is around to
see it, for instance. Or when seen by strangers to our civilization
who have no idea what to make of it. Signhood is conferred on
a sign – on what *thereby becomes* a sign – if and when human
beings (or other semiotically competent creatures) attach a signification to it that goes beyond its intrinsic physical properties,
whether in furtherance of a particular programme of activities, or
to link different aspects or phases of their activities, to enrich their
understanding of their local circumstances or general situation.
Harris's key term here is *integration*:

> Signs, for the integrationist, provide an interface between
> different human activities, sometimes between a variety of
> activities simultaneously. They play a constant and essential
> role in integrating human behaviour of all kinds ... Signs are
> not given in advance, but are made. The capacity for *making*
> signs, as and when required, is a natural human ability.
>
> (Harris 2000: 69)

Signhood is a transient, not a permanent, property of a sign.
Nor is the nature of its signhood – its semiotic value – fixed, either
for all sign-makers or for all occasions of their use of it in
sign-making. The speed-limit 'sign', irrelevant as such for bus
passengers, may none the less function for them as a landmark
by which they orient themselves in relation to their usual
bus stop (perhaps they come to know that if they leave their
seat as the bus passes the thirty m.p.h. 'sign', they will be standing ready at the exit as it draws to a halt), and thus as a sign by
which they integrate their bus journey with what happens next

(compare Whorf's comment on the workman for whom an electric heater 'had the meaning of a convenient coathanger' – Chapter 4 above).

All this applies to the linguistic sign no less than to any other kind. The linguistic sign, whether spoken, written or manifest in any other medium, is not an object, or a permanent property of an object. It has no fixed or determinate semiotic value. It becomes a sign as and when used as such, and its signification is a function of that use. According to Harris, it is doubtful whether a definite boundary between linguistic and non-linguistic signs can be drawn: to say that linguistics is a branch of semiology is not necessarily to say that it is a well-defined or sharply demarcated branch. In a given communicational episode what counts as linguistic and what does not may not be decidable:

> In order to understand the currency exchange rates in this morning's newspaper, I have to understand a table in which there occur the graphic forms (i) *US*, (ii) *$*, (iii) *France*, (iv) *Fr*, and (v) *5.659*. Furthermore, I have to work out that (v), which occurs in the bottom row of a column headed by (iii), gives me information about how many francs I can expect to get for a dollar. (But I also have to understand that, in Berkeley's sense, there 'is no such thing as' six hundred and fifty-nine thousandths of a franc.) How much of all this is *verbal* information I have no way of telling. *Nor does it matter.* It does not prevent me from working out what I want to know. To ask what the status of the table is as regards the distinction between verbal and non-verbal communication is just a nonsense question. For a start, I have to understand the significance of the relationship between columns and rows. And in what compartment of human knowledge does that belong?
>
> (Harris 1997: 271)

In fact, Harris denies that 'language' is to be equated or deemed co-terminous with verbal behaviour: 'If, when asked to repeat what I said, I repeat it, that is certainly a (partial but relevant) manifestation of my linguistic proficiency. But equally if, when asked to sit down, I sit down, that is no less a manifestation of my linguistic proficiency ... If the former is, then the latter is too' (Harris 1997: 268). Sitting down, in these circumstances, is an act whose integration with the preceding request to do so involves a use of language (understanding the request) on all fours with, e.g. saying 'no, I won't, thanks'.

So what, if anything, is special about language? Is there any place, or particular need, for a distinct integrational *linguistics* within integrational semiology?

Linguistic signs are the most important means by which we elaborate and articulate an understanding of the world and all that therein is. Language is our great general medium of concerted and systematic inquiry. It can be used to investigate and talk about anything under the sun, not to mention the sun itself. But what about language itself? A particular kind of use of language to talk about language – a particular way of exploiting the reflexivity of language – we call 'linguistics'. And the fact that linguistics is language about language has often made linguists uneasy. Firth remarks that 'the reflexive character of linguistics, in which language is turned back on itself, is one of our major problems' (Firth 1948: 147). But Firth never attempted to solve the problem, or even state precisely what he took it to be. In Harris's bolder and more positive formulation, that it necessarily relies on the reflexivity of language 'makes linguistics fundamentally different from all other forms of inquiry into human affairs' (Harris 1998: 26).

Why? Because in turning the medium of inquiry back on itself it becomes an *object* of inquiry, and to envisage treating linguistic phenomena as 'objects' is, in and of itself, to propose a distorted account of them. There are no (first-order) linguistic objects. Language is a temporally situated, ongoing *process* – the process of making and re-making signs in contextualized episodes of communicative behaviour. And if that is accepted, then, apart from the provision of anecdotal accounts of the specifics of particular communicative episodes, one might be inclined to conclude that pointing this much out is where linguistics ought to stop. Whatever it might be to go further, if going further implies engaging in the kind of retrospective talk about linguistic signs that requires that they be identified *in abstracto*, it is not and cannot be a matter of reporting on objectively given first-order realities. In a sense, therefore, linguistics is logically impossible. Identifying a sign involves decontextualizing the unique communicative episode within which and for purposes of which the sign was created, abstracting and reifying some aspect of that episode, and presenting the reification for inspection and analysis as 'the sign' in question. But whatever is thus presented *cannot* be the sign in question. For the sign has no existence outside its unique communicative episode.

None the less, logically impossible or not, linguistics undeniably exists. Moreover, the decontextualizing and reifying of linguistic signs that linguistics is based on has specific roots in the first-order communicational process itself.

The reflexivity of language is the *sine qua non* not just for the organized inquiry we call 'linguistics', but for any metalinguistic discourse at all:

> The point about verbal metalanguage is that without it language as we know it would *not* be possible.
>
> Try to imagine English shorn of all its metalinguistic equipment. At first sight it might seem as though little has changed. We should still apparently be able to say 'Hello!', 'Goodbye!', 'The cat sat on the mat', and many other things. We could even get by without dictionaries and grammars, as many civilizations in the past have done. But we are overlooking something much more fundamental. In non-reflexive English it would be impossible to ask anyone to repeat what they had just said, let alone ask them what it meant. We have to realize that 'repetition' and 'meaning' are metalinguistic concepts, every bit as much as 'name' or 'word' or 'sentence'. And unless such notions were available to us, we should have to make sense of our own linguistic experience in a very different way from that to which we are accustomed. It is even arguable that, shorn of reflexivity, we should be unable to make much sense of language at all.
>
> (Harris 1998: 28)

The key metalinguistic concept is *repetition*. An utterance, once uttered, is an item in the human environment, and, like any other such item, may be referred to and talked about. Specifically, it can be repeated:

Q. 'Did you say *bat*?'
A. 'No, I said *hat*.'

The point of raising this question is that the questioner is uncertain and seeks confirmation. But the confirmation is not about the existence of any English word, nor about the acoustic 'data'. It is about what the interlocutor said. The signs that occur in first-order communication are those the participants construe as occurring, and what is signified is what the participants construe as having been signified . . .

The great error here would be to suppose that the phonologist's analysis of the acoustic 'data' as an utterance of the English sequence of phonemes /hat/ is a 'scientific' confirmation or translation into 'scientific' language of the participant's assertion 'I said *hat*'. Nothing could be more mistaken. If my interlocutor asks what I said and I reply 'I said *hat*' I am not proposing an analysis of the utterance: I am just repeating what I had previously said.

(Harris 1998: 145)

So repetition is just repetition, and counts as repetition in so far as the interlocutors agree that that is what has happened.

However, it is no great intellectual leap to suppose that in repeating what I said I am not just producing another, similar, utterance (although, in a sense, that is all I *could* be doing), but producing a second instantiation of something more abstract than either utterance itself. Such an interpretation is hinted at in an ambiguity that attends our normal use of the word 'repeat': if someone talks of repeating some action twice, many English-speakers will be in doubt whether that means they did it twice or three times in all. The former reading suggests that the 'action itself' is being envisaged as something over and above any particular instance of it. In the specifically linguistic case, it seems implicit not only in Harris's perhaps unfortunate (given the point he is making) use of italics (the typographical convention in linguistics for distinguishing an abstract linguistic unit from an utterance) when citing the repeated 'hat' in his example, but also in the very terms in which the matter is discussed: if I repeat *what* I said, does that not automatically conjure up a 'that' which has now been said twice? If so, then the 'that' in question is some sort of abstract invariant underlying actual utterances, and the door is open to the kind of thinking about language that not only characterizes the whole Western tradition but also lies at the heart of modern linguistic science.

It is important to see that the door is first opened, not by some linguist's arbitrary postulation that signs are abstract invariants existing in advance of any utterance in which they are brought into play, but simply because the very idea of repetition conduces to the reification of a repetitum.

But the process of reification will remain a nebulous and uncertain affair if it has to be done strictly through the oro-aural medium. So long as language is purely spoken language, there is no possibility of drawing the distinction between utterances and what they are utterances of in any concerted or systematic way, because purely spoken language cannot yield the consistently reliable metalinguistic discourse required for articulating it. When attempting to abstract from unique spoken utterances, a pre- or non-literate culture faces the difficulty that there is nothing to do it in except unique spoken utterances. Talk about utterances stable and thoroughgoing enough to permit the concept of a language as a complete and coherent set of abstract units requires a radical development. That new development was the use of writing as a linguistic medium. Writing meets the need for a consistently reliable concrete correlate of the idea of apprehending a unique spoken utterance as an instance of something, by providing a means of citing the something in question in a medium other than oral utterance itself. In its role as an analogue of speech, writing automatically and necessarily abstracts from the phonic specificities of the individual utterance simply by not existing in the spoken medium itself: 'writing achieves the object of fixing the identification of utterances (in the limited sense of providing them with something outside speech itself to which they can be referred) by simply laying it down what it is your utterance was an utterance of. If you write it *CAT*, then *that* is what you said' (Love 1998: 106; cited by Harris 1998: 124).

This is the sense in which, as Firth puts it, 'written words are more real than speech itself' (see Chapter 5 above). Derrida makes a similar point when he says that 'there is no linguistic sign before writing' (see Chapter 13 above).

If there is no linguistic sign before writing then, before writing, there can be no conception of a language as a set of linguistic signs, and no linguistics (*qua* descriptive analysis of linguistic signs) either. Both the 'lay' concept of a language as a (more or less) determinately identifiable linguistic system and the linguistics that articulates a theorization of that concept are, in the first place, products of literacy.

Secondly, in their modern Western form, they are bolstered by a particular kind of linguistic education derived from a Graeco-

Roman tradition as adapted to meet the political needs of post-
Renaissance Europe

> and the rigid political divisions into autonomous nation-states
> that are a feature of that period of European history. 'One
> country – one language' was the ideal to which all the major
> centralising monarchies aspired. Compiling dictionaries and
> grammars of one's mother tongue became a patriotic enter-
> prise. In certain instances academies were established, some-
> times under royal patronage, in order to give authoritative
> rulings on linguistic matters, so that there should be no doubt
> about what the proper form of the national language was.
> Under such regimes it became increasingly difficult to defend
> publicly the linguistic rights of minorities or to treat linguistic
> non-conformity of any kind as other than a deviation from an
> officially sanctioned norm.
>
> (Harris 1998: 31)

The founding text of modern linguistics is usually taken to be
Saussure's *Cours de linguistique générale* (Saussure 1916). It is
based on an explicit appeal to the reader's sense of what languages
are like for the individual language-user. Saussure's objection
to the nineteenth-century historical linguistics that he hoped to
supersede was that it dealt in diachronic changes operating
over such long time spans that they do not impinge on the
individual's linguistic experience. Although the individual unconsciously participates in bringing about such changes, they
are not real to him or her. So what then *is* real to him or her,
where language is concerned? Saussure's answer is that the individual experiences a language as a synchronic totality of
decontextualized signs. Given that the world does not on inspection appear to contain any such things, why should that be?
Because of a culture-specific background of ideas about language
shared by Saussure and his readers.

There can be few who have encountered the *Cours de linguistique générale* without prior exposure to what some linguists
disparagingly refer to as 'traditional grammar'. And it is traditional grammar that has bequeathed to modern linguistic science
its commitment to the idea that behind the manifold vagaries of
speech there are fixed objects called languages. The network of
ideas underlying traditional grammar involves imposing on the

continuum of linguistic differences between people at different times and places an analysis in terms of discrete linguistic systems. It abstracts from the communicational behaviour deemed to involve a given system what it sets up as the strictly linguistic aspects of that behaviour. It then projects this abstraction as a body of knowledge which, if acquired by a learner, might be put to use in communicational episodes involving existing speakers of the language in question. This conception of languages is indeed primarily a pedagogical tool, in use in Western educational institutions since classical antiquity for teaching them.

The traditional pedagogue's idea of what a language is has a number of features worth stressing in the present context.

First, it emphasizes the idea of a language as an object: language-use as a form of behaviour is treated as secondary to the object – indeed, as being founded on, and possible only because of, knowledge of the object. This feature is the basis for the well-known distinctions, in Saussurean and Chomskyan versions of linguistic science, between *langue* and *parole* on the one hand, and 'competence' and 'performance' on the other.

Second, a language as presented by the grammarian is a synchronic object. Learning English, French or Swahili is not the same thing as learning the history of English, French or Swahili. And this is where the idea of the synchronic language system gets its plausibility. We are inclined to think of languages in this way, not because that accords with our day-to-day experience as language-users but because we (many of us) have undergone an overt training in languages that presents them thus.

Third, traditional linguistic pedagogy treats a language as a fixed and determinable system. Take the largest dictionary and the most detailed grammar book and there, for practical purposes, you have it – the whole language. Chomsky's idea of a language as something that might be (conceived of as being) known 'perfectly' is a projection or transposition of the idea that one might, in principle, come to have exhaustive knowledge of a language, taken as the totality of the information contained in the grammar book in combination with the dictionary.

Fourth, the fixed synchronic system upheld by the traditional language teacher does not allow for dialectal and regional variation. If the language in question is French, say, it is a homogeneous, monolithic standard Parisian literary French that is taught. This idea, too, is simply taken over by the modern structuralist science of language: both Saussure and Chomsky assume, for all theoretical purposes, a homogeneous speech community.

In all these ways, says Harris, what purports to be a culture-neutral science of language embodies a conceptualization of languages that was already in daily use for purposes of formal linguistic education in the culture whose product that science is. Given this conceptualization, and its logical and historical background, it is profoundly ironic that modern linguistics claims to be primarily concerned with the descriptive analysis of *speech*, writing being conventionally treated as no more than an ancillary notation.

Observing that orthodox linguistics seems to be in the business of describing things that do not exist, Harris proposes the axioms of his integrational semiology as a new foundation for theorizing about language, and on that basis sets out to explain how and why languages come into being, how and why it comes to seem plausible to treat them as fixed codes, and how and why there emerges a science of language dedicated to treating fixed codes as linguistic realities. In doing so he transcends and explains not only the orthodoxy but also its uneasy coexistence with a common-sense view that seems to contradict it. Putting it in terms of a specific point that puzzled Firth (see Chapter 5 above), he resolves the tension between our sense that words are fixed, institutionalized objects and our sense that every word when used in a new context is a new word.

Starting from close analytical attention to the circumstances in which we communicate with one another, Harris has elaborated a comprehensive linguistic philosophy capable in principle of illuminating all aspects of our situation *vis-à-vis* language, including our modes of apprehending it. He has himself applied his ideas to many aspects of linguistic thought in the Western tradition. Their implications for the future of that tradition remain to be seen.

Chapter 15

Kanzi on human language

It becomes our duty to warn the valiant disciples of Mr. Darwin that before they can claim a real victory, before they can call man the descendant of a mute animal, they must lay a regular siege to a fortress which is not to be frightened into submission by a few random shots: the fortress of language, which as yet, stands untaken and unshaken on the very frontier between the animal kingdom and man.

(Müller 1873: 230)

Savage-Rumbaugh *et al.* (1993) . . . present a longitudinal study comparing the development of word and sentence comprehension in a human child and a bonobo (Kanzi), raised and tested in settings that are as comparable as ethics and common sense will allow. In contrast with many previous studies of primate language, blind testing procedures are used to ensure against the kind of cuing that proved to be responsible for the supposed linguistic and arithmetic comprehension of the infamous horse Clever Hans. In all honesty, I cannot think of anything else that the authors could have done to convince their audience that this is a fair test of the hypothesis that apes are capable of at least some language comprehension, at both the lexical and structural levels.

I, for one, am convinced. Indeed, it seems fair to conclude from this work that the bonobo (or at least one bonobo) is capable of language comprehension that approximates (in level if not detail) the abilities of a human 2-year-old on the threshold of full-blown sentence processing.

(Bates 1993: 222–3)

The central message of the ape-language work is clear. Not only can apes acquire a capacity for symbolic communication through . . . structured experience . . . but also they can acquire it spontaneously through casual exposure to language, just as human infants do. It has been easy for Kanzi to comprehend language; the key was in his early exposure to speech and the pairing of the speech with symbols. His comprehension skills are so extensive as to make it implausible to offer a conditioning account. His younger sister . . . Panbanisha has followed in his footsteps, revealing that it is the rearing experiences Kanzi received, not Kanzi himself, that permitted him to understand simple language. If Kanzi can acquire language so readily, we must conclude that the ape brain is capable of a primitive language.

(Savage-Rumbaugh and Lewin 1994: 248)

It has nothing to do with language, and nothing to do with words.

(Thomas Sebeok, quoted in
The Indianapolis Star, 7 April 1991)

Kanzi and his half-sister Panbanisha are bonobos, *Pan paniscus*, a species of ape native to central Africa. They were raised in the 1980s and 1990s by Sue Savage-Rumbaugh and Duane Rumbaugh, in the United States near Atlanta, Georgia. Before they reached the age of ten Kanzi and Panbanisha had acquired a wide variety of language skills. Because the bonobo's vocal organs do not allow them to produce human-sounding vowels and consonants, they did not learn to speak, but rather to use an artificial language consisting of abstract lexigrams embossed on a computerized keyboard designed specially for this purpose. Kanzi and Panbanisha know and make communicational use of over 250 such signs. These include not only signs for concrete, manipulable objects and foods but also the signs for *bad, now, dessert, tummy, away, slap, observation room, Panbanisha, Karen, river, bottom, Group room, A-frame, carry, shop, thank you, draw* and many other words. They are said to use the signs for a wide variety of communicational purposes, performing such speech acts as announcing their intentions (such as where they are going or what they plan to do), reporting on a past event, playing games of pretence, warning and accusing others (Savage-Rumbaugh *et al.* 1998). Moreover, the results of comprehensive experimental tests have shown both Kanzi and Panbanisha to understand a great deal of spoken English, including sentences with a variety of grammatical structures. What perhaps is most distinctive of Kanzi and Panbanisha's linguistic accomplishments is that neither their productive nor their receptive competence is limited to sentences of which they have had previous experience. In other words, their linguistic ability has the property of creativity that most linguists have long held to be uniquely human.

However, the claims made for Kanzi and Panbanisha's linguistic abilities have proved highly controversial. Linguists have argued that, although Kanzi and his siblings have developed impressive communicational skills, these skills lack one or more of the essential properties of human language. This was the position argued forcefully by generative linguists, such as Steven Pinker and Noam Chomsky. Other linguists, for instance Bickerton (1990) and Wallman (1992), granted that Kanzi and Panbanisha had acquired some 'primitive' linguistic abilities; however, they denied that the bonobos had mastered any syntax, the *sine qua non* claimed to be characteristic of human language. And a few went even further, such as the semiotician Thomas Sebeok, who is quoted above from an interview in the *Indianapolis Star*.

The controversy raging at the end of the twentieth century had roots that begin far back in the history of Western linguistic thought. The standard view in the ancient world was expressed by the Greek rhetorician Isocrates, who claimed that *logos* – the rational capacity for articulate discourse, translated here as 'speech' – is the faculty that distinguishes humans from animals. It is also the source of all the other social, moral, political, technological and intellectual characteristics that are uniquely human.

> In most of our abilities we differ not at all from the animals; we are in fact behind many in swiftness and strength and other resources. But because there is born in us the power to persuade each other and to show ourselves whatever we wish, we not only have escaped from living as brutes, but also by coming together have founded cities and set up laws and invented arts, and speech has helped us attain practically all of the things we have devised. For it is speech that has made laws about justice and injustice and honor and disgrace, without which provisions we should not be able to live together. By speech we refute the wicked and praise the good. By speech we educate the ignorant and inform the wise.

We regard the ability to speak properly as the best sign of intelligence, and truthful, legal and just speech is the reflection of a good and trustworthy soul.

(Isocrates (436–338 BC), quoted in Kennedy 1963: 8–9)

The dominant figure in this long debate is the French philosopher and mathematician René Descartes (1596–1650). In his 1637 *Discourse on Method* (Descartes 1637), Descartes claimed that there is a fundamental difference in type between humans and animals. In other words, humans should not be thought to be smarter, more skilled or better equipped animals; we are an entirely different category of being. Humans are endowed with a rational soul (or 'mind'); animals are not. Because humans have a rational soul, we are conscious and may direct our bodily and mental actions freely and purposefully. Animals cannot do this and are merely 'sentient machines'. They experience sensations – they feel heat, see colours, sense pain, hear sounds etc. However, they cannot be consciously aware of these sensations, for this would require a rational soul (or mind: Descartes uses the expressions interchangeably: cf. Baker and Morris 1996). Unlike those of a human, an animal's actions are not freely directed (volitional); rather, they are passive reactions to external causes – like the actions of a machine when someone pushes its 'on' button. For this reason, the actions of animals may be given purely mechanical, causal explanations.

Significantly, Descartes argued that it is because an animal does not have a rational soul that it does not have language. For Descartes took language to be a form of telementation: the expression of thoughts (or 'judgements') in vocal or written form so that they may be understood by others (see Volume I, p. 33). And yet, an animal has no thoughts to express or communicate. Animals cannot think, because thinking is a mental action directed by a conscious and purposive – in other words, rational – soul. It is because we humans have rational souls that we can think and form judgements and that we therefore have judgements to express and communicate to others. Simply put, no animal has language because no animal has thoughts.

Descartes did not deny that an animal might conceivably learn to make the sounds or gestures that humans make in using language. He acknowledged, for instance in the *Discourse on*

Method (Descartes 1637), that there are parrots that can do this quite well. But this is not language. When a parrot vocalizes and gestures, it cannot be doing what we humans do when speaking: that is, expressing thoughts. Their actions, including vocalizing and gesturing, are merely mechanical responses to stimuli. Although the vocalizations and gestures that such an animal might be taught to produce sound or look like human language, those vocalizations and gestures could not really be language – because they could not really be the expression of the animal's thoughts. And yet, 'There are no men so dull and stupid, not even idiots, as to be incapable of joining together different words, and thereby constructing an utterance by which to make their thoughts understood . . . On the other hand, there is no other animal, however perfectly and happily circumstanced, which can do the like' (Descartes 1637: 43).

The logic of Descartes' argument is clear: any being that truly has language must be expressing its thoughts, and this in turn means that it must have the means of forming thoughts, that is, a rational soul (or 'mind'). Along with Isocrates' argument, made two thousand years before Descartes, the argument made in the *Discourse on Method* puts in emphatic form the place that language has had in the Western conceptualization of the distinctiveness of humanity and of the human's difference from animals: the animal's lack of linguistic ability is the mark, the proof, of its categorial difference from the human. Because the human being is categorically distinct, it is not therefore possible for any creature to possess just a bit of, or a rudimentary version of, the human's linguistic or mental faculties. As Descartes describes them, the rational soul, the will, consciousness, thinking and language are not faculties that one could logically have *simplified* or *reduced* versions of. There is an unbridgeable gap between humans and animals, and language is the measure of that gap.

For the next two hundred years Descartes' picture of linguistic ability as the distinguishing mark of difference between animals and humans held sway in Western thought. In turn, it gave increased importance to questions about the origin of language (see Volume I, Chapter 11). Was language simply a gift from God or could humans have invented it? If it was an artificial (i.e. human-made) invention, how could humans have progressed from lacking language – like animals – to having language? Many European philosophers, such as Condillac, Herder and Rousseau, assumed that it was humans' rational or reflective endowment that enabled them to invent language, and that it was because animals lacked this that they could neither invent language nor learn a human one. In this case, an answer to the question of how humans first invented language would necessarily give insight into the essential nature of the human mind or rational soul. In other words, Cartesian-inspired speculation on the origin of language was not primarily directed at working out how primitive humans might have succeeded in distinguishing themselves, historical step by historical step, from the animals, but rather in identifying and casting an analytical light on the rational properties that constituted human uniqueness. Linguistic ability provided this light.

Descartes' view of language as the exclusive property of humans and as proof of humans' sole possession of reason continued to influence linguistic thought at the end of the twentieth century. But it has had an uncomfortable relationship with another of the most influential ideas of modern Western thought: the evolutionary theory of Charles Darwin (1809–82). In his *Origin of Species* (Darwin 1859), Darwin rejected the Cartesian claim that humans are categorially distinct from animals. On the contrary, we humans are animals – apes, in particular – whose cognitive and behavioural abilities are the result of a continuous evolutionary development from the abilities possessed by our ape ancestors, some of whom would also have been the ancestors of apes living today. Evolution proceeds by means of small modifications in descent and selective adaptation to environmental conditions. But in Darwin's day, as in our own, this has been seen to raise a puzzling question: How could such a gradual, incremental process have produced humans, who – according to the main lines of the Western tradition – are unique in possessing reason and language? If humans did not somehow emerge full-born with their rational and linguistic powers, but were instead the result of small modifications accumulating over millennia, how could something so complex and wonderful and distinctive as the human's capacity for language and reason ever have resulted?

Max Müller, a contemporary of Darwin and one of the most influential linguists of the period, argued that linguistics has a 'veto' over the claims of evolutionary theory (see Volume I, Chapter 14). For the linguist studies the complexities of language in great detail and so necessarily appreciates how language is completely unlike any of the communicational or cognitive abilities possessed by non-human animals. The linguist knows that language cannot possibly have evolved by the slow incremental steps postulated by evolutionary theory.

> There is to my mind one difficulty which Mr. Darwin has not sufficiently appreciated, and which I certainly do not feel able to remove. There is between the whole animal kingdom, on one side, and man, even in his lowest state, on the other, a barrier which no animal has ever crossed, and that barrier is – Language. By no effort of the understanding, by no stretch of imagination, can I explain to myself how language could have grown out of anything which animals possess, even if we granted them millions of years for that purpose. If anything has a right to the name of *specific difference*, it is language, as we find it in man, and in man only.
>
> (Müller 1873: 182)

Indeed, Müller's belief, that human language poses an awkward, perhaps unsolvable problem for evolutionary theory, continued to have its advocates at the end of the twentieth century. 'Human language is an embarrassment for evolutionary theory because it is vastly more powerful than one can account for in terms of selective fitness' (Premack 1985: 218).

Darwin knew that humanity's possession of language raised serious questions for his theory of evolution, and he responded to this threat in Chapter 3 of *The Descent of Man* (Darwin 1871). The fact that only humans possess language had been claimed by many of Darwin's contemporaries to be proof not only that humans have rational powers that distinguish them categorially from all animals, but that humanity must therefore have required a 'special act of creation', as recounted in Genesis (see Volume I, Chapter 3). In *The Descent of Man* Darwin voiced his fear that humanity's sole possession of 'the faculty of articulate speech' might be thought to provide 'an insuperable objection to the belief that man has developed from some lower form' (Darwin 1871: 467) – in other words, as Müller called it, a linguistic 'veto' to the theory of natural selection. However, Darwin maintained that his theory could, in principle, explain the evolution of linguistic ability in the hominid line and thus neutralize the threat posed by humanity's unique possession of language. Still, although he speculated about the outlines of such an explanation in *The Descent of Man* –

treating linguistic expression as having evolved from the expression of emotions in apes – his ideas were not convincing and had little effect on twentieth-century linguistic thought. So, although Darwinian theory remained at the end of the twentieth century the most powerful force in thinking about animal and human abilities, none the less there is as yet no generally accepted application of evolutionary theory to language.

And yet at the same time, although most linguists support the Cartesian assumption that language is uniquely human and unrelated to the abilities of any non-human animal, the conflict between this view and evolutionary theory has become more of an embarrassment to linguists than it is a threat to evolutionists. For neo-Darwinian evolutionary theory has become the dominant method of explaining the nature of human abilities. At the beginning of the twentieth century's last decade, one pair of generative linguists conceded that, in view of this conflict, 'one could hardly blame anyone for concluding that it is not the theory of evolution that must be questioned but the theory of language' (Pinker and Bloom 1990: 708). After all, it requires no stretch of the imagination to interpret the linguist's insistence that human language is unrelated to any animal ability as confirmation of the claims of present-day creationists: that is, those who, as Max Müller did, continue to maintain what was for centuries the dominant view in the Western tradition – that human language and reason are the gifts of God. Faced with this prospect, some linguists (e.g. Bickerton 1990 and Chomsky 1991, 1998) have opted for what may seem no less of a question-begging assumption: that at some point in hominid evolution a genetic mutation of catastrophic proportions occurred, giving humans, and only humans, language. Chomsky, for instance, speculates that at one time there must have existed 'an ancient primate with the whole human mental architecture in place, but no language faculty'. Eventually 'a mutation took place in the genetic instructions for the brain, which was then reorganized in accord with the laws of physics and chemistry to install a faculty of language' (Chomsky 1998: 17). Can *Homo loquens* have been the product of such a single and powerfully transformative mutation? Or, on the other hand, will it eventually be possible for evolutionary theory to explain how the human linguistic abilities could have resulted from by small incremental modifications to abilities once possessed by the common ancestor to humans and non-human apes? How can these questions be addressed? 'Now the fact is that not a single instance has ever been adduced of any animal trying or learning to speak, nor has it been explained by any scholar or philosopher how that barrier of language, which divides man from all animals, might effectually be crossed' (Müller 1873: 188).

It is within this context that we may make sense of the twentieth century's growing interest in primate communicational abilities and, in particular, of its repeated attempts to teach captive primates the rudiments of human language. For instance, many have thought that if, say, a chimpanzee could be brought up to acquire rudimentary linguistic skills, this would show that chimpanzees have at least some natural linguistic capacity – even though, perhaps owing to the lack of facilitating environmental circumstances, that capacity is never realized in the wild. Furthermore, if chimpanzees have this capacity, as we know humans do, it would then seem plausible to claim that the common ancestors of chimpanzees and humans must also have had this capacity, even though it came to fruition only in the hominid line. In other words, if a chimpanzee could be taught to use even a simplified form of a human language, then it would seem that Darwin was right and that those who maintain a creationist or catastrophic-mutationist position are wrong: the human capacity for language *is* related to the capacities possessed by at least one ape species. Accordingly, the possession of language would no longer be citable as proof of the Cartesian claim that humans are categorially distinct from animals.

> I am inclined to conclude from the various evidences that the great apes have plenty to talk about, but no gift for the use of sounds to represent individual, as contrasted with racial, feelings or ideas. Perhaps they can be taught to use their fingers, somewhat as does the deaf and dumb person, and thus helped to acquire a simple, nonvocal 'sign language'.
>
> (Yerkes 1925: 180)

There have been a number of projects with the aim of teaching language to apes. The first few of these attempted to teach chimpanzees actually to speak (Witmer 1909, Furness 1916, Hayes and Hayes 1951). But, although in some cases the apes concerned were able, with assistance, to produce a handful of words, it eventually became clear that no ape possesses a vocal tract that is capable of producing anything like the range of sounds that humans require to produce speech (see Lieberman 1975). Thereafter the efforts shifted to non-vocal means of producing language. The most noteworthy of these was the 1960s attempt by Allen and Beatrice Gardner to teach their female chimpanzee Washoe the manual signs of American Sign Language (Gardner and Gardner 1969, 1971). By her sixth year Washoe, who had been raised in a trailer in the Gardners' backyard, was said to have learned over 130 individual signs. Apparently, she used signs to refer to a variety of objects and events and to name pictures and objects that were presented to her. She was also said to generalize the meanings of particular signs, spontaneously extending the use of a particular sign in referring to objects or events that were in some way similar to the referent for which she had originally learned the sign. She was even said to have invented her own expressive metaphors.

In the 1970s similar claims were made concerning projects involving other language-trained chimpanzees (Sarah, Lana, Loulis etc.), gorillas (Koko, Michael), and one orang-utan (Chantek). Some, like Washoe, were taught the signs of American Sign Language (ASL), while others were trained to use artificially constructed languages of various types and construction. These studies attracted a great deal of public attention, as they were felt to hold out the possibility of eventually producing a 'talking ape' – an animal that could tell us what an animal thinks about, what its experiences are and, generally, what it is like to be a non-human animal.

However, these studies also generated strong criticism within the scientific community. This criticism came to a head in 1979 with various publications reporting on a failed attempt by the psychologist Herbert Terrace to teach ASL to a male chimpanzee named Nim Chimpsky (see Terrace 1979a; Terrace *et al.* 1979). Terrace claimed that although at one stage he had thought that Nim had learned how to use signs linguistically – referring, requesting and constructing grammatical sentences – upon further investigation, he had to reject this conclusion. Furthermore, when he studied the films of the Gardners' Washoe, he came to the same disillusioning conclusion. Terrace claimed that, if one looked closely at the circumstances in which Nim and Washoe produced signs, they only did so when they were in the presence of the objects concerned. They never referred to objects that were absent from their field of vision, something that children naturally do as soon as they acquire their first words. Nim and Washoe, according to Terrace, primarily used signs imitatively: that is, producing a given sign only when it had already been produced by one of their trainers. Crucially, when they produced sequences of signs, these were apparently devoid of the grammatical properties and functions that are distinctive of human sentences.

> Given that apes have been observed to produce sequences such as 'Washoe more eat', 'water bird', 'Mary give Sarah apple', 'please machine give Lana apple', it is natural to ask whether such sequences were generated by a grammar ... The sequences of words that looked like sentences were subtle imitations of the teacher's sequences. I could find no evidence confirming an ape's grammatical competence, either in my own data or those of others, that could not be explained by simpler processes.
>
> (Terrace 1979b: 67)

Terrace's conclusion, which came to be widely accepted in the scientific community, was that although Nim, Washoe – and, by implication, the other 'signing apes' – had certainly developed new skills, what they had acquired was not *what* human children acquire – that is, it was not *language*. 'Nim's and Washoe's use of signs suggests a type of interaction between chimp and trainer that has little to do with human language' (Terrace 1979b). Furthermore, *how* Nim and Washoe had acquired their skills was not how human children acquire language. Instead, as a result of explicit training, modelling, stimulus reinforcement and conditioning (which is not how children learn language), the 'signing apes' had picked up a variety of collateral, *non-linguistic* skills. What they were doing may have *looked* like language, but – like the vocalizations of a trained parrot – there really was nothing genuinely linguistic about it. In the same way that a parrot draws on collateral skills to give the false appearance of saying something, say, in English, the 'signing apes' had drawn on their considerable cognitive endowments to acquire ways of behaving – hand gestures, key-punches etc. – that superficially seemed similar enough to language to fool their human trainers into thinking it really was. 'Washoe and her peers, though they may have simulated conversation, acquired neither a human language nor something crucially like one, but rather a system of habits that are crude facsimiles of the features of language' (Wallman 1992:

150). In other words, Descartes was right: an animal might be able to produce behaviour that was *similar* in appearance to language, but it lacked whatever was required to make it truly language. For Descartes, what the animal was missing was a 'rational soul' or mind; for the language theorists of the late twentieth century, it was a uniquely human endowment – the language faculty (see Chapter 9 above). 'Clearly, in *any* species, the language faculty must be supplemented by a certain level of functioning in other mental domains for manifestation of normal language. What appears to be the case is that the ape is competent in some or all of the collateral areas but devoid of a language faculty' (Wallman 1992: 112).

This criticism by Terrace and others seemed to write an end to the ape language story, until the first few reports appeared in the mid-1980s about the bonobo named Kanzi that the Rumbaughs were raising at the Language Research Center outside Atlanta, Georgia. According to these reports, Kanzi had acquired an impressive range of language skills without undergoing any of the repetitive training and conditioning that most of the earlier projects had used. He had been brought up in a very human-like, language-rich environment, in which lexigram signs and English speech were used to facilitate, regulate and comment upon each of his countless daily interactions with the Rumbaughs and their assistants. By the time Kanzi was two years old, it had become clear that he had mastered the use of a number of the lexigram signs. Yet he had not been explicitly taught. In other words, like a human child, he had simply 'picked up' these linguistic skills as a part of his socialization into the small, family-like environment in which he was nurtured. He made use of the signs spontaneously and purposefully, without any hint of the imitation or cuing that had been detected in the Nim and Washoe videos. Moreover, he employed the signs for a variety of communicational purposes, including referring to objects, places and events that were absent from the immediate context. As he grew, he had added 250 of these lexigram signs to his productive repertoire. As each of the abstract signs on the keyboard has the meaning of an English word, this was taken to mean that Kanzi had learned over 250 words. He demonstrated his mastery of these signs in a variety of controlled tests.

Perhaps the most significant claim made for Kanzi was that he had learned how to understand a surprising amount of spoken

English: both words and grammar. And yet, spoken English comprehension had not been one of the Rumbaughs' goals with Kanzi, so they had put no effort or attention into it. He had acquired an understanding of spoken English more or less as a human child does, that is, by being brought up in an interactional environment which is mediated by the use of speech. When he was eight years old, the Rumbaughs put Kanzi through a battery of tests to compare his comprehension ability with that of a two-and-a-half-year-old girl (Savage-Rumbaugh *et al.* 1993). Each was tested on 650 English sentences, none of which they had ever heard before. Under controlled experimental conditions Kanzi was found to be slightly better at understanding the sentences than the child. Because one of the primary goals of the tests was to determine which syntactic structures Kanzi could understand, many of the sentences he was tested on had unlikely or even bizarre meanings. This was to ensure that their meanings could not be derived from semantic or contextual predictability. For instance, he was asked to 'Pour the lemonade into the Coke', to 'Take the television outside' and to 'Put the pine needles in the refrigerator', all sentences to which he responded correctly. The sentences exhibited a variety of syntactic patterns, including subordination, passivization, complementation and relativization (Savage-Rumbaugh *et al.* 1993). Similar results were reported for Kanzi's sister Panbanisha at five and a half years (Williams *et al.* 1997). The results apparently confirmed that, although these bonobos' grasp of spoken English structures was not that of an adult human and would probably never progress that far, nevertheless, it was in crucial ways the equal of that of a normal two-and-a-half- to three-year-old human child.

> Certainly most humans understand more complex language than does Kanzi, but there no longer can be said to exist any real differences between the way Kanzi learns and employs language and the way we do the same thing. Of course, it remains possible to impugn the validity of the data and the honesty of the experimenters, and such continues to be frequently done. Yet Kanzi continues to demonstrate that these abilities are real, as does his sister Panbanisha . . .
>
> 1. They have learned to differentiate English phonemes, and they understand combinations of these phonemes to be words.

2. They understand words spoken rapidly and in sentential contexts, where the use/meaning of the word differs from sentence to sentence . . .
3. They know the written symbol that corresponds to many of the spoken words. They can use this symbol to communicate even though they cannot speak.
4. They comprehend the syntactic aspects of utterances. They understand that pronouns such as 'it' refer to previous sentences. They understand that word order can be used to signal a different sort of relationship so that Kanzi biting Sue is not the same thing as Sue biting Kanzi. They understand pronouns of possession such as 'mine' and 'yours'. They understand expressions relating to time, such as 'now' or 'later'. They understand qualifications of state such as 'hot' and 'cold'. They understand that one clause within a sentence can modify another portion of the same sentence, for example, 'Get the ball that is outdoors, not the one that is here'.
5. They follow the thread of conversations that they hear around them, even if they are not participating in such conversations.

(Savage-Rumbaugh *et al.* 1998: 207)

However, at the end of the century, there remained strong resistance to such claims about Kanzi and Panbanisha and as yet no consensus in favour of extending attribution of the capacity for language to non-human apes. The resistance took various forms, but there were two general critical points which stand out. The first of these concerns syntax. Although Greenfield and Savage-Rumbaugh (1990) claim there to be some word-order rules underlying Kanzi's use of lexigrams, few commentators have felt there was any real evidence of syntactic structure in Kanzi or Panbanisha's lexigram production. And yet, the critics claim, syntactic structuring is a universal – indeed an essential – feature of human language use.

Just as hotly disputed is the claim, based on the results discussed above (Savage-Rumbaugh *et al.* 1993), that Kanzi manifests a grasp of some syntactic rules in his responses to spoken English. For instance, discussing the claim that Kanzi grasps the syntactic-functional difference between 'Grab Jeannine' and 'Give the trash to Jeannine', one critic argues:

It is certainly true that Kanzi did something different with Jeannine depending upon whether he heard 'Grab Jeannine' or 'Give the trash to Jeannine', but responding correctly to these commands requires no syntactic competence whatsoever. Given that Kanzi knows the meaning of these words, or at least has formed appropriate associations between these words and their corresponding things and actions, and given that he is able to 'select the critical words' and 'respond appropriately', there is only one way we should expect Kanzi to respond to the coupling of 'grab' with 'Jeannine' or to the combination of 'give', 'trash', and 'Jeannine'. There is, in other words, only one pragmatically sensible way in which to combine the act of giving with the two entities Jeannine and trash, and that is to give the moveable, inanimate one to the one that is capable of being given things, the animate one. No ability to decipher syntactic structure is required in order to respond appropriately.

(Wallman 1992: 103)

The testing of Kanzi's sentence comprehension, in summary, demonstrates that he is able to put together the object or objects and the action mentioned in the way that is appropriate given the properties of the objects involved, what he typically does with them, or both. His performance provides no evidence, however, that he was attending to even so simple a syntactic feature as word order ... What is not new in the Kanzi project is the penchant of the experimenters for over-interpreting the achievements of their subjects, according them a linguistic competence that is simply not warranted by the data.

(Wallman 1992: 104)

The second passage here gives an idea of the tenor of the debate, which often descends below the level expected of mature scientific debate. In any case, it remains unclear how the critics of the comprehension studies can otherwise account for Kanzi and Panbanisha's ability to understand sentences in which word order is reversed but meaning remains the same – that is, sentences such as 'Give Sue the dog' and 'Give the dog to Sue', or in which understanding depends on determining which noun after the verb is the direct object and which the indirect object. Another problem for the critic is the many sentences used in the test in which there is more than one semantic or pragmatic interpretation possible, as in 'Kanzi, make the (toy) dog bite the (toy) snake'. For, both dog and snake could bite or be bitten; moreover, so could Kanzi. Yet Kanzi produces the syntactically correct response all the same. It seems clear that at least some 'primitive' grasp of syntactic properties is needed to understand these sentences correctly, and simple reliance on word order or on semantic/ pragmatic plausibility would not be enough. Kanzi and Panbanisha's syntactic abilities still await detailed analysis and a more considered response from linguists (although see Kako 1999).

Other critics continue to maintain that Kanzi and Panbanisha are relying on collateral skills to do what looks like language but really is not. A key feature in this critique is the claim that, even though Kanzi and Panbanisha may produce signs and respond correctly to spoken sentences, they do not understand what they are doing – not as we humans understand it. In other words, they do not understand that what they produce or that to which they respond *is language*.

> What impresses one the most about chimpanzee signing is that fundamentally, deep down, chimps just don't 'get it'. They know that the trainers like them to sign and that signing often gets them what they want, but they never seem to feel in their bones what language is and how to use it ... They do not even clearly get the idea that a particular sign might refer to a kind of object. Most of the chimps' object signs can refer to any aspect of the situation with which the object is typically associated ... Also, the chimps rarely make statements that comment on interesting objects or actions; virtually all their signs are demands for something they want, usually food or tickling.
>
> (Pinker 1994: 340)

It is hard to imagine what testing procedure could prove that Kanzi and Panbanisha 'get it'. How can it be shown that they know what they are doing in producing and responding to language – that they see verbal behaviour as we humans do, that is, as language? What operational criterion could be used to determine whether anyone – human or bonobo – sees what they do in producing and responding to words *as language*? Perhaps this kind of criticism can be effectively rebutted only by means of eye-witness observations of Kanzi and Panbanisha, something that none of the ape language critics has yet done. Even so, the widely available video presentations provide potential counter-instances to these critical claims. For example, in one hour-long video produced by Japanese television Kanzi is shown spontaneously teaching his half-sister, Tamuli, the meaning of the spoken English command 'Groom Kanzi'. Kanzi grasps Tamuli's hand, puts it into the appropriate form for grooming, brings it up under his own chin (prime bonobo grooming territory) and works her fingers together in a standard grooming movement. All through this, Kanzi's eyes are fixed on Tamuli's, and at the end, he claps her on the back in a gesture which, if produced by a human, would unhesitatingly be glossed as 'Your turn now'. It is hard to watch these scenes and yet not to acknowledge that Kanzi knows what 'Groom Kanzi' means, that he is aware that his half-sister Tamuli does not, and that he is trying to teach her what it means – in other words, that Kanzi knows quite well what at least this bit of language means. Moreover, not only does Kanzi show here that he does indeed 'get it', but also that he knows that young Tamuli does not.

If the claims made about Kanzi and Panbanisha are correct, then it will have to be accepted that there are two bonobos who have at least some capacity for language: in other words, that the capacity for language is not a uniquely human endowment. Other bonobos are currently being raised in linguistic surroundings at Savage-Rumbaugh's Language Research Center, and they may soon have to be admitted into the domain of the language-competent as well. Furthermore, Savage-Rumbaugh and her colleagues have already shown that some 'common' chimpanzees (*Pan troglodytes*) have no less of a claim to possessing some linguistic competence (Brakke and Savage-Rumbaugh 1995, 1996). And yet, at the same time, it is certain that the debates over the proper interpretation of these studies will continue for a long time to come.

The highly controversial character of ape language research and of Kanzi and Panbanisha's claims to have broken into the human linguistic fortress reflects the fact that there is much more at stake in these debates than purely linguistic matters. As Isocrates realized at the beginning of the fourth century BC, the claim that language is uniquely human implies that it is only humans who inhabit a world in which there is morality, justice, dignity, knowledge and rationality. For how could a being without language distinguish between true and false, good and evil, or justice and injustice? And how could it acquire true knowledge or communicate it to others? The conclusion would seem to be, as Descartes insisted, that linguistic humans are categorially distinct from non-linguistic animals. Given this reasoning, the claim that some higher primates have rudimentary linguistic abilities therefore amounts to affirming that this categorial divide has somehow been bridged and that questions concerning the morality, justice, dignity, knowledge and reason of non-human animals should be reopened, with the expectation that the old cultural certainties will no longer prevail. Whether the human race is ready for this kind of cognitive, legal, moral, and indeed theological, revolution may become clear as we make our way into the twenty-first century.

Suggestions for further reading

Chapter 1

A biography of Sapir, *Edward Sapir: linguist, anthropologist, humanist* (Darnell 1990), contains a complete bibliography, as does *Selected Writings in Language, Culture and Personality* (Sapir 1949). All of Sapir's writings are in the process of being reissued as *The Collected Works of Edward Sapir* (Sapir 1990–).

On the American linguistic tradition before Sapir, see *Linguistics in America* (Andresen 1990a). 'The immediate sources of the "Sapir–Whorf hypothesis" (Joseph 1996) offers a critical appraisal of Sapir's connection to various strains of European linguistic thought.

For an overview of the development of American linguistics in the structuralist period, see *American Structuralism* (Hymes and Fought 1981). A more idiosyncratic view is put forward in *Theory Groups and the Study of Language in North America: a social history* (Murray 1994).

Chapter 2

Jakobson's *Selected Writings* (Jakobson 1962–88) are available in several volumes. The best one-volume anthology of his work is *On Language* (Jakobson 1990). The *Dialogues* (Jakobson and Pomorska 1983) provide a fascinating auto-perspective on his life and work.

The definitive study of the development of the concept of the mark is *La notion de «marque» chez Trubetzkoy et Jakobson* (Viel 1984). Its place in the broader perspective of Western linguistic thought is examined in Chapter 6 of *Limiting the Arbitrary:*

linguistic naturalism in Plato's Cratylus *and modern theories of language* (Joseph 2000). Edna Andrews's *Markedness Theory: the union of asymmetry and semiosis in language* (Andrews 1990) covers many of the theory's later developments.

Jakobson's early career is described in Jindrich Toman's *The Magic of a Common Language: Jakobson, Mathesius, Trubetzkoy and the Prague Linguistic Circle* (Toman 1995). Interesting further perspectives are offered by the papers in the volume *Jakobson entre l'Est et l'Ouest, 1915-1939: un épisode de l'histoire de la culture européenne* (Gadet and Sériot 1997) while *Roman Jakobson: life, language, art* (Bradford 1994) takes a still wider view.

The development of 'structuralism' in linguistics is chronicled by E. F. K. Koerner in 'European structuralism – early beginnings' (Koerner 1975). As a critical analysis, Fredric Jameson's *The Prison-House of Language: a critical account of structuralism and Russian formalism* (Jameson 1972) remains essential three decades on.

Chapter 3

The 1987 re-edition of *Nineteen Eighty-Four* (Orwell 1949), cited here in the Penguin Twentieth-Century Classics edition of 1989, corrects significant mistakes in earlier published versions, including the omission of the number '5' from Winston's final tracing in the dust of $2 + 2 = 5$. 'Politics and the English language' (Orwell 1946) and *The English People* (Orwell 1947) are both available, along with all of Orwell's known writings, in the twenty-volume *Complete Works of George Orwell* (Orwell 1986–98).

Michael Shelden's excellent *Orwell: the authorised biography* (Shelden 1991) provides a wealth of background information on Orwell's writings.

Stuart Chase's *The Tyranny of Words* (Chase 1938) was reviled in its day by academic linguists quite as much as by Orwell, but is a lively and fascinating document that deserves a better fate than the near-total oblivion into which it has fallen.

For a fuller history of Ogden's Basic project, see John E. Joseph's 'Basic English and the "debabelization" of China' (Joseph 1999).

Chapter 4

J. B. Carroll's collection *Language, Thought and Reality: selected writings of Benjamin Lee Whorf* (Whorf 1956) borrows the title that Whorf, had he lived, would have used for a book of his own. As it is, his thinking has to be reconstructed from the short and often repetitious articles that Whorf published in his lifetime, plus a fragmentary and heterogeneous *Nachlass*. All references to Whorf's writings in this chapter are to Carroll's edition, which gives full details of the bibliographical history of previously published material.

J. H. Hill's article 'Language, culture and world view' (Hill 1988) includes a useful conspectus of subsequent discussion and further exploration of the Sapir–Whorf hypothesis. For a recent thorough reappraisal, see *The Whorf Theory Complex: a critical reconstruction* (Lee 1997).

Chapter 5

Nearly all Firth's published writings are to be found in one or another of three volumes. *Papers in Linguistics 1934–1951* (Firth 1957) is a collection of papers which Firth himself compiled for publication. P. D. Strevens reprinted in one volume (Firth 1964) two short books, *The Tongues of Men* and *Speech*, first published in 1937 and 1930 respectively. *Selected Papers of J. R. Firth 1952–59* (Firth 1968) is a posthumous collection edited and introduced by F. R. Palmer.

The Philological Society's *Studies in Linguistic Analysis* (Firth *et al.* 1957) is a collection of Firthian papers, including one by Firth himself. *In Memory of J. R. Firth* (Bazell *et al.* 1966) is a larger and more wide-ranging miscellany. *Prosodic Analysis* (Palmer 1970) gives detailed exemplifications of Firthian phonological procedures. Despite its title, *Principles of Firthian Linguistics* (Mitchell 1975) is not an account of the principles of Firthian linguistics but a collection of Mitchell's own Firth-inspired papers. It does however include a general introductory chapter.

Other introductory material is to be found in *Schools of Linguistics: competition and evolution* (Sampson 1980). *The London School of Linguistics: a study of the linguistic theories of B. Malinowski and J. R. Firth* (Langendoen 1968) is a longer critical discussion. *Phonology: an introduction to basic concepts* (Lass 1984) includes an introduction to Firthian phonology.

The 'systemic-functional' linguistics developed by M. A. K. Halliday and his school develops certain precepts of Firth's, particularly that linguistics should deal with 'meaning' at all levels of analysis, that meaning is a function of choice and that 'texts' should be dealt with in their 'context of situation'. See *Explorations in the Functions of Language* (Halliday 1973), *Learning How to Mean* (Halliday 1975) and *Language as a Social Semiotic* (Halliday 1978).

Chapter 6

Wittgenstein's most important works are the *Philosophical Investigations* (Wittgenstein 1953) and the *Tractatus Logico-Philosophicus* (Wittgenstein 1922). Among his other posthumously published works, *The Blue and Brown Books* (Wittgenstein 1958) most explicitly concerns language. An excellent introduction to Wittgenstein's thought – 'early' and 'late' – can be found in Ray Monk's wonderful biography: *Ludwig Wittgenstein: the duty of genius* (Monk 1990). The best and most accessible introduction to Wittgenstein's later philosophy is Marie McGinn's *Wittgenstein and the* Philosophical Investigations (McGinn 1997). Gordon Baker and Peter Hacker's four-volume commentary is the standard work on the *Philosophical Investigations* (Baker and Hacker 1980, 1985; Hacker 1990, 1996a). An excellent account of Wittgenstein's philosophical influence can be found in Hacker's *Wittgenstein's Place in Twentieth-Century Analytical Philosophy* (Hacker 1996b). The best discussion of Wittgenstein's rhetorical method is in a series of articles by Gordon Baker (Baker 1991, 1992, 1998, 1999).

Chapter 7

Of the three slim volumes that contain almost all we have of Austin's work, only half of one of them, *Philosophical Papers* (Austin 1961), consists of writings that Austin himself published during his lifetime. Six of the thirteen papers in that collection, as well as the whole of the other two books, have been subjected to varying degrees of editorial intervention. *Sense and Sensibilia* (Austin 1962a) is G. J. Warnock's reconstruction from lecture notes that were by no means fully written out. *How to do Things with Words* (Austin 1962b) is more incontrovertibly Austin's: the text we have under that title is substantially that which he used in giving the William James Lectures at Harvard in 1955, which were themselves based on notes for lectures delivered in Oxford from 1952 onwards.

Like Firth, Austin is a thinker whose tremendous reputation among, and influence on, those who knew him personally is not altogether explained by the published writings. The prosopographical contributions to two collections of essays, *Symposium on J. L. Austin* (Fann 1969) and *Essays on J. L. Austin* (Berlin *et al.* 1973) are therefore especially valuable. Both also include critical discussions of the work. Book-length discussions, hostile and broadly sympathetic respectively, are *J. L. Austin: a critique of ordinary language philosophy* (Graham 1977) and *J. L. Austin* (Warnock 1989).

The best-known and (many would say) the best systematic attempt to apply the linguistic method to an important philosophical problem is *The Concept of Mind* (Ryle 1949). *Philosophy and Ordinary Language* (Caton 1963), *The Linguistic Turn: recent essays in philosophical method* (Rorty 1967) and *Philosophy and Linguistics* (Lyas 1971) are collections of essays which, although not confined to linguistic philosophy as understood here, together provide a comprehensive conspectus of the movement. *A Critique of Linguistic Philosophy* (Mundle 1970) criticizes the movement from a narrowly professional point of view. *Words and Things: an examination of, and an attack on, linguistic philosophy* (Gellner 1959) is a more panoptic polemic. It contains a fascinating and famously offensive explanation of the attractiveness of linguistic philosophy to its practitioners in terms of the sociology of their academic milieu. To the extent that the phrase 'linguistic philosophy' appears in these works at all, the precise sense assigned to it does not always accord with the usage of the present chapter, which follows *Speech Acts: an essay in the philosophy of language* (Searle 1969) – a book which, along with *Words and Deeds: problems in the theory of speech acts* (Holdcroft 1978), may be cited as prominent among post-Austinian explorations of speech-act theory. 'Searle on language' (Love 1999) is a critical discussion of Searle's philosophy of language.

For Austin's relevance to cognitive semantics, see the first-named editor's contribution to *Language and the Cognitive Construal of the World* (Taylor and MacLaury 1995).

Chapter 8

Besides *Verbal Behavior* (Skinner 1957), B. F. Skinner's best-known works include *The Behavior of Organisms: an experimental analysis* (Skinner 1938), *Walden Two* (Skinner 1948) and *Beyond Freedom and Dignity* (Skinner 1971). The three volumes of his superb autobiography are: *Particulars of My Life* (Skinner 1976), *The Shaping of a Behaviorist* (Skinner 1979) and *A Matter of Consequences* (Skinner 1983). These were republished in a uniform edition by the New York University Press in 1984.

The journal *Behavioural and Brain Sciences* (1984) reproduces six of Skinner's key papers from 1945–81, followed by peer commentary and replies from Skinner. *B. F. Skinner: consensus and controversy* (Modgil and Modgil 1987a), contains twenty-six original essays critical or supportive of Skinner, with interchange among the authors and a brief reflection from Skinner.

Leonard Bloomfield's *Language* (Bloomfield 1933) has emerged from decades of excoriation by Chomsky and his students to general acclaim as the single greatest work of twentieth-century American linguistics.

Noam Chomsky's review of *Verbal Behavior* (Chomsky 1959) was published in the journal *Language*. Julie T. Andresen's 'Skinner and Chomsky thirty years later' (Andresen 1990b) is a pro-Skinnerian critical reading of the review. In 1971 Chomsky reviewed Skinner's *Beyond Freedom and Dignity*, in 'The case against B. F. Skinner' (Chomsky 1971).

Chapter 9

Chomsky not only has published voluminously on language, but is well known to a wider public for his numerous writings on political issues; serious bibliographies of his works are books in themselves. One that is comprehensive up to the date of publication is *Noam Chomsky: a personal bibliography 1951–1986* (Koerner and Tajima 1986).

The specifics of his thinking about syntax have twisted and turned over the years in ways that cannot be tracked in an introductory essay; moreover, much of his writing is forbiddingly abstruse and irritatingly graceless. The following selection includes works that are both salient and fairly readable, and would collectively provide a useful point of entry into a serious study of his ideas: *Syntactic Structures* (Chomsky 1957), 'Review of B. F. Skinner, *Verbal Behavior*' (Chomsky 1959), *Aspects of the Theory of Syntax* (Chomsky 1965), *Cartesian Linguistics: a chapter in the history of rationalist thought* (Chomsky 1966), *Language and Mind* (Chomsky 1968), *Rules and Representations* (Chomsky 1980), *Knowledge of Language: its nature, origin and use* (Chomsky 1986), and *The Minimalist Program* (Chomsky 1995). If taken in chronological sequence, these texts also offer a sketch of how the ideas have developed (although it must be borne in mind that *Syntactic Structures* (Chomsky 1957) is, according to its author, a written-up version of lecture notes distilling work published in full only in *The Logical Structure of Linguistic Theory* (Chomsky 1975)). *The Sound Pattern of English* (Chomsky and Halle 1968) is the landmark text on the phonological ('morphophonemic') component of a generative grammar, a topic on which Chomsky himself has not subsequently contributed much and which has been passed over here.

But Chomsky is a prime example of a thinker perhaps best approached via the interpretations of others. *The Language Instinct* (Pinker 1994) is a controversial but eminently readable presentation of a broadly Chomskyan psychology of language. More directly focused on Chomsky himself is *The Chomsky Update: linguistics and politics* (Salkie 1990), which deals with his politics as well as his linguistics. *The Linguistic Wars* (R. A. Harris 1993) is an entertaining, scholarly history of Chomsky's personal and intellectual relations with other labourers in the academic vineyard which he himself created, and offers a good introductory overview of some aspects of 'generativism'. *Grammatical Theory in the United States from Bloomfield to Chomsky* (Matthews 1993) is more soberly technical. It traces in detail the development of Chomsky's grammatical thought and places it in the context of twentieth-century linguistics.

From the outset Chomsky attracted much critical attention both within and outside linguistics. *Noam Chomsky: consensus and controversy* (Mogdil and Mogdil 1987b) is a useful collection of readings. *Challenging Chomsky: the generative garden game* (Botha 1989) is an idiosyncratic and deeply ambivalent account of Chomsky's relations with his critics, helpful in drawing attention to some of the philosophical issues that arise from his work.

Chapter 10

The article 'Empirical foundations for a theory of language change' (Weinreich *et al.* 1968) provides a comprehensive introduction to the principles of Labovian quantitative sociolinguistics, including a summary of his work in New York City. Labov's MA dissertation on vowel changes on Martha's Vineyard was first published in *Word* (Labov 1963) and subsequently reprinted in *Sociolinguistic Patterns* (Labov 1972a), a collection of Labov's papers on social stratification and language change. *Sociolinguistic Patterns* also includes theoretical chapters on language change ('On the mechanism of linguistic change') and sociolinguistics ('The study of language in its social context' and 'The social setting of linguistic change'). The New York City study was published six years earlier under the title *The Social Stratification of English in New York City* (Labov 1966). A thorough discussion of Labov's reservations about introspection and his emphasis on the observation of naturally occurring speech can be found in *What is a Linguistic Fact?* (Labov 1975). *Language in the Inner City: studies in Black English Vernacular* (Labov 1972b) is a collection of papers relating to Labov's work on African American Vernacular English (AAVE), including two seminal papers: 'The logic of non-standard English', which argues for the recognition of AAVE as an independent linguistic system whose expressive qualities equal those of other dialects of English, and 'Contraction, deletion and inherent variability of the English copula', in which Labov introduces the concept of variable rules. More recently he has published the first volume of *Principles of Linguistic Change* (Labov 1994), which draws together different aspects of his work on language variation and change.

Chapter 11

Most of the books published in Goffman's lifetime are still in print. One of the most accessible and most popular is *The Presentation of Self in Everyday Life* (Goffman 1959). Goffman's book with the most explicit focus on language is his *Forms of Talk* (Goffman 1981). 'On face-work' (Goffman 1955) is reprinted in Goffman's *Interaction Ritual* (Goffman 1967). An abridged version of 'Felicity's condition' (Goffman 1983) is available in *The Goffman Reader* (Lemert and Branaman 1997), as are a representative selection of Goffman's writings and two helpful introductory essays by the editors. *Erving Goffman: exploring the interactional order* (Drew and Wootton 1988) is a collection of specially commissioned articles on Goffman's work by specialists in interactional analysis. *Garfinkel and Ethnomethodology* (Heritage 1984) is an excellent presentation of related work by the ethnomethodological school of interaction analysis and in many ways the best introduction to the subject.

Chapter 12

Bruner's *Child's Talk: learning to use language* (Bruner 1983) is the most developed presentation of his ideas on the role of social interaction in language acquisition. His *Acts of Meaning* (Bruner 1990) gives a good account of his later views on the role of culture and narrative in the child's development. A useful and up-to-date survey of Bruner's impact on the study of language acquisition is available in *Jerome Bruner: language, culture, self* (Bakhurst and Shanker 2001). This also includes Tomasello's very helpful explanation and assessment of Bruner's work. Tomasello's closely related views on the child's development of mind and language are presented in *The Cultural Origins of Human Cognition* (Tomasello 1999). A good and up-to-date overview of the various topics and issues in the study of language acquisition is the *The Handbook of Child Language* (Fletcher and MacWhinney 1995).

Chapter 13

The three books of Derrida's *annus mirabilis*, 1967, are *De la grammatologie* (Derrida 1967a; English translation *Of Grammatology*), *L'Écriture et la différence* (Derrida 1967b; English translation *Writing and Difference*) and *La Voix et la phénomène* (Derrida 1967c; English translation *Speech and phenomena*).

Glas (Derrida 1974) appeared in an English translation with the same title in 1978, followed a few years later by a very useful volume of commentary by John P. Leavey entitled *Glassary* (Leavey 1986).

Derrida's *dialogue des sourds* with Searle began in 1977 in the first issue of *Glyph*, which included an English translation by Alan Bass of Derrida's 'Signature event context', followed by Searle's

'Reiterating the differences: a reply to Derrida'. Derrida's counter-reply originally appeared as a long article (in English), 'Limited Inc a b c . . .' (Derrida 1977), then was republished as a book, *Limited Inc.*, in 1988.

The first book of interviews with Derrida, *Positions* (Derrida 1972), was followed by an English translation with the same title by Alan Bass in 1981.

Books on Derrida and deconstruction are now legion. The gentlest introduction is Christopher Johnson's brief *Derrida* (Johnson 1997), which focuses on his critique of the traditional concept of writing, particularly in Lévi-Strauss. More encompassing is Michal Ben-Naftali's 'Deconstruction: Derrida' (Ben-Naftali 1999), while *Jacques Derrida: opening lines* by Marian Hobson (Hobson 1998) goes beyond a survey of Derrida's work to attempt a systematic reading of his thought across, and in spite of, his deliberate life-long efforts to thwart any such reading. Among older studies, Jonathan Culler's *On Deconstruction: theory and criticism after structuralism* (Culler 1982) is useful for its situating of Derrida's work within contemporary developments in Anglo-American literary theory.

For a fuller consideration of Derrida's position within the history of structuralism and post-structuralism, see John E. Joseph, 'The exportation of structuralist ideas from linguistics to other fields: an overview' (Joseph 2001).

Chapter 14

Harris's oeuvre is large, but there is some repetition from work to work. A bibliography of his writings complete up to 1995 is to be found in *Linguistics Inside Out: Roy Harris and his critics* (Wolf and Love 1997).

What has been called Harris's 'wholesale onslaught' on 'orthodox' linguistics is largely contained in three books, *The Language-Makers* (Harris 1980), *The Language Myth* (Harris 1981), and *The Language Machine* (Harris 1987). His main works on writing are *The Origin of Writing* (Harris 1986), *La Semiologie de l'écriture* (Harris 1993b) and *Signs of Writing* (Harris 1995). *Rethinking Writing* (Harris 2000) is a reformulation in English (rather than a translation) of parts of *La Sémiologie de l'écriture*. The most comprehensive source for his integrational theory of the sign is *Signs, Language and Communication* (Harris 1996). The integrational linguistics that Harris thinks might follow from acceptance of his semiological theory is best approached via *Introduction to Integrational Linguistics* (Harris 1998) and the readings in *Integrational Linguistics: a first reader* (Harris and Wolf 1998).

'Transcending Saussure' (Love 1989) and the Introduction to *The Foundations of Linguistic Theory: selected writings of Roy Harris* (Love 1990) are exegetical essays. The papers collected in *Linguistics Inside Out: Roy Harris and his critics* (Wolf and Love 1997) offer a critical examination of various aspects and implications of Harris's views, together with a long response from Harris ('From an integrational point of view' (Harris 1997)) that both engages with his critics and develops some of the major themes of his work. The reflexive character of language is discussed in Taylor 1992, 1997 and 2000.

Chapter 15

A fascinating account of Kanzi and Panbanisha's upbringing and accomplishments is given in *Kanzi: the ape at the brink of the human mind* (Savage-Rumbaugh and Lewin 1994). The implications of this work for issues in philosophy, linguistics, anthropology and cognitive science are discussed in *Apes, Language and the Human Mind* (Savage-Rumbaugh, Shanker and Taylor 1998). The story of Herbert Terrace's failed experiment with the chimpanzee Nim is told in *Nim* (Terrace 1979a). The most comprehensive account of the various arguments against ape language research is *Aping Language* (Wallman 1992). *The Origins of Language* (King 1999) offers a well-balanced collection of articles on the implications of primate studies for inquiry into language origins and evolution. Richard Sorabji's *Animal Minds and Human Morals* (Sorabji 1993) provides an interesting account of the history of Western thinking about the status of animals in a human world.

Bibliography

Andresen, J. T. (1990a) *Linguistics in America 1769–1924*. London: Routledge.

Andresen, J. T. (1990b) 'Skinner and Chomsky thirty years later', *Historiographia Linguistica* 17, 145–65.

Andrews, E. (1990) *Markedness Theory: the union of asymmetry and semiosis in language*. Durham and London: Duke University Press.

Archangeli, D. (1997) 'Optimality theory: an introduction to linguistics in the 1990s', in D. Archangeli and D. T. Langendoen (eds), *Optimality theory: an overview*, 1–32. Malden, Mass. and Oxford: Blackwell.

Austin, J. L. (1961) *Philosophical Papers* (ed. J. O. Urmson and G. J. Warnock). Oxford: Oxford University Press. Page references to 1979 edition.

Austin, J. L. (1962a) *Sense and Sensibilia* (ed. G. J. Warnock). London: Oxford University Press

Austin, J. L. (1962b) *How to do Things with Words* (ed. J. O. Urmson and M. Sbisa). London: Oxford University Press. Page references to 1975 edition.

Baker, G. P. (1991) 'Section 122: neglected aspects', in *Wittgenstein's Philosophical Investigations: text and context*, 35–68 (ed. R. Arrington and H. J. Glock). London: Routledge.

Baker, G. P. (1992) 'Some remarks on "Language" and "Grammar"', *Grazier Philosophishe Studies* 42, 107–31.

Baker, G. P. (1998) 'The private language argument', *Language & Communication* 18, 325–56.

Baker, G. P. (1999) 'A vision of philosophy', in *Figuras do racionalismo*. Campinas, Brazil: ANPOF.

Baker, G. P. and Hacker, P. M. S. (1980) *Wittgenstein: understanding and meaning*. Oxford: Blackwell.

Baker, G. P. and Hacker, P. M. S. (1985) *Wittgenstein: rules, grammar and necessity*. Oxford: Blackwell.

Baker, G. P. and Morris, K. (1996) *Descartes' Dualism*. London: Routledge.

Bakhurst, D. and Shanker, S. (2001) *Jerome Bruner: language, culture, self*. London: Sage.

Baron, N. (2000) *Alphabet to Email*. London: Routledge.

Barthes, R. (1963) *Sur Racine*. Paris: Seuil (Engl. transl., *On Racine*, by R. Howard, New York: Hill & Wang, 1964).

Bates, E. (1993) 'Comprehension and production in early language development', in E. S. Savage-Rumbaugh *et al.*, *Language Comprehension in Ape and Child*, Monographs of the Society for Research in Child Development 58, 222–42.

Bazell, C. E., Catford, J. C., Halliday, M. A. K. and Robins, R. H. (eds) (1966) *In Memory of J. R. Firth*. London: Longman.

Ben-Naftali, M. (1999) 'Deconstruction: Derrida', in S. Glendinning (ed.), *The Edinburgh Encyclopedia of Continental Philosophy* 653–64, Edinburgh: Edinburgh University Press.

Berlin, I., Forguson, L. W., Pears, D. F., Pitcher, G., Searle, J. R., Strawson, P. F. and Warnock, G. J. (1973) *Essays on J. L. Austin*. Oxford: Clarendon Press.

Bickerton, D. (1990) *Language and Species*. Chicago: University of Chicago Press.

Bloomfield, L. (1933) *Language*. New York: Holt, Rinehart and Winston.

Boas, F. (ed.) (1911) *Handbook of American Indian Languages*. Washington, D.C.: Smithsonian Institution.

Boas, F. (1920) 'The classification of American Languages', *American Anthropologist* (n.s.) 22, 367–76. Reprinted in Boas 1940, 211–28.

Boas, F. (1940) *Race, Language and Culture*. New York: Macmillan.

Botha, R. P. (1989) *Challenging Chomsky: the generative garden game*. Oxford: Blackwell.

Bradford, R. (1994) *Roman Jakobson: life, language, art*. London and New York: Routledge.

Brakke, K. and Savage-Rumbaugh, S. (1995) 'The development of language skills in bonobo and chimpanzee – 1. Comprehension', *Language & Communication* 15, 121–48.

Brakke, K. and Savage-Rumbaugh, S. (1996) 'The development of language skills in Pan – II. Production', *Language & Communication* 16, 361–80.

Breitner, C. *et al.* (1966) 'An academically oriented preschool for culturally deprived children', in F. M. Hechinger (ed.), *Pre-School Education Today*. New York: Doubleday.

Bruner, J. S. (1974) 'Nature and uses of immaturity', in K. J. Connolly and J. S. Bruner (eds), *The Growth of Competence*, 687–708. London and New York: Academic Press.

Bruner, J. S. (1975) 'The ontogenesis of speech acts', *Journal of Child Language* 2, 1–19.

Bruner, J. S. (1977) 'Early social interaction and language acquisition', in H. Schaffer, ed., *Studies in Mother–Infant Interaction*, 271–89. London: Academic Press.

Bruner, J. S. (1983) *Child's Talk: learning to use language*. Oxford: Oxford University Press.

Bruner, J. S. (1984) *In Search of Mind: essays in autobiography*. New York: Harper and Row.

Bruner, J. S. (1990) *Acts of Meaning*. Cambridge, Mass.: Harvard University Press.

Bruner, J. S. (2000) 'Tot thought', *New York Review of Books*, 9 March 2000, 27–30.

Cameron, D. (1990) 'Demythologizing sociolinguistics: why language does not reflect society', in J. E. Joseph and T. J. Taylor (eds), *Ideologies of Language*, 79–95. London and New York: Routledge.

Cameron, D. (1995) *Verbal Hygiene*. London and New York: Routledge.

Caton, C. E. (ed.) (1963) *Philosophy and Ordinary Language*. Urbana: University of Illinois Press.

Chase, S. (1938) *The Tyranny of Words*. New York: Harcourt, Brace; London: Methuen.

Chomsky, N. (1957) *Syntactic Structures*. The Hague: Mouton.

Chomsky, N. (1959) 'Review of B. F. Skinner, *Verbal Behavior*', *Language* 35, 26–58.

Chomsky, N. (1964) *Current Issues in Linguistic Theory*. The Hague: Mouton.

Chomsky, N. (1965) *Aspects of the Theory of Syntax*. Cambridge, Mass.: M.I.T. Press.

Chomsky, N. (1966) *Cartesian Linguistics: a chapter in the history of rationalist thought*. New York: Harper and Row.

Chomsky, N. (1968) *Language and Mind*. New York: Harcourt, Brace, Jovanovich. Page references to 1972 edition.

Chomsky, N. (1971) 'The case against B. F. Skinner,' *New York Review of Books* 17, 18–24.

Chomsky, N. (1975) *The Logical Structure of Linguistic Theory*. New York: Plenum Press.

Chomsky, N. (1980) *Rules and Representations*. Oxford: Blackwell.

Chomsky, N. (1986) *Knowledge of Language: its nature, origin and use*. New York: Praeger.

Chomsky, N. (1991) 'Prospects for the study of language and mind', in A. Kasher (ed.), *The Chomskyan Turn*. Oxford: Blackwell.

Chomsky, N. (1995) *The Minimalist Program*. Cambridge, Mass.: M.I.T. Press.

Chomsky, N. (1998) 'Language and mind: current thoughts on ancient problems: Part I and Part II' lectures presented at Universidad de Brasilia, published in *Pesquisa Linguistica* 3, 4. Page reference to English manuscript.

Chomsky, N. and Halle, M. (1968) *The Sound Pattern of English*. New York: Harper and Row.

Culler, J. (1975). *Structuralist Poetics: structuralism, linguistics, and the study of literature*. Ithaca, N.Y.: Cornell University Press.

Culler, J. (1982) *On Deconstruction: theory and criticism after structuralism*. Ithaca: Cornell University Press.

Darnell, R. (1990) *Edward Sapir: linguist, anthropologist, humanist*. Berkeley: University of California Press.

Darwin, C. (1859) *On the Origin of Species* (Facsimile edn, 1964). Cambridge, Mass.: Harvard University Press.

Darwin, C. (1871) *The Descent of Man*. London: John Murray. Page references to Modern Library edition, New York: Random House.

Derrida, J. (1962) *Introduction à 'L'origine de la géométrie' de Husserl*, second edn, Paris: Presses Universitaires de France. Page references to 1974 edition (Engl. transl., *Edmund Husserl's 'Origin of Geometry': an introduction*, by J. P. Leavey, New York: Harvester Press, 1978).

Derrida, J. (1967a) *De la grammatologie*. Paris, Minuit (Engl. transl., *Of Grammatology*, by G. C. Spivak, Baltimore: The Johns Hopkins University Press, 1976).

Derrida, J. (1967b) *L'Écriture et la différence*. Paris: Seuil (Engl. transl., *Writing and Difference*, by D. A. Bass, Chicago: University of Chicago Press, 1978).

Derrida, J. (1967c) *La voix et la phénomène*. Paris: Presses Universitaires de France (Engl. transl., *Speech and Phenomena*, by D. B. Allison, Evanston, Ill.: Northwestern University Press, 1973).

Derrida, J. (1972) *Positions*. Paris: Minuit (Engl. transl., *Positions*, by A. Bass, Chicago: University of Chicago Press, 1981).

Derrida, J. (1974) *Glas*. Paris: Galilée (Engl. transl., *Glas*, by J. P. Leavey and R. Rand, Lincoln: University of Nebraska Press, 1978).

Derrida, J. (1977) 'Limited Inc a b c . . .', *Glyph* 2, 1–79 (repl., *Limited Inc.*, ed. by G. Graff, Evanston, Ill.: Northwestern University Press, 1988).

Derrida, J. (1987) *Psyché: inventions de l'autre*. Paris: Galilée (Engl. transl., by J. Lye from www.brocku.ca/english/courses/4F70/deconstruction.html, 1996).

Descartes, R. (1637) *Discourse on Method*. Page references to 1992 edition. London: J. M. Dent.

Drew, P. and Wootton, A. (1988) *Erving Goffman: exploring the interactional order*. Cambridge: Polity Press.

Ehrenburg, I. (1963) *Men, Years – Life*, Vol. 3, *Truce*, transl. by T. Shebunina in collaboration with Y. Kapp, London: MacGibbon & Kee, 1921–23.

Fann, K. T. (ed.) (1969) *Symposium on J. L. Austin*. London: Routledge & Kegan Paul.

Firth, J. R. (1948) 'The semantics of linguistic science', *Lingua* 1 (reprinted in J. R. Firth (ed.), *Papers in Linguistics 1934–1951*, London: Oxford University Press, 1957).

Firth, J. R. (1957) *Papers in Linguistics 1934–1951*. London: Oxford University Press.

Firth, J. R. (1964) The Tongues of Men *and* Speech (ed. P. D. Strevens). London: Oxford University Press.

Firth, J. R. (1968) *Selected papers of J. R. Firth 1952–59* (ed. F. R. Palmer). London: Longman.

Firth, J. R. *et al.* (1957) *Studies in Linguistic Analysis* (special volume of the Philological Society). Oxford: Blackwell.

Fletcher, P. and MacWhinney, B. (1995) *The Handbook of Child Language*. Oxford: Blackwell.

Foucault, M. (1971) *L'Ordre du discours*. Paris: Gallimard (Engl. transl., in R. Young (ed.), *Untying the Text*, 48–78 (London: Routledge and Kegan Paul, 1981).

Fowler, J. (1986) 'The social stratification of *r* in New York City department stores, 24 years after Labov'. New York University, MS.

Fowler, R. (1974) *Understanding Language: an introduction to linguistics*. London: Routledge and Kegan Paul.

Furness, W. H. (1916) 'Observations on the mentality of chimpanzees and orang-utans', *Proceedings of the American Philosophical Society* 55, 281–90.

Gadet, F. and Sériot, P. (1997) *Jakobson entre l'est et l'ouest, 1915–1939: un épisode de l'histoire de la culture européenne*. Lausanne: Institut de Linguistique et des Sciences du Langage, Université de Lausanne.

Gardner, A. and Gardner, B. (1969) 'Teaching sign language to a chimpanzee', *Science* 165, 664–72.

Gardner, B. and Gardner, A. (1971) 'Two-way communication with an infant chimpanzee', in A. Schrier and F. Stollnitz (ed.), *Behavior of Non-Human Primates*, vol. 4, 117–84. New York: Academic Press.

Gellner, E. (1959) *Words and Things: an examination of, and an attack on, linguistic philosophy*, London: Routledge and Kegan Paul. Page references to 1979 edition.

Gethin, A. (1990) *Antilinguistics: a critical survey of modern linguistic theory and practice*. Oxford: Intellect.

Gipper, H. (1976) 'Is there a linguistic relativity principle?', in R. Pinxten (ed.), *Universalism versus Relativism in Language and Thought*. The Hague: Mouton.

Goffman, E. (1955) 'On face-work: an analysis of ritual elements in social interaction', in *Psychiatry: Journal for the Study of Interpersonal Processes* 18, 3, August, 213–31.

Goffman, E. (1959) *The Presentation of Self in Everyday Life*. New York: Anchor Books.

Goffman, E. (1967) *Interaction Ritual*. New York: Pantheon Books.

Goffman, E. (1974) *Frame Analysis*. New York: Harper and Row. Page references to 1986 edition.

Goffman, E. (1981) *Forms of Talk*. Oxford: Basil Blackwell.

Goffman, E. (1983) 'Felicity's condition', in *American Journal of Sociology* 89, 1, Chicago: University of Chicago Press, 1–3, 25–51.

Graham, K. (1977) *J. L. Austin: a critique of ordinary language philosophy*. Hassocks: Harvester.

Greenfield, P. M. and Savage-Rumbaugh, S. (1990) 'Grammatical combination in *Pan paniscus*; processes of learning and invention in the evolution and development of language', in S. Parker and K. Gibson (eds), *Comparative Developmental Psychology of Language and Intelligence in Primates*, 540–78. Cambridge: Cambridge University Press.

Grice, H. P. (1989) *Studies in the Way of Words*. Cambridge, Mass.: Harvard University Press.

Gumperz, J. (ed.) (1982) *Language and Social Identity*, Cambridge: Cambridge University Press.

Haas, W. (1957) 'Zero in linguistic description', in Firth *et al.* (1957), 33–53. Oxford: Blackwell.

Hacker, P. M. S. (1986) *Insight and Illusion*, second edn. Oxford: Blackwell.

Hacker, P. M. S. (1990) *Wittgenstein: meaning and mind*. Oxford: Blackwell.

Hacker, P. M. S. (1996a) *Wittgenstein: mind and will*. Oxford: Blackwell.

Hacker, P. M. S. (1996b) *Wittgenstein's Place in Twentieth-Century Analytical Philosophy*. Oxford: Blackwell.

Halliday, M. A. K. (1973) *Explorations in the Functions of Language*. London: Arnold.

Halliday, M. A. K. (1975) *Learning How to Mean*. London: Arnold.

Halliday, M. A. K. (1978) *Language as a Social Semiotic*. London: Arnold.

Harris, R. (1980) *The Language-Makers*. London: Duckworth.

Harris, R. (1981) *The Language Myth*. London: Duckworth.

Harris, R. (1986) *The Origin of Writing*. London: Duckworth.

Harris, R. (1987) *The Language Machine*. London: Duckworth.

Harris, R. (1990) 'On redefining linguistics', in H. G. Davis and T. J. Taylor (eds), *Redefining Linguistics*, 18–52. London: Routledge.

Harris, R. (1993a) 'Integrational linguistics', in A. Crochetiere, J.-C. Boulanger and C. Ouellon (eds), *Actes du quinzieme congrès international des linguistics*. 321–3. Sainte-Foy: Presses de l'Université Laval.

Harris, R. (1993b) *La Sémiologie de l'écriture*. Paris: CNRS.

Harris, R. (1995) *Signs of Writing*. London: Routledge.

Harris, R. (1996) *Signs, Language and Communication*. London: Routledge.

Harris, R. (1997) 'From an integrational point of view', in G. Wolf and N. Love (eds), *Linguistics Inside Out: Roy Harris and his critics*. 229–318. Amsterdam: Benjamins.

Harris, R. (1998) *Introduction to Integrational Linguistics*. Oxford: Pergamon Press.

Harris, R. (2000) *Rethinking Writing*. London: Athlone Press.

Harris, R. and Taylor, T. J. (1989) *Landmarks in Linguistic Thought I: the Western tradition from Socrates to Saussure*. London: Routledge. Page references to 1997 edition.

Harris, R. and Wolf, G. (eds) (1998) *Integrational Linguistics: a first reader*. Oxford: Pergamon Press.

Harris, R. A. (1993) *The Linguistics Wars*. New York: Oxford University Press.

Harris, Z. S. (1951) *Methods in Structural Linguistics*. Chicago: University of Chicago Press.

Hayes, K. and Hayes, C. (1951) 'The intellectual development of a home-raised chimpanzee', *Proceedings of the American Philosophical Society* 95, 105–9.

Heritage, J. (1984) *Garfinkel and Ethnomethodology*. Cambridge: Polity.

Hill, J. H. (1988) 'Language, culture and world view', in F. J. Newmeyer (ed.), *Linguistics: the Cambridge survey. Volume 4: Language: the socio-cultural context*. Cambridge: Cambridge University Press.

Hobson, M. (1998) *Jacques Derrida: opening lines*. London and New York: Routledge.

Hockett, C. F. (1958) *A Course in Modern Linguistics*. New York: Macmillan.

Holdcroft, D. (1978) *Words and Deeds: problems in the theory of speech acts*. Oxford: Clarendon Press.

Hollenbach, B. (1977) 'Reversal of Copala Trique temporal metaphors through language contact,' *International Journal of American Linguistics* 43, 150–4.

Hymes, D. and Fought, J. (1981) *American Structuralism*. The Hague: Mouton.

Jakobson, R. (1962) *Selected Writings*. The Hague: Mouton.

Jakobson, R. (1971) 'The sound laws of child language and their place in general phonology', (transl. R. Sangster), in R. Jakobson, *Studies on Child Language and Aphasia*. The Hague: Mouton.

Jakobson, R. (1978) *Six Lectures on Sound and Meaning*, transl. J. Mepham. Cambridge, Mass.: M.I.T. Press.

Jakobson, R. (1990) *On Language* (ed. L. R. Waugh and M. Monville-Burston). Cambridge, Mass: Harvard University Press.

Jakobson, R. and Pomorska, K. (1983) *Dialogues*, transl. C. Hubert. Cambridge, Mass: M.I.T. Press.

Jakobson, R. and Waugh, L. R. (1979) *The Sound Shape of Language*. Bloomington: Indiana University Press; Hassocks: Harvester

Jameson, F. (1972) *The Prison-House of Language: a critical account of structuralism and Russian formalism*. Princeton: Princeton University Press.

Johnson, B. (1977) 'The frame of reference: Poe, Lacan, Derrida', *Yale French Studies* 55/6, 457–65.

Johnson, C. (1997) *Derrida*. London: Phoenix.

Joseph, J. E. (1996) 'The immediate sources of the "Sapir–Whorf hypothesis"', *Historiographia Linguistica* 23.

Joseph, J. E. (1999) 'Basic English and the "Debabelization" of China', in H. Antor and K. L. Cope (eds), *Intercultural Encounters: studies in English literatures*, 51–71. Heidelberg: C. Winter.

Joseph, J. E. (2000) *Limiting the Arbitrary: linguistic naturalism in Plato's* Cratylus *and modern theories of language*. Amsterdam and Philadelphia: John Benjamins.

Joseph, J. E. (2001) 'The exportation of structuralist ideas from liguistics to other fields: an overview', in S. Auroux, E. F. K. Koerner, H. Niederehe and K. Versteegh (ed.), *History of the Language Sciences: an international handbook on the evolution of the study of language from the beginnings to present*. Berlin and New York: Walter de Gruyter.

Kako, E. (1999) 'Elements of syntax in the systems of three language-trained animals', *Animal Learning & Behavior* 27, 1.

Kennedy, G. (1963) *The Art of Persuasion in Greece*. Princeton: Princeton University Press.

King, B. J. (ed.) (1999) *The Origins of Language: what nonhuman primates can tell us*. Santa Fe, N.M.: School of American Research Press.

Koerner, E. F. K. (1975) 'European structuralism – early beginnings', in T. A. Sebeok (ed.), *Current Trends in Linguistics*, 13: *Historiography of Linguistics*, 717–827. The Hague: Mouton.

Koerner, E. F. K. and Tajima, M. (eds) (1986) *Noam Chomsky: a personal bibliography 1951–1986*. Amsterdam: Benjamins.

Kurzweil, E. (1980) *The Age of Structuralism: Lévi-Strauss to Foucault*. New York: Columbia University Press.

Labov, W. (1963) 'The social motivation of a sound change', *Word* 19, 273–309.

Labov, W. (1966) *The Social Stratification of English in New York City*. Washington, D.C.: Center for Applied Linguistics.

Labov, W. (1972a) *Sociolinguistic Patterns*. Philadelphia: University of Pennsylvania Press.

Labov, W. (1972b) *Language in the Inner City: studies in Black English vernacular*. Philadelphia: University of Pennsylvania Press.

Labov, W. (1972c) 'Some principles of linguistic methodology', *Language in Society* 1, 97–120.

Labov, W. (1975) *What is a Linguistic Fact?* Lisse: Peter de Ridder Press.

Labov, W. (1994) *Principles of Linguistic Change, Volume 1: External Factors*. Oxford: Blackwell.

Langacker, R. W. (1987) *Foundations of Cognitive Grammar, Volume 1*. Stanford: Stanford University Press.

Langacker, R. W. (1991) *Foundations of Cognitive Grammar, Volume 2*. Stanford: Stanford University Press.

Langendoen, D. T. (1968) *The London School of Linguistics: a study of the linguistic theories of B. Malinowski and J. R. Firth*. Cambridge, Mass.: M.I.T. Press.

Lasnik, H. (2000) *Syntactic Structures Revisited: contemporary lectures on classic transformational theory*. Cambridge, Mass.: M.I.T. Press.

Lass, R. (1984) *Phonology: an introduction to basic concepts*. Cambridge: Cambridge University Press.

Leavey, J. P. (1986) *Glassary*. Lincoln: University of Nebraska Press.

Lee, P. (1997) *The Whorf Theory Complex: a critical reconstruction*. Amsterdam: Benjamins.

Lemert, C. and Branaman, A. (1997) *The Goffman Reader*. Oxford: Blackwell.

Lévi-Stauss, C. (1955) *Tristes tropiques*. Paris: Plon.

Lieberman, P. (1975) *On the Origins of Language*. New York: Macmillan.

Locke, J. (1690) *An Essay Concerning Human Understanding* (ed. P. Nidditch). Oxford: Oxford University Press. Page references to 1975 edition.

Longacre, R. E. (1956) Review of W. M. Urban, *Language and Reality* and B. L. Whorf, *Four Articles on Metalinguistics, Language* 32, 298–308.

Love, N. (1989) 'Transcending Saussure', *Poetics Today* 10, 793–818.

Love, N. (ed.) (1990) *The Foundations of Linguistic Theory: selected writings of Roy Harris*. London: Routledge.

Love, N. (1998) 'Integrating languages', in R. Harris and G. Wolf (eds), *Integrational Linguistics: a first reader*, 96–110. Oxford: Pergamon Press.

Love, N. (1999) 'Searle on language', *Language and Communication* 19, 9–25.

Lyas, C. (ed.) (1971) *Philosophy and Linguistics*, London: Macmillan.

McGinn, M. (1997) *Wittgenstein and the* Philosophical Investigations. London: Routledge.

Malinowski, B. (1935) *Coral Gardens and their Magic* (2 vols). London: Allen and Unwin.

Malotki, E. (1979) *Hopi-Raum*. Tübingen: Narr.

Malotki, E. (1983) *Hopi Time*. Berlin: Mouton de Gruyter.

Martinet, A. (1955) *Economie des changements phonétiques*. Berne: Francke.

Matthews, P. H. (1993) *Grammatical Theory in the United States from Bloomfield to Chomsky*. Cambridge: Cambridge University Press.

Merleau-Ponty, M. (1964) 'La conscience et l'acquisition du langage', *Bulletin de Psychologie*, 236, XVIII 3–6, 226–59. (Engl. transl., *Consciousness and the Acquisition of Language*, by H. J. Silverman, Evanston, Ill.: Northwestern University Press, 1973).

Mitchell, T. F. (1975) *Principles of Firthian Linguistics*. London: Longman.

Mogdil, S. and Mogdil, C. (eds) (1987a) *B. F. Skinner: consensus and controversy*. New York: Falmer Press.

Mogdil, S. and Mogdil, C. (eds) (1987b) *Noam Chomsky: consensus and controversy*. New York: Falmer Press.

Monk, R. (1990) *Ludwig Wittgenstein: the duty of genius*. London: Jonathan Cape; New York: The Free Press.

Müller, F. M. (1873) 'Lectures on Mr. Darwin's philosophy of language', *Fraser's Magazine* 7 and 8. Page references to reprinting in R. Harris (ed.), *The Origin of Language*, 147–233. Bristol: Thoemmes Press, 1996.

Mundle, C. W. K. (1970) *A Critique of Linguistic Philosophy*, Oxford: Clarendon Press.

Murray, S. O. (1994) *Theory Groups and the Study of Language in North America: a social history*. Amsterdam: Benjamins.

Ogden, C. K. and Richards, I. A. (1923) *The Meaning of Meaning*. London: Routledge and Kegan Paul.

Orwell, G. (1934) *Burmese Days*. New York: Harcourt Brace.

Orwell, G. (1937) *The Road to Wigan Pier*. London: Gollancz.

Orwell, G. (1938) *Homage to Catalonia*. London: Secker and Warburg.

Orwell, G. (1945) *Animal Farm: a fairy story*. London: Secker and Warburg.

Orwell, G. (1946) 'Politics and the English language', *Horizon* 13, 76, 252–65.

Orwell, G. (1947) *The English People*. London: Collins. Reprinted in S. Orwell and I. Angus (eds), *The Collected Essays, Journalism and Letters of George Orwell* 3, 1–38. London: Secker & Warburg, 1968.

Orwell, G. (1949) *Nineteen Eighty-Four*. London: Secker and Warburg. Page references to the Penguin Twentieth-Century classics edition, 1989.

Orwell, G. (1986–98) *Complete Works of George Orwell*. London: Secker and Warburg.

Palmer, F. R. (ed.) (1970) *Prosodic Analysis*. London: Oxford University Press.

Pinker, S. (1994) *The Language Instinct*, New York: William Morrow and Co.; London: Allen Lane (The Penguin Press).

Pinker, S. and Bloom, P. (1990) 'Natural language and natural selection', *Behavioural and Brain Sciences*, 13, 707–27.

Plato (1995) *Opera*, Volume I, (ed. E. A. Duke *et al.*), Oxford: Clarendon Press. (transl. from Joseph 2000).

Premack, D. (1985) 'Gavagai! or the future history of the animal language controversy', *Cognition* 19, 207–96.

Romaine, S. (1981) 'The status of variable rules in sociolinguistic theory', *Journal of Linguistics* 17, 93–119.

Rorty, R. (ed.) (1967) *The Linguistic Turn: recent essays in philosophical method*. Chicago: University of Chicago Press.

Ryle, G. (1949) *The Concept of Mind*. London: Hutchinson.

Salkie, R. (1990) *The Chomsky Update: linguistics and politics*. London: Unwin Hyman.

Sampson, G. R. (1980) *Schools of Linguistics: competition and evolution*. London: Hutchinson.

Sapir, E. (1907) 'Herder's "Ursprung der Sprache"', *Modern Philology* 5, 109–42.

Sapir, E. (1917) 'Do we need a "superorganic"?', *American Anthropologist* 19, 441–7.

Sapir, E. (1921) *Language: an introduction to the study of speech*. New York: Harcourt Brace.

Sapir, E. (1929) 'The status of linguistics as a science', *Language* 5.

Sapir, E. (1931) 'Conceptual categories in primitive languages', *Science* 74.

Sapir, E. (1933) 'Language', in *Encyclopedia of the Social Sciences*, vol. 9, 155–69, New York: Macmillan.

Sapir, E. (1949) *Selected Writings in Language, Culture and Personality* (ed. D. G. Mandelbaum). Berkeley: University of California Press.

Sapir, E. (1990) *The Collected Works of Edward Sapir* 16 volumes. Berlin: Mouton de Gruyter.

Sapir, E. (1994) *The Psychology of Cultures: a course of lectures* (ed. J. T. Irvine). Berlin: Mouton de Gruyter.

Saussure, F. de (1916) *Cours de linguistique générale*. Paris: Payot. Page references to 1922 edition.

Savage-Rumbaugh, E. S., Murphy, J., Sevcik, R., Brakke, K., Williams, S. and Rumbaugh, D. M. (1993) *Language Comprehension in Ape and Child*, in Monographs of the Society for Research in Child Development, Serial no. 233, 58, 304.

Savage-Rumbaugh, S. and Lewin, R. (1994) *Kanzi: the ape at the brink of the human mind*. New York: Wiley.

Savage-Rumbaugh, S., Shanker, S., and Taylor, T. J. (1998) *Apes, Language and the Human Mind*. New York: Oxford University Press.

Scaife, M. and Bruner, J. S. (1975) 'The capacity for joint visual attention in the infant', *Nature* 253, 265–6.

Scollon, R. and Scollon, S. B. (1981) *Narrative, Literacy and Face in Interethnic Communication*, Norwood N.J.: Ablex.

Searle, J. R. (1969) *Speech Acts: an essay in the philosophy of language*. Cambridge: Cambridge University Press.

Shelden, M. (1991) *Orwell: the authorised biography*. London: Heinemann.

Skinner, B. F. (1938) *The Behavior of Organisms: an experimental analysis*. New York and London: Appleton-Century.

Skinner, B. F. (1948) *Walden Two*. New York: Macmillan.

Skinner, B. F. (1957) *Verbal Behavior*. New York: Appleton-Century-Crofts; London and New York: Methuen.

Skinner, B. F. (1971) *Beyond Freedom and Dignity*. New York: Knopf; London: Cape (1972).

Skinner, B. F. (1976) *Particulars of my Life*. New York: Knopf.

Skinner, B. F. (1979) *The Shaping of a Behaviorist*. New York: Knopf.

Skinner, B. F. (1983) *A Matter of Consequences*. New York: Knopf.

Sorabji, R. (1993) *Animal Minds and Human Morals: the origins of the Western debate*. London: Duckworth.

Taylor, J. R. and MacLaury, R. E. (eds) (1995) *Language and the Cognitive Construal of the World*. Berlin: Mouton de Gruyter.

Taylor, T. J. (1992) *Mutual Misunderstanding*. Durban, N.C.: Duke University Press and London: Routledge.

Taylor, T. J. (1997) *Theorizing Language: analysis, normativity, rhetoric, history*. Oxford: Pergamon.

Taylor, T. J. (2000) 'Language constructing language: the implications of reflexivity for linguistic theory'. *Language Sciences* 22, 483–99.

Terrace, H. (1979a) *Nim*. New York: Columbia University Press.

Terrace, H. (1979b) 'The trouble with ape-language studies', *Psychology Today*, November, 1979, 63–76.

Terrace, H., Petito, L., Sanders, R. and Bever, T. (1979) 'Can an ape create a sentence?', *Science* 206, 892–902.

Toman, J. (1995) *The Magic of a Common Language: Jakobson, Mathesius, Trubetzkoy and the Prague linguistic circle*. Cambridge, Mass.: M.I.T. Press.

Tomasello, M. (1999) *The Cultural Origins of Human Cognition*. Cambridge, Mass.: Harvard University Press.

Tomasello, M. (2001) 'Bruner on Language Acquisition', in D. Bakhurst and S. Shanker (eds), *Jerome Bruner: language, culture, self*, 31–49. London: Sage.

Tooke, J. H. (1857) *The Diversions of Purley* (ed. R. Taylor). London: William Tegg.

Trevarthen, C. (1979) 'Instincts for human understanding and for cultural cooperation: their development in infancy', in M. von Cranach *et al.* (eds), *Human Ethology: claims and limits of a new discipline*, 530–71. Cambridge: Cambridge University Press.

Viel, M. (1984) *La notion de «marque» chez Trubetzkoy et Jakobson*. Paris: Didier Érudition.

Voegelin, C. F., Voegelin, F. M. and Jeanne, L. M. (1979) 'Hopi semantics', in A. Ortiz (ed.), *Handbook of North American Indians*. Volume 9: *Southwest*. Washington, D.C.: Smithsonian Institution.

Wallman, J. (1992) *Aping language*, Cambridge: Cambridge University Press.

Warnock, G. J. (1989) *J. L. Austin*, London: Routledge.

Weinreich, U., Labov, W. and Herzog, M. (1968) 'Empirical foundations for a theory of language change', in W. P. Lehmann and Y. Malkiel (eds), *Directions for Historical Linguistics*. Austin: University of Texas Press.

Whorf, B. L. (1956) *Language, Thought and Reality: selected writings of Benjamin Lee Whorf* (ed. J. B. Carroll). Cambridge, Mass.: M.I.T. Press.

Williams, S., Brakke, K. and Savage-Rumbaugh, S. (1997) 'Compre-hension skills of language-competent and nonlanguage-competent apes', *Language & Communication* 17, 4.

Witmer, L. (1909) 'A monkey with a mind', *The Psychological Clinic* 3, 179–205.

Wittgenstein, L. (1922) *Tractatus Logico-Philosophicus* (transl. C. K. Ogden and F. Ramsey) London: Routledge.

Wittgenstein, L. (1953) *Philosophical Investigations*. Oxford: Blackwell.

Wittgenstein, L. (1958) *The Blue and Brown Books* (second edn 1969). Oxford: Blackwell.

Wittgenstein, L. (1993) *Philosophical Occasions* (eds, J. Klagge and N. Nordmann). Indianapolis and Cambridge: Hackett.

Wolf, G. and Love, N. (eds) (1997) *Linguistics Inside Out: Roy Harris and his critics*. Amsterdam: Benjamins.

Yerkes, R. (1925) *Almost Human*. New York: Century Company.

Index